Plume of Bees

Plume of Bees

a literary biography of C.K.Stead

Judith Dell Panny

CAPE CATLEY LTD

To Rolf, meinem guten Mann an meiner Seite,
and to the memory of Terry Sturm,
respected friend and colleague.

creative nz
Arts Council of New Zealand *Toi Aotearoa*

This book has been published with the assistance of a grant from Creative New Zealand.

First published September 2009

Cape Catley Ltd
Ngataringa Road
P O Box 32-622
Devonport, Auckland
New Zealand

Email: cape.catley@xtra.co.nz
Website: www.capecatleybooks.co.nz

Typeset in Sabon 10.5/14
Designed and typeset by Kate Greenaway, Matakana
Cover design by Trevor Newman, North Shore City
Cover photographs *New Zealand Herald*
Printed by Publishing Press Ltd, North Shore City

ISBN: 978-1-877340-23-9

Contents

Acknowledgements

Warm thanks to family members and good friends who have provided help and encouragement or who have read and constructively criticised sections of the text in draft: Rolf Panny, David Boldt, Anne Austin, Liz and Barry Chisholm, Mary McKenzie, Pete Marsden, Kevin Penberthy, Vanessa Seymour, Ilse and Bryan Surgenor, John Wareham, Axel Vieregg, Frieder Voit.

I am grateful to Kay Stead for access to her comprehensive bibliography of C. K. Stead's publications. To Karl Stead, sincere thanks for the granting of copyright, allowing the many quotations from his poetry, fiction, critical writing, and letters lodged in the Turnbull Library to be reproduced in this book, and also for making available a range of family photographs for inclusion.

Thanks are due to Bill Worsfold and family at Kaiwaka for their assistance. I remember with respect Josephine Worsfold whom I interviewed in February 2006. She died in January 2007.

To the New Zealand High Commissioner to London, Jonathan Hunt, many thanks for hospitality and for facilitating my attendance at the London launch of *My Name Was Judas*.

I acknowledge the help and expertise of staff of the Massey University Library, the Takapuna Library, the National Library and the Alexander Turnbull Library.

To Copyright Licensing Limited, grateful acknowledgement and thanks are extended for the Writing Award granted to me in October 2006.

Judith Dell Panny
Ashhurst, Manawatu,
New Zealand
June 2009

Introduction
The Stead Phenomenon

"C.K." is a self-portrait. The poem appeared in *Metro*, in *New Zealand Books* and later in *The Black River*, C. K. Stead's fourteenth volume of poetry. The poet contrasts C. K., the man he is reputed to be, with Karl, the person he believes himself to be.

C.K.[1]
for Margo White

There's a Stead I
recognise only by
his picture

in the papers
and what's said of him
behind the lines –

has my name, my
face, my (such as they are)
achievements –

doesn't smile
often, and when he does (they
say) watch out! –

doesn't suffer fools
(or anyone)
gladly … 'No, no,'

I protest

'this is not the man
who eats my lunch, reads

'my newspaper, sleeps
in my bed' – but who's
listening?

The world's sure it
knows you better than
you know yourself.

One day I'll meet
the bastard, surprise
him, introduce

myself. 'Hullo, C.K.
I'm Karl. We haven't
met.' 'Let's

'keep it like that,'
he says, unfriendly,
and turns away.

The poem reiterates two widely held impressions: the quietly spoken, personable fellow, and the brusque, prickly intellectual. At the same time, Stead mocks those who would claim to know him better than he knows himself.

"C.K." and "Karl" form what could be termed 'the Stead phenomenon', a personality that includes contradictory elements. Contrasting extremes also characterise his reception as a writer in New Zealand. Despite prestigious awards, including a CBE for services to New Zealand literature in 1985, and the Order of New Zealand in 2007, and despite the honour of being one of only two New Zealanders to become a Fellow of the Royal Society of Literature, Stead has not always been admired in his own country. Journals, newspapers, radio and television have revealed a man embroiled in controversy.

Fiction writers critical of their society tend to be cautious, speaking through jesters, fools, the mentally deranged or children. They can hide behind allegory, parody, or the personae of various characters. A covert approach has not been favoured by Stead. Controversial views have been stated unequivocally in his articles and critical essays, sometimes provoking intense disfavour. University of Auckland colleague Terry Sturm has defended him, maintaining that Stead's most provocative pieces of writing present well-reasoned arguments, directed against lack of intellectual rigour, a parroting of populist views, and uncritical adherence to political correctness. Sturm is convinced that Stead has been unfairly pilloried by the media and critics in this country.[2] Poet and novelist Kevin Ireland protests at "people who call [Stead's] principles into question": "I think he's wrong quite often, but he's never unprincipled." Ireland has described him as "one of the bravest and sincerest liberals in New Zealand life".[3]

There has been no need for advocacy of this kind in Britain, where Stead is highly esteemed. In 2001, the degree Doctor of Letters was conferred on Professor Karl Stead by the University of Bristol. At the ceremony, Professor Andrew Bennett described him as "an internationally renowned critic, poet and novelist, and one of New Zealand's leading writers and critics".[4] The accolade acknowledges the extent and diversity of Stead's published work. In addition to fourteen books of poetry, he is the author of eleven novels, two collections of short stories, and seven volumes of literary criticism. Novels and stories have been translated into many languages. His first novel, *Smith's Dream,* source of the film *Sleeping Dogs,* has sold tens of thousands of copies. His first critical text, *The New Poetic,* in print through several editions since its first issue in 1964, has sold well over 100,000 copies.

Despite this evidence of success, Kim Hill, the well-known New Zealand radio interviewer and commentator, observed in a 1994 radio interview, "Your books aren't judged like other people's books any more." Referring to the New Zealand reception of Stead's publications, she asked, "Is it that we're a small country?"[5] The implication can only be that his unpopular views as a critic would be well-known, prejudicing critics against his literary work.

Sturm is convinced that Stead's significance as an author has not been fully recognised here.[6] More positive and better balanced appraisal has been offered in Britain than in New Zealand. Reviews of *Pound, Yeats, Eliot and the Modernist Movement* provide a vivid example. John Chalker in the Oxford journal, *The Year's Work in English Studies,* describes Stead's text as "the most important and engaging book of the year",[7] whereas the *Landfall* review by Professor K. K. Ruthven of Canterbury University scorns the work: "Now and again the buzz-words of yesteryear congregate to fashion banalities which ought to have induced a melt-down in Stead's crap-detector."[8] To Ruthven's question, "Who ... is going to read this absurdly priced book?" Stead, in the next *Landfall*, reported that it "has been published on both sides of the Atlantic and was reprinted (still in hardcover) six months after publication".[9]

A man of ambition and robust ego, Stead positioned himself from the 1960s, academically and creatively, at the very heart of New Zealand's literary scene. He returned from England to contribute to the literature, and has done so abundantly. Over the years he has disclosed ambivalence toward his decision to stay in this country, rather than accept invitations to take up positions abroad. His 1979 poem "Walking Westward" begins with a tone of regret as the poet's eye looks to the horizon from New Zealand's western shore: "Out there is the world/ (...) /the hook of Maui is in your guts/ here is all the beauty of Lackland/ ... /in Paradise are no legends."[10] While "Walking Westward" is equivocal, implying that one and the same place can be viewed as paradise or hell, the opening mood is certainly dour, with the narrator seemingly trapped in a place referred to as "Lackland". The poem proposes an attitude that some fellow countrymen and women, rightly or wrongly, have interpreted as Stead's disdain for his homeland. John Needham is one who has inferred that the land and the people of New Zealand are "meaningless" to the poet: "his poem exaggerates the bareness of 'Lackland'."[11] Immediately after the poem's publication, the merits of "Walking Westward" were fiercely debated in reviews and letters to journals, demonstrating Stead's ability to engage with readers and provoke a reaction.

It was Stead's poetry that drew my attention to his work thirty years ago. My earliest interest was fired by the discovery of "SCORIA", published in *Islands* in 1979. The long poem celebrates Auckland's history, geology, mythology and the poet's memories of childhood in the suburb of Mt Eden. The poem's musical quality appealed to me. Having imagined it spoken in a way that would bring out the richness of its sound patterns, I gathered a group of four and directed a concert reading, making the most of tonal contrasts offered by two male and two female voices. A pianist provided accompaniment for sections located at Stead's boyhood home, where his mother taught or practised the piano. Gary Brain, then chief timpanist for the New

Zealand Symphony Orchestra, improvised a percussion backing for sections involving the volcanic heritage of the Auckland Isthmus and the Maori myths and legends of the region. Our trial audiotape led to an invitation to record in Wellington for Radio New Zealand. The reading by four amateurs, and Elizabeth Alley's interview with Karl Stead, formed a Concert Programme item on October 15, 1983, which was repeated in 1984.[12]

Alert to Stead's work thereafter, I noted that novels appeared at regular intervals, as did new volumes of poetry. It did not escape my notice that Stead was a literary figure who generated controversy, although from provincial Manawatu, or from universities in Germany, I was not party to exchanges that revealed the polarisation of Stead's supporters and detractors in the late 1980s and into the 1990s.

Early in 2005, as I reflected on Stead's achievements through more than five decades, it seemed that opposing responses to this high-flying author presented a set of contradictions worthy of investigation. When I proposed a literary biography and provided an outline, Stead agreed to a book that would place emphasis on his writing rather than on his life. There was an initial interview and answers by e-mail to questions relating to his early years, after which my work proceeded independently. I have relied on resources available in the public arena – Stead's many publications, public lectures, letters to Sargeson and Curnow lodged in the Alexander Turnbull Library, and interviews conducted by journalists, radio personalities and colleagues. Detachment on my part has been essential in confronting the breadth of response to his writing, and in recording the findings impartially.

What temperament does this man bring to his art, and, conversely, what does the art reveal of his idiosyncrasies and preoccupations? The inquiry begins with an account of his childhood to seek influences and talents that may have predisposed him to become a foremost writer and a man of ambition.

1 C. K. Stead, "C.K.", *The Black River*, Auckland University Press, 2007, pp. 63-4.

2 Terry Sturm, interview with author, 20 December 2005.

3 Kevin Ireland, cited by Stephen Stratford, in "Blaspheming Against the Pieties: Why the Literati Hate C. K. Stead", *Metro*, April 1990, p. 81.

4 Andrew Bennett, from an address to 'Mr Vice-Chancellor' at the conferring of the degree Doctor of Letters on Professor Karl Stead, 12 July 2001. *Speeches Delivered in*

Commendation of Honorary Graduates, University of Bristol, 9-13 July 2001, p. 26.

5 Kim Hill, “Nine to Noon”, *National Radio*, 6 July 1994.

6 Sturm, interview with author, 20 December 2005.

7 John Chalker, “Review of *Pound, Yeats, Eliot and the Modernist Movement*”, *The Year's Work in English Studies* 67, Oxford, 1986, p. 538.

8 K. K. Ruthven, “*Pound, Yeats, Eliot and the Modernist Movement*, C. K. Stead”, *Landfall* Volume 40 (4), December 1986, p. 510.

9 C. K. Stead, “Correspondence”, *Landfall* Volume 41 (1), March 1987, p. 108.

10 C. K. Stead, “Walking Westward”, *Walking Westward*, Auckland, The Shed, 1979, p. 32.

11 John Needham, “Letter of reply to C. K. Stead”, *Comment*, September 1979, pp. 10-11.

12 The readers were Fiona Poole, Marianne Tremaine, Brian Finch and Terry Skelsey. The pianist was Glenys Robertson. Apart from Marianne Tremaine, who was on the Massey University staff, and NZSO timpanist Gary Brain, we were members of staff teaching in the English Department at the Palmerston North Teachers' College.

CHAPTER ONE

The Rhythm of the Garden

In the Suburb of Mt Eden

As a child, C. K. Stead received a musical education through listening and through playing the piano. His mother Olive was a gifted pianist, who sang with a clear, true voice. His maternal grandmother's rich and melodious singing often filled the house. Stead's own talents include a fine singing voice, perfect pitch, a facility with words and an ear for the music of language.

Piano playing provided solace for Stead's mother between the ages of five and seven, when her parents sailed abroad without her. Loneliness, she claimed, made her a musician. It is not as easy to account for her son's impulse to become a writer. He believes he was endowed with creativity and the will to excel. Sensory alertness, nurtured in the terraced garden of his Mt Eden home, was further sharpened through exploring nearby volcanic hills and spending long holidays on a farm near Kaiwaka.

Christian Karlson Stead was born in October 1932, when his sister Norma Nellie was two years old. Five years later, a second sister arrived prematurely, living only a few hours, a loss that caused grief in the family and confusion in the boy's mind.

> Many tears were shed.
> To me she was a puzzle –
> a sibling coming
> and then gone.[1]

A third sister, Frances Caroline, was born when her brother was seventeen.

Christian Karlson was the name of Stead's Swedish grandfather, a man revered by his wife Caroline and by Olive, their only child. The grandfather's family history remained a mystery until the early 1960s. After writing letters to Sweden, Olive Stead discovered that her father was born after his mother had become a widow. So that she could retain her respectability and remarry, the baby was placed in the care of a foster mother. It was believed that the boy's father was an army officer named Karl, but those who responded from Sweden to the inquiries did not know the man's surname.

Christian Karlson left Sweden as a young man, gained Master Mariner qualifications in Bristol, and later became a sea captain. Stead writes:

> He died before I was born, but he was a very strong presence in the house. He'd obviously been a very dominating and much-loved character. My grandmother lived with us so he was referred to constantly. So I felt as though he was in the house even though he wasn't. The house was full of photographs of sailing ships and the islands where he worked and spent a lot of his life.[2]

A few years before his death Christian Karlson came ashore planning to retire, though he was persuaded several times by ship owners to make 'one last voyage'. Between these final voyages he constructed a villa on half an acre in the suburb of Mt Eden, using the local scoria stone for terraces, boundary walls and the outer walls of the basement. Carl Christianson in *The Singing Whakapapa*, whose career parallels Christian Karlson's, "built the house ... and spent many months landscaping it, building rock walls, rockery gardens, ornamental pagodas over which roses were trained, planting fruit trees and laying out flower and vegetable gardens."[3]

In 1930, the sixty-year-old Captain Karlson accepted a contract from a French company to take a ship from New Caledonia, transporting a team to prospect for phosphate deposits on the coast of the New Hebrides. He fell ill on the voyage and was hospitalised in Noumea. "He has suffered a serious bout of malaria, has managed to bring the ship back to port, but as a consequence of his effort is now gravely ill. There are complications... Fears are held..."[4] This account from *The Singing Whakapapa* reflects what actually happened. Caroline Karlson planned to sail to New Caledonia from Wellington, but before the ship's departure, she received news of her husband's death. Karl Stead's parents and their baby daughter had by then come to live in the Karlson home in Mt Eden. The Kensington Road property, a good suburban location only a hundred metres or so from Maungawhau School, became the Stead family home.

The life of Ethel Grady, née Christianson, from *The Singing Whakapapa*, is patterned on that of Stead's mother, who received no formal secondary schooling, spending most of her girlhood sailing with her parents. Nevertheless she completed her Licentiate in Pianoforte before the age of twenty. In Auckland, working as a teacher of piano, she met James Walter Ambrose Stead, whom she married in 1929.

The eldest of five children, James Stead worked on the Kaiwaka farm of his mother's relatives instead of receiving a secondary education. There he was known as Jim. His uncle, Bill Bowmar, welcomed the young nephew at a time of labour shortage during World War I, when Northland farmers were struggling to improve the productivity of land formerly mined by gum-diggers. In those days, lack of secondary schooling was commonplace. Unusual was the fact that Jim's grandfather, Walter Collins Stead, had studied at Oxford University, winning a pewter mug as a member of a successful Oxford rowing team.[5]

Walter's second son, Jim's father, was James Bond Read Stead, born in Surrey, England. He married in Auckland, and the occupation 'storeman' was recorded on his marriage certificate. The Stead relatives today know little of his career, but, given that he was unable to provide education beyond primary schooling for Jim, it is assumed that the family met with hard times. In his later years he was thought to have worked on the waterfront. He makes a grandfatherly appearance in Stead's poem "The Rower", as "a tall man/ /'wellspoken'," who gives his grandson half a crown at Christmas. He concludes his life, according to the poem, with "everything he'd/ ever owned lost or/ spent –".[6]

Jim's mother died of pernicious anaemia, following a long illness, when he was nineteen. A year earlier Jim's farm work had come to a sudden halt after a day hunting rabbits. He injured an arm when his rifle discharged as he climbed through a fence. His cousin Josephine Worsfold, five years old at the time, recalled her father's alarm as a neighbour galloped toward them at high speed to fetch help. While searching for a missing cow, he had come upon the eighteen-year-old collapsed and close to death.

Jim was hauled on a horse-drawn sled to the farmhouse. A local doctor travelled twenty miles by train from the township of Maungaturoto to Kaiwaka and rode the remaining three miles to the farm on horseback. The patient was eventually sent on a five-hour train journey to Auckland in the guard's van and transported to Auckland Hospital, where he almost died of pneumonia. Since he was too ill for the arm to be amputated, he subsequently kept it, but the right hand was paralysed. In *The Singing Whakapapa*, James Grady endures a similar accident. Like the fictional character, the right-handed Jim Stead learnt to use his left hand for all precise manoeuvres such as tying shoelaces.

Jim Stead aspired to a parliamentary career. He tried unsuccessfully to become a Labour Party candidate, a failure that may have followed from lack of skill or training in public speaking. Nevertheless his political roles, as secretary and later chairman of the Auckland Labour Party, were valued highly. He was also secretary of two trade unions. At home, he and his friends punctuated political debates by thumping fists on the kitchen table of an evening. A photograph of Labour's Michael Joseph Savage, Micky Savage, whom Karlson Stead as a small child confused with Mickey Mouse, hung on the kitchen wall beside his high chair.

At the age of seven Karlson asked to join the Labour Party. Though his parents laughed, they took the request seriously. His father paid the subscription and the boy received a badge and membership card. His youthful contribution to electioneering was to remove National Party leaflets from letterboxes and replace them with Labour Party leaflets. He acquired from his father's involvement in the Labour cause a "commitment to the traditional socialist ideals of the welfare state, the general good. The profit motive not figuring as something that's very important."[7]

> My father was political
> a revolutionary of sorts
> a forty-a-day man
> with a gunshot arm
> and paralysed hand.[8]

In the depths of the Great Depression, the Stead family would have suffered less hardship than most as Jim Stead retained his job as a

Post Office accountant and Olive Stead continued teaching piano. In addition, the Mt Eden property supported a fine vegetable garden and an orchard of fruit trees. Hens produced a regular supply of eggs as well as chicken for the table.

"The Eden we are all cast out from"[9]

The fowls were also valuable as a source of entertainment for the young boy, who observed them closely. In the long lyrical poem "SCORIA", which recreates childhood experiences, he discovers a relationship between cock and hen. The cock is "the black knight strutting and shining"; his conquest of the hen is swiftly made, resulting in her "shuddering/ a moment only/ ruffling" before she returns to "picking and scratching".[10]

It was Karlson's boyhood task to ensure that the fowls were given fresh water each day. This responsibility features in his novel *The Secret History of Modernism*. In a dream the authorial narrator is relieved to discover that the hens have not been neglected. After making his descent to the deepest level of the garden, he finds everything as it should be: "the birds have survived and are well."[11] For this character, the dream, when it recurs, usually marks the onset of a new book:

> ... there is pleasure (the lower garden is a hidden, orderly, green and fertile place, even beautiful, with rich volcanic soil and a dark loamy smell); but there is also an inexplicable sadness, only ever to be assuaged by words on a page.[12]

The dream of a return to the childhood garden is comparable to a dream Stead himself has known, signalling on several occasions, though not inevitably, the inception of a new novel. The "inexplicable sadness" is for the loss of child-like wonder, in keeping with T. S. Eliot's understanding:

> And the end of all our exploring
> Will be to arrive where we started
> And know the place for the first time.
> Through the unknown, remembered gate[13]

Re-entry through the "unknown, remembered gate" allows a naïve view to be recaptured. Stead's mature reflection is that "the Eden we are all cast out from is that of the world fresh to our awakening senses. For me one of the most important functions of poetry was to take us back there."[14]

"SCORIA" remakes Stead's first Eden. Memory transports him into the walled property with its many levels and "impossible gate" that was firmly "shut".[15] To the child, the place is at once a prison and a paradise. Each item is named and brought into being: "there was beyond the lemon/ asparagus/ beyond asparagus/ beans."[16] The rock wall is bound by "hairy arms", the lilac has "wrists" and the scoria is "bearded".[17] This is poetry that "invites the reader's imagination to work like a child's".[18] Tactile and visual exploration comes naturally to the small boy:

> Dry
> its pores edged
> sharp to the touch
> bearded often
>   with a white lichen
> hard on palms
>   on bare knees
> but a warm refuge
>   my friend the rock
> SCORIA[19]

"SCORIA" progresses from the confines of the garden to the encompassing view from Mangawhau/Mt Eden across isthmus and harbours and westward to the Waitakere Ranges. While gathering berries on volcanic hillsides, the boy observed "dripping cave mouths" and imagined resounding voices, "saying/ We are your neighbourhood gods/ Vulcan/ Matuahou."[20]

In contrast with the garden and nearby hills, the interior of the house was dark and oppressive. His childhood, Stead claims, was characterised by "two more or less continuous states of feeling ... intellectual boredom (which lasted until I went to secondary school) and aesthetic distaste".[21] He was aware of distaste long before he encountered homes he found attractive. The aversion sprang from a particular atmosphere, "a dead man's gloom alive/ his 'Sang aus dem Exil'/ in the redwood panels".[22] The house was indeed a mausoleum, a monument to the grandfather, retaining his presence in photographs recalling his career, on walls that he had lined with dark timber. The high expectations of Stead's mother and grandmother would have been very clear to a boy named after the exceptional Christian Karlson.

Pianist or Poet

"SCORIA" offers a joyless indoor image of piano practice, as the young Karlson looks through windows at the green world out of doors: "Clean hands on cold keys/ cold feet on clean linoleum".[23] During Stead's boyhood, music filled the house and garden. "Czerny ... Mozart ... Liszt" mingled with the elements – air (fragrant with daphne and lilac), earth with its "tamed foundation stones", and water that "ran warm from the tap".[24] It is scarcely surprising that, as Stead explained to interviewer Margo White, a writing career was not his first choice: "You know, my great ambition as a child was to be a concert pianist." His mother, acknowledged as an excellent musician, "was talented, musically and intellectually", but "didn't have any outlet."[25] Lodged in the mind of her son at an early age was the idea that he should perform before audiences – surely a reflection of the mother's ambition. It did not follow from the achievement of a boy whose coordination let him down.

> '*Third* finger! *Third* finger!'
> That was the voice
> from two rooms away.
> I'd used second finger
> or fourth.
>
> That's how it was
> having your teacher in the house
> while you practised.
>
> Not that the note was wrong,
> just the finger.
> How could she tell?
>
> I was her worst pupil,
> her biggest disappointment –
> perfect pitch
> and some failure of hand and eye.

Never mind, Mum,
you trained my ears.
They're listening still.[26]

Stead's music tuition honed his alertness to the mood of each key and to the way sound, rhythm and pace can reflect feeling. At the same time, his failure as a pianist frustrated him, distressed his mother and caused tension. At the age of seventy-two, Stead in conversation remarked that his limitations should have been clear to his mother much sooner. He spoke of his regret at not having learnt a different instrument. Because the goal was excellence as a soloist, no thought was given to the pleasure he might have gained as a member of an orchestra. His lifelong sensitivity to music has taken the form of passion for work by composers such as Richard Strauss and Richard Wagner, and it found expression in his ability to sing.

Stead remembers singing with Grandmother Karlson from the time he was very young, without inhibition, for the joy of it. Grandmother Christianson in *The Singing Whakapapa* also has a superb singing voice. The youthful hero of this novel, Hugh Grady, laments that no one ever imagined his voice should be trained, "that he must not stop singing, must go on, learn more, study, travel, win fame, sing at La Scala, Covent Garden, the Met. No one did."[27] While Stead's singing voice was likewise taken for granted and untrained, talent of a different kind was fostered unwittingly. His grandmother sang ballads, folk songs, arias from opera, theme songs from films, traditional lyrics and whatever was currently popular. Learning the words of songs, and combining language and melody from an early age offered the very finest of preparation for a future poet.

A poem in *The Black River* suggests that sensitivity toward words being sung began before birth. In "The Art of Poetry (ii)", Stead is surely speaking personally in referring to the "secret ways" of words:

Even under
a blue-eyed day
they can be the dark
living of the leaves –

as they were once
when you first

heard them in the womb
singing.[28]

Norma, like their father, could not sing in tune; she was "*Daddy's Girl*".[29] Olive's ambitions were focused on her son, who had promised such musical talent as a small child. She concluded eventually that Karlson was not especially bright. Although Norma took Latin at secondary school, Stead reports, "it was thought that Latin would be too difficult for me."[30]

Stead was, nevertheless, closer to his mother than his father in temperament. The poem "Speaking Plain" finds his father, a man then in his sixties, at work in the garden.

He has his back to me.
Something's unresolved
between us.[31]

What is unresolved is not disclosed, but conflict between father and son is hinted at in a letter from Stead to Sargeson, which speaks of his father's "inability to admit gracefully when he has been proved wrong". Stead's debating skills may have been honed through exchanges with his father, who is also characterised as a sentimentalist "under the rough exterior – but likeable in many ways too".[32] Elsewhere there is recollection of the "handsome father" who, Stead recalls in a poem, "winked at me from the school steps at prize-giving".[33] One prize Stead secured at Mount Albert Grammar was the school's chess trophy. At secondary school he showed brilliance in subjects that interested him, especially chemistry and English.

Olive Stead's potential as a concert pianist was not realised and Jim Stead's political ambitions were not fulfilled. Despite the disappointments of his parents, and despite years of failing to master the piano, Stead became certain that he could accomplish whatever he set out to do. To him, his self-confidence seemed innate: "There must have been belief in myself, yet when I look back on it I don't know where it came from."[34] He believed that he needed only to redirect his abilities toward achievement in a field of endeavour of his own choice.

A mother's love
Is what a son learns guilt and selfhood rejecting.

When we sat at the piano I wanted to get it right
But stole your music instead and took a path

Where you couldn't follow, couldn't judge me a failure.[35]

On his thirty-fifth birthday, he could refer to a talent that was publicly recognised.

Mother, you expelled me with
A silver tongue
A country in my cry
A trenching tool
To seed fresh furrows.
Long, long I've crouched
In the kitchens of art
Over the hot stove of letters.
Hear me now.
Before the fingers are bone
Hear me.[36]

The discovery of Rupert Brooke's collected works first led Stead to write his own poetry in Form Three.

> My initiation as a poet came a year or two after the end of the war. New Zealanders sent food parcels to Britain and my sister corresponded with the daughter of a family in Rugby to whom our food parcels had been sent. This girl sent my sister a copy of the Collected Poems of one of Rugby School's most celebrated old boys – Rupert Brooke. My sister didn't read the poems but I did, and I began at once to write Brookish imitations. The effect was immediate, compulsive, and long-lasting. My long boredom was over, and you might say I've never looked back.[37]

In class, Keats's "Ode to a Nightingale" was as much of a revelation to him as it was to Bill Harper, the authorial narrator of *Sister*

Hollywood. In that novel, the schoolboy continues reading the poem after class, when he should have been on his way to soccer practice.

> I wasn't hanging back for lack of keenness on soccer. It was more serious than that. I had entered another world. It was the fifth stanza that took me away – the one in which the poet, following the sound of the nightingale, enters a garden he can't see in darkness. Because he can't see, he invents the garden as he goes.
>
> (...)
>
> The poet stops imagining the garden. He simply listens to the nightingale until he's all ears – nothing but hearing. Gradually he's extinguished by the song.
>
> Still wouldst thou sing, and I have ears in vain –
> To thy high requiem become a sod.
>
> What on earth did that mean? I didn't know – I didn't need to know. It meant exactly what it said. It was a kind of magic I hadn't encountered before, and would probably never feel so keenly again.[38]

Stead's reaction to hearing "The Waste Land" read aloud by his English teacher was just as intense. The lines beginning "The river's tent is broken" and concluding "The nymphs are departed" led him to wonder, "'What is this?' It made my scalp tingle."[39]

As a young writer of both poetry and stories, Stead applied dedication and focus. "I was purposeful ... the energy came out of passionate interest, first of all having discovered works of literature at school and second having discovered the wish to write things of that kind."[40] His father subscribed to the *New Statesman*, which includes book reviews and poems. These the son read with interest: "It gave me my first sense of an ongoing literary world in London that I wouldn't otherwise have known about until I met Frank Sargeson."[41] At school, the traditional class texts and library books made an impact but John Mulgan's novel *Man Alone* provided a significant local example. "I began writing at the age of thirteen under the influence of English writers – first Rupert Brooke and John Buchan, then Keats and Wordsworth, Dickens and Sir Walter Scott. Soon I was discovering New Zealand poets and fiction writers who were mapping our country in literature."[42]

In his focused approach to writing, Stead used the Zen discipline that he had already applied to the sport of high-jumping at which he excelled, winning the Mount Albert Grammar championship at sixteen, and becoming a member of the senior athletic team. The high-jumper, suspended in flight and at one with the action of jumping, seemed to offer an image of the Zen-self. Stead discovered his own Zen technique, preparing himself by lying on the ground in the right position and imagining a successful jump. The Zen quest for perfection appealed to Stead. "Writing is the Zen which replaced high-jumping. The principles are the same, but one has so much more time ... to learn them, and to bring oneself nearer to getting them right."[43]

The Kaiwaka Farm

Asked bluntly by journalist Kamala Jackson whether his childhood was happy, Stead's answer was evasive. Claiming to have "an affirmative temperament" and to be "an optimist" he said that "a happy or an unhappy childhood doesn't have so much to do with what happened to you so much as your temperament. If I wanted to be autobiographical, and tell the truth, it would be possible to present some aspects of my childhood as unhappy, but in fact I *feel* as though I was relatively happy as a child, but I was extremely bored."[44] The final words redirected the discussion away from happiness.

Boredom during his primary school years was relieved by mentally revisiting his favourite holiday place, the Kaiwaka farm a hundred kilometres north of Auckland, where the farmer's wife was Jim Stead's cousin, Josephine Worsfold. Her husband, Hamlyn Worsfold, had special regard for Jim, and took an interest in his young son Karlson. The farm was run by Josephine and her sisters while Hamlyn was overseas with the armed forces. Karlson became one of their helpers during holidays in those years. To the joy and relief of everyone, Hamlyn survived. Respected by family and friends for his even temper and natural wisdom, he had previously studied medicine at Otago University, until the Depression years forced him to leave before graduating. He told his young relative of opportunities that followed from a university education. With his encouragement, the city boy developed skills and independence, burning off patches of scrub, helping with milking, fishing for eels, hunting rabbits, riding horses and searching for fossil gum that could be sold later in Auckland. Each summer he returned to Kaiwaka with fresh enthusiasm. The farm offered wide horizons, undulating hills, bush, orchard, crops and pasture.

Stead's earliest memory, as a two-year-old, is of watching and listening from the knee of his mother, who was seated on a three-legged stool in the farm's milking shed.[45] From the age of eight he made the train journey to Kaiwaka alone to be met at the station by cousins, who found his smart corduroy shorts amusing.

Represented as the Beaumont farm, later the Mangold farm, in *The Singing Whakapapa*, it was the source of life-informing experiences for Stead. One involved a swarm of bees.

> No one would ever guess
> You rode once hell-for-leather
> Bareback
> Bees in your hair.[46]

Ten-year-old Karlson rode Bos'n to the farm gate to collect a package of meat. As he leant toward the box used for deliveries, he was attacked by bees that had swarmed there. In the very manner described in *The Singing Whakapapa*, he and the terrified horse raced back to the farmhouse, "behind them a widening plume of bees".[47] Not mentioned in the novel is the fact that the stings were treated with blue-bags only, a home remedy of doubtful benefit. The muslin bags, each the size of an eggcup, contained a block of alkaline powder. In those days, one or two would be routinely added to laundry water to whiten linen. To treat bee-stings, they were partly dissolved and placed on the swelling. "Next day, and for days afterwards, the stings ached and burned and itched, and [the boy's] eyes looked out of holes small as nostrils in a moon of a face." Not only for Hugo (or Hugh) from *The Singing Whakapapa*, but for Stead himself, the event assumes the significance of a myth that has continuing relevance:

> Life since had seen repetitions of that moment – the blind reaching for something, the fury of the response, the wildness of the ride, the tranquillity of the dam and the vastness and indifference of the sky.[48]

On the farm, Stead developed a sense of closeness to the earth, the weather, the crops, trees and streams through the bush. When the cows move toward their bails for milking in *The Singing Whakapapa*, his character Hugo enjoys "the herd smell, the piss-and-shit smell, the smell and taste and feel of milk squirted hot from the teat. He liked the bristle feel of the cows' bony backs as he slapped them into their bails, the softness and roundness of their noses, the dreaminess of their eyes." Sounds made by the pigs are recalled: "their deepest oink-notes, like a double-bass in an echo chamber, were incomparable and thrilling."[49] Incorporating this harvest of sensations into his writing decades later needed no new visit to the childhood farm to refresh impressions that were secure in his memory.

Stead's poetry and novels show his appreciation of animals. According to Josephine Worsfold, the Kaiwaka relatives remember how good he was with dogs and horses, managing Bos'n, a tricky horse, particularly well. Karlson and his cousins rode bareback, and in later years they all recalled having fallen off the same horse. Remounting called for ingenuity, with Stead writing, "I used the ruts worn deep/ by the cream sledge – stood him in the hollow/ and leapt from its edge."[50] Josephine also remembered that the lad regularly freed the farm dogs because he didn't like to see them chained up.

"Dogs 2 (Calvus replies)" conveys a sense of affinity between humans and dogs.

> it has to do with childhood
> the feel of fur
> smell of it wet
>
> [...]
>
> No I don't think they're human
> or that I'm a dog
> but isn't there a kind
> of planetary kinship --
> all of us in the same lovely boat
> under the same harsh sentence?[51]

The natural world provided a store of images, like the clear pool at the foot of a waterfall, where the boy marvelled at "small brown fish" suspended "in shafts of light".[52] Fernstars at the water's edge shone in the darkness, to the astonishment of the observer. He chose to know the stone-rimmed pool at night by standing in it, feeling its chill, registering its sound and noticing the paradoxes of "audible" silence and cold "burning" fernstars. Experiences of this kind retained their impact, whenever they were called to mind. In his poetry Stead names these discovery events "first things/ as fernstars for example".[53]

knee-deep in stone
          cold
audible–silent
          rush
and deaf
and blind
        but for
fernstars'
          white
burning.[54]

The same pool in native bush on the Kaiwaka farm appears in *The End of the Century at the End of the World*, where it is "one of the holy places"[55] for character Maurice Scobie. Stead became aware of fundamental truths of birth, life and death at Kaiwaka. Five decades later, he links the concept of death to the farm's quietude and stillness, a quality he had always marvelled at:

        and death will come
in the guise of just this stillness
or another

        but that was always the case.[56]

The Singing Whakapapa conjures up a boy named Hugo at primary school and Hugh at secondary school. There are parallels between this boy and Karlson, who, at the same stage, shortened his name to Karl. Actual events and exchanges of dialogue have found their way into the novel. Stead has admitted that the three sisters who ran the farm during the war have been transformed – but not much.[57] Aged eighty-nine, Josephine Worsfold recalled her indignation when she learnt that her sister, on meeting Stead after an interval of fifty years, really did exclaim, "God, I've had to wait *all these years* to tell you what *a little bugger of a kid* you were." These are the very words spoken by Greta in the novel.[58]

The furious swarm of bees was part of Stead's rich experience on the Northland farm. In his career, he would encounter fury from readers, critics and other writers, without losing his equilibrium, his self-confidence, or his impulse to write.

1 C.K. Stead, "Speaking Plain", *The Red Tram*, Auckland University Press, 2004, p. 19.

2 Kamala Jackson, "C. K. Stead: Poet, Novelist, Academic, Activist and Aucklander on his Origins", *Metro*, February 1985, p. 124.

3 C. K. Stead, *The Singing Whakapapa*, Auckland, Penguin Books, 1994, p. 266.

4 ibid, p. 267.

5 Stead's poem "The Rower", published in 2007, see footnote 6, indicates that Grandfather Stead rowed for Oxford, though family members I questioned were uncertain as to whether it was Oxford or Cambridge – or both. My own investigation failed to locate the pewter mug that would have settled the matter. Despite the wording of the poem, which implies that Grandfather Stead was the rower, the Oxford/Cambridge rower was Stead's great-grandfather, Walter Collins Stead.
The following family tree locates the members referred to in this chapter.

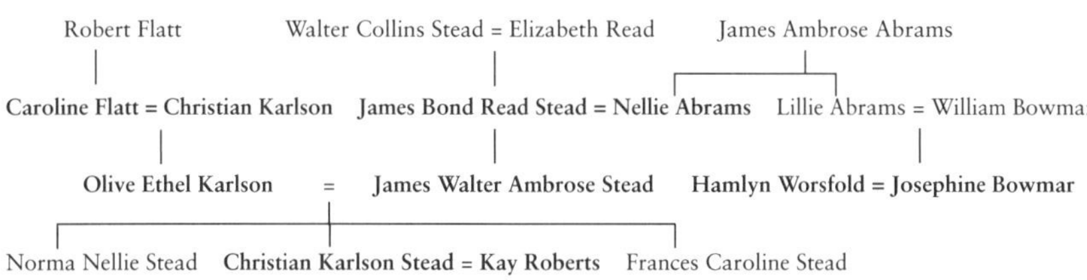

6 C. K. Stead, "The Rower", *The Black River*, Auckland University Press, 2007, p. 20.

7 Jackson, *Metro*, February 1985, p. 124.

8 Stead, "Africa: An Autobiography", *The Red Tram*, p. 39.

9 C. K. Stead, *Kin of Place: Essays on 20 New Zealand Writers*, Auckland University Press, 2002, p. 308.

10 C. K. Stead, "SCORIA", *Geographies*, Auckland University Press/Oxford University Press, 1982, p. 12.

11 C. K. Stead, *The Secret History of Modernism*, London, Vintage, 2001, p. 68.

12 ibid, p. 68.

13 T. S. Eliot, "Little Gidding V", *Four Quartets*, London, Faber and Faber, 1951, p. 43.

14 Stead, *Kin of Place*, p. 308.

15 Stead, "SCORIA", *Geographies*, p. 11.

16 ibid, p. 9.

17 ibid, pp. 10 and 11.

18 Stead, *Kin of Place*, p. 204.

19 Stead, "SCORIA", *Geographies*, p. 10.

20 ibid, p. 11. At Maungawhau Primary School, Stead and his classmates were introduced to Maori myths and legends. At secondary school he encountered Greek and Roman myths and legends.

21 C. K. Stead, *The Writer at Work: Essays*, Dunedin, University of Otago Press, 2000, p. 214.

22 Stead, "SCORIA", *Geographies*, p. 21.
23 ibid, p. 21.
24 ibid, p. 14.
25 Margo White, "Mr Congeniality", *Metro*, August 2005, p. 60.
26 Stead, "Speaking Plain", *The Red Tram*, p. 20.
27 Stead, *The Singing Whakapapa*, p.76.
28 Stead, "The Art of Poetry (ii)", *The Black River*, p. 30.
29 Stead, "My Sister and M.S.", *The Black River*, p. 60.
30 Stead, *The Writer at Work*, p. 233.
31 Stead, "Speaking Plain", *The Red Tram*, p. 21.
32 C. K. Stead, letter to Frank Sargeson, 3 June 1958, Turnbull Library Papers.
33 C. K. Stead, *Poems of a Decade*, Dunedin, Pilgrim South Press, 1983, p. 36.
34 Stead, *The Writer at Work*, p. 232.
35 C. K. Stead, "Sonnet 17", *Walking Westward*, Auckland, The Shed, 1979, p. 26.
36 C. K. Stead, "Birthday Poem", *Crossing the Bar*, Auckland, Auckland University Press/Oxford University Press, p. 35.
37 C. K. Stead, *In the Glass Case: Essays on New Zealand Literature*, Auckland, Auckland University Press/Oxford University Press, 1981, p. 261.
38 C. K. Stead, *Sister Hollywood*, London, Collins, 1989, pp. 28-29.
39 Stead, "With Fleur Adcock, 1991", *The Writer at Work*, Dunedin, University of Otago Press, 2000, p. 259.
40 Stead, "With Dennis McEldowney", *The Writer at Work*, p. 233.
41 ibid, pp. 234-5.
42 Stead, "The View from Mt Eden", *The Writer at Work*, p. 198.
43 C. K. Stead, "Picture Perfect", *North and South*, October 1998, p. 80.
44 Jackson, *Metro*, February 1985, p. 124.
45 ibid.
46 C. K. Stead, "Bald Caesarian", *Crossing the Bar*, Auckland University Press/Oxford University Press, 1972, p.43. This eight-line poem reappears, with a change to the spelling of the title, in C. K. Stead, "Bald Caesarion", *Dog*, Auckland, Auckland University Press, 2002, pp. 47-48. The poem, extended to 33 lines, retells the story of the bees' attack and its aftermath.

> You had trailed a plume of demons over the land.
> Pride with an indignity was joined
> and bald Caesarion, lacking Caesar's glory,
> would gather to himself
> a mythic story.

The same event is retold in Stead, "Sonnet 15 (for Sam Hunt)", *Walking Westward*, p. 25, which concludes with the lines,

> I galloped hell for leather, bees in my hair,
> Trailing across that sky a dark and angry plume.

The parallel between Stead's own boyhood experiences at Kaiwaka and those of Hugo Grady was confirmed by C. K. Stead in an interview with the author, 28 August 2005.

47 Stead, *The Singing Whakapapa*, p. 16.
48 ibid, p. 16.
49 ibid, p. 26.
50 C. K. Stead, "After the Wedding", *Straw into Gold*, Auckland, Auckland University Press, 1997, p. 102.
51 Stead, "Dogs 2 (Calvus replies)", *Straw into Gold*, p. 154.
52 Stead, "After the Wedding", *Straw into Gold*, p. 102.
53 Stead, "Walking Westward", *Walking Westward*, p. 49.
54 ibid, pp. 37-38.
55 C. K. Stead, *The End of the Century at the End of the World*, Auckland, HarperCollins, 1992, p. 141.
56 Stead, "After the Wedding", *Straw into Gold*, p. 105.
57 C. K. Stead, interview with author, 28 August 2005.
58 Josephine Worsfold, interview with author, 2 February 2006. Greta's words appear in Stead's *The Singing Whakapapa*, p. 25.

CHAPTER TWO

Marriage, Tragedy, Satire

Takapuna

In January 1955, two months after his twenty-second birthday, Stead married twenty-one-year-old Kay Roberts. He then embarked on a masters programme. Until his marriage he had lived at home, as expected of university students whose families lived in town. The flat to which the young couple moved was part of an old house on Takapuna Beach. Its enclosed verandah, a long narrow living/dining/workroom with a kitchen beyond a partition, became their "glassed-in shell":

> Our glassed-in shell is busy trapping sun.
> My work is done: matting covers the boards,
> Books and our pottery dishes upright in
> Their standing frames of smooth-grained furniture.
> Cushions have captured cocks of strutting red –
> A low divan suggests you sprawl among them:
> Composite image of bright concupiscence![1]

Steps from the beach to the former front lawn remain today but the house has been demolished. The area is now a public reserve with views of the sea-lane and vessels sailing south to the port of Auckland or north to the wider world.

Bus and ferry transported the Steads to and from the foot of Queen Street, within walking distance of the University of Auckland, where Kay worked in the university library and Stead attended classes while receiving a post-primary teachers' bursary. He completed a Master's degree in English with first class honours in one year. As an undergraduate he had majored in English, studied French and history to stage two and passed units in geography and philosophy. A fourth year was devoted to teacher training. In university holidays, compulsory military training was completed and various holiday jobs were undertaken in wool stores, freezing works, post office, a food warehouse, a machine factory and in a hospital as an orderly, a job that included a few days in the morgue. Some of this experience has found its way into novels and stories.

Death, Poetry and Fiction

Stead was eighteen, his first year at university underway, when his good friend Ian Lamont was killed. It was 1951. After attending primary school together, the two became friends at secondary school. Lamont, who left a year earlier than Stead to become a mechanic, bought a powerful Norton motorbike. One Friday night, he cruised round the local shopping area in search of his friend, but he did not see Stead's wave and accelerated away. The following morning a phone call informed the Stead family that Ian Lamont had run into the back of a parked truck in a dark street and been killed.

The Mt Eden home, the roads along which the youths sped on the Norton, their holiday jobs, the situation that led to the death of one of them – these facts are included in the story, "A New Zealand Elegy", but Stead has placed them in a new context. An imaginary scandal involves a woman living next-door, tartly named "maid Marion"[2] by the narrator's mother. The two lads are intrigued by a drama that begins to unfold in the well-lit lounge over the fence. The story explores, with some insight, the desires and imaginings of young fellows keen to have their way with girls. The enthusiasm for experience, the relish for speed, and enjoyment of wrestling, camping, fishing, swimming is abruptly lost for one, while the other is left to deal with grief.

The trauma of Ian Lamont's death has stayed with Stead a lifetime. "A New Zealand Elegy" was not written until 1979. The experience enters "The Clodian Songbook/15", published 1982, addressed to "Ianus ... the one who took the last blow first".

> I wish you manuka on the eternal winds.
> 'So long' we used to say, not knowing what it meant.[3]

Talking About O'Dwyer, published in 1999, conveys the same sense of loss. The central character Mike Newall endures consequences that follow from the death of his boyhood friend Frano Panapa. There, too, a young man buys a Norton motorcycle and rides it fast. Late one night he is killed after crashing into a wall. The shock suffered by Mike, his solitary walking and reflecting, and his reaction to viewing the body, draw on the author's 1951 experience.

At the time, Stead came to terms with the tragedy through writing poetry. His earliest surviving poem was written in response to the death of Ian Lamont:

> I wrote a sequence of poems about him called 'Fragments of a Saturday Night', which I sent to Charles Brasch. He turned it down with some kind comments about its 'freshness', and it was later destroyed along with a lot of other stuff when I had one of those big necessary burn-ups that young writers have. But I can still remember the last poem in the sequence, which went as follows:
>
> Earth you are frozen now
> The dead-cold centre of a doom-darkened winter
> Yet from this spiny row
> Of waxen, wasted willow-sticks will grow
> New life in spring.
> The sun will be warmer then
> And velvet leaves will spin
> A net of new-born comforts round old signs.
> Persistent sapling shoots in lines
> Of contradicting green
> Will not admit
> That dead-brown death has ever been.[4]

The University of Auckland

Early in 1951, Stead had felt anticipation and excitement on arriving at the University of Auckland.

> In the library of the old arts building there was a room – not a large room – which housed English literature. English literature seemed of manageable proportions. But more important, there was in that room a small case for which the key could be obtained from the lending desk, which contained the work of New Zealand poets. ...
>
> And finally, as if the existence of the books wasn't itself

> sufficient, some of the poets could be seen walking about. Allen Curnow had just given up his job on the Christchurch *Press* and come to lecture in Auckland. An absurdly youthful-looking and very emphatic Robert Chapman, who wrote verses in those days, was my Stage I tutor in History. Keith Sinclair, whose poem 'Strangers or Beasts' I used to quote to girls at parties with varying effect, was a lecturer. M. K. Joseph in the English Department was just beginning to be known as a poet. Rex Fairburn had transferred from a tutorship in English to a lectureship in the History of Fine Art, and he, like Frank Sargeson, put in occasional appearances at Somervell's Coffee Bar. R. A. K. Mason was a remoter figure. And later there were others – notably Kendrick Smithyman and Maurice Duggan.
>
> ... I'm trying to communicate the particularity and vividness with which both – the books and the writers – materialised for me in 1951. I studied the books in that glass case more intensively than anything set down in the courses I enrolled for.[5]

Poetry became a significant part of university life from Stead's first day there, when a student approached him saying, "I write poetry. You look as though you do, too." This story, related by Stead years later, seemed so unlikely that he added, "I don't know whether I've invented that, but I do remember it as though it really happened. His name is Rob Dyer and he was a very brilliant young man who had come first of all from Whangarei and then King's College and had a scholarship."[6] He and Stead formed a poetry group that met and shared poems, reading them aloud. The university's annual literary magazine, *Kiwi*, was edited by Stead and Dyer in 1954 and published in 1955.

Rob Dyer and Stead were friends during and beyond university years. Stead's "Letter (to R.R.D.)", is addressed to him from the Takapuna flat in 1955:

> And you have chosen Greece, alone,
> While I, a husband grateful where
> Your blessings on us both have shone,
> Watch from this shell the breeding storm.[7]

From Rob Dyer, son of Major, later Lt Colonel Humphrey Dyer, Stead learnt of the military man's wartime exploits, some of which he later incorporates into *Talking About O'Dwyer.* Stead has also acknowledged that the character of Tusker in "A Quality of Life" owes its starting point to the person of Rob Dyer.[8]

The most significant setting for "A Quality of Life" is a home Stead knew well, with rugs on timber floors, fine paintings and substantial furniture. It belonged to the parents of a fellow student and friend, Diane Henderson. He formed an enduring friendship with her mother, artist Louise Henderson, a Frenchwoman, and her father Hubert, Director of Education for the Auckland region. Both were liberal, and sensitive toward young people. In "A Quality of Life" it is the father who is French and an artist. The home in the story is hospitable and aesthetically pleasing, reflecting the atmosphere of the Henderson home. Stead writes:

> It was a high bourgeois household of a kind one read about in European literature but didn't expect to meet in New Zealand. When I declared myself Left of Labour, Hubert asked had I read the Communist Manifesto. I hadn't. He took a copy from his shelves and gave it to me – this at the height of the Cold War and McCarthyism – not to convert me, but because he thought it better I should know what I was talking about.[9]

Stead's reading as a student included the work of the most significant poets of the day, Eliot, Pound, Yeats, Auden, Spender, Day-Lewis, MacNeice, and the modern American poets. At the same time he was reading Baxter, Fairburn and particularly the work of Allen Curnow.

> In the last years at secondary school I had discovered his poetry and his Caxton anthology and so I already greatly admired him. I'd seen his photograph in the *Listener* and I very clearly remember, before the university year started, before I'd ever heard him lecture, seeing him walking up through Albert Park and getting a tremendous feeling of excitement that there he was in reality.[10]

Stead first saw Curnow in enrolment week, March 1951, and he spoke at the launch of Curnow's final book of poetry in March 2001, the year of his death. Curnow became Stead's stage two tutor in 1952, and a mentor and friend from 1955. Stead recounts his reaction to being asked by Curnow to comment on some of his poems.

> In fact, from 1955, when I was a MA student, I must've seen 80 percent at least of his poetry. I remember very clearly he came into the old student caff, with the typescript of a new poem, and he said, 'Would you like to read this?' I was absolutely astonished, and honoured. I thought, 'It's not good enough just to say things. I've got to write them down.' And really that went on over the years.[11]

Curnow also commented on some of Stead's poetry from that time on. It was a fortunate liaison that encouraged, challenged and advantaged them both.

A significant number of Stead's poems were published while he was still a student, the first appearing in the Australian *Jindyworobak Anthology* in 1952. In the same year, four poems appeared in the Auckland University Literary Club's journal, *Kiwi*, and the following year, three poems were published in the *Literary Supplement* of *Craccum* and two in the *New Zealand Poetry Yearbook*. This achievement was surpassed in 1954, when the *Yearbook* published three poems, the *New Zealand Listener* published one, and *Landfall* published three. "Of course I wanted to be published in *Landfall*. Monte Holcroft's *Listener*, and Lou Johnson's *Poetry Yearbook* were important starting places." Stead has observed that "a young New Zealand poet of the Fifties whose work was smiled upon by Charles Brasch could consider himself launched."[12] In those days, Brasch, *Landfall*'s editor, was a leader among arbiters of literary taste. Stead was able to "consider himself launched" at the age of twenty-one.

During student years in Auckland, Stead's activities included a role in an Oscar Wilde play and parts in three student revues, one of which was "The Plotters", a parody of Shakespeare's *Julius Caesar*, performed in 1954. He also played soccer. While on the field, Stead applied a particular strategy for testing the strength of a poem.

> I used to put my latest poem to the test by dismissing it from my thoughts and then suddenly surprising myself with the recollection of it in the middle of a soccer field during a game

> (I played centre-forward for University). If it didn't seem at that instant to fade into 'literariness', it might be worth working at.[13]

Enter Sargeson

As a committee member of the university's Literary Club, Stead suggested inviting Frank Sargeson to speak to the group. A shy Sargeson agreed. Later he wrote to Stead, praising his *Landfall* poems and inviting him to visit some day. Stead took up the invitation early in 1955, after he and Kay had moved to the North Shore. Throughout their stay in Takapuna, where they lived for just over a year, the couple visited Sargeson at least once a week. He called on them frequently, bringing fruit and vegetables from his garden.

Stead received encouragement from Sargeson, who made a point of reading and commenting on each newly published poem.

> I had come under Sargeson's influence while still a student. He was a mentor, a teacher, different from, but as important as those at the university. It has been said often enough: in the constricting provincial suburban society that was New Zealand in the 1950s, Sargeson opened a magical space for younger writers. He created an environment in which literature was not only studied as a thing of the past but became a way of life, a total commitment. As well as seeming at the very centre of the NZ literary web, he had lines out to a wider world –[14]

To Sargeson, it seemed inevitable that commitments to family and the workplace would undermine a person's capacity to find fulfillment as a writer. "Frank always had that view that the whole life of the artist should be devoted to his art, or her art, and that marriage was counter-productive and so was academic life. ... In general his attitude was that writers were better not to marry."[15] Sargeson's opinion was coloured by the fact that he was gay. However, once he got to know Kay, he admired her, lent her books he thought she should read and then discussed them with her. At a time when Stead's reading was governed by the requirements of his university study, Kay was enjoying a reading programme devised by Frank Sargeson.

That very year, Janet Frame was living in an army hut on Sargeson's property. The Steads, Janet Frame and Frank Sargeson discussed literature, read poetry and listened to music together. Stead describes the relationship that developed among the four of them.

> We talked about books and writers, and about ourselves. There were reminiscences, verbal games, jokes, gossip. We swam together and went for walks. Once the four of us went to a literary party together. We'd been there I suppose ten minutes when Sargeson noticed that Janet was missing. She hadn't been able to cope with so many people, and had run home.
>
> On another occasion we took the bus along the eastern bays of the Hauraki Gulf to swim at a beach overlooked by a headland in which there were gun emplacements. Frank wreathed himself in seaweed, used a stick as a pipe, and did a Pan-dance in the shallows, lifting his knees high like a figure on an ancient urn or bas relief. Suddenly the guns boomed over our heads. The army was doing a practice shoot out to sea – blanks no doubt, but the sound was huge. Frank dropped his pipe; Janet shrieked, panicked ... rushed from the water and had to be soothed and reassured.[16]

Janet Frame has written that she greatly valued her friendship with the young couple. In *An Angel At My Table*, she describes Kay and Karl. "Both were in the golden glow of youth and love and Karl was writing poetry and stories, and both became drawn with Frank into my web of worship. ... The friendship of Karl and Kay filled my life ... "[17] Her remarks drew the following response from Stead.

> One is enormously touched by that and by the fact that she remembers so vividly and it was obviously so important to her. But what you maybe don't get so clearly from the autobiography is just how funny everything was when the four of us were together. We're all highly verbal people, Kay and I, Frank and Janet, and in different ways all of us could be quite funny and we would set one another off.
>
> And in addition to that, the sense of the importance of books and the whole thing of a life in literature. Four people with that kind of idea reinforcing one another.[18]

Satire in *All Visitors Ashore*

In a letter to Janet Frame, August 1979, Stead put forward a suggestion.

> I had an idea in the weekend that you and I should write a novel together. I would write the first 20 pages and send it to you and then you would write the next 20 and send it back. I thought I (it would be first person – two characters) would be Curl Skidmore; you would be Cecelia Skyways. Frank would figure as Melior Farbro, or the old master.[19]

Stead explains that "a little later, it took hold of me, took off, took its own course ... . It was written very fast; and then, once completed, was something I couldn't bring myself to re-read. It was consigned to an iron trunk and remained there until some time in 1983 when I met a London publisher, Carol O'Brien, who ... asked whether I had a novel to offer her."[20] When Stead confessed that there was one he couldn't bear to re-read, O'Brien assured him that there was no need; *she* would read it. The result was the book's publication the following year.

All Visitors Ashore was launched in London first, because Stead imagined that New Zealand critics might be less concerned with reading it as a work of fiction than engaging in a game of 'Who's Who?' The novel playfully satirises New Zealand life in 1951 and refers to actual writers by name. It does, indeed, include Cecelia Skyways and Melior Farbro who bear resemblances to Janet Frame and Frank Sargeson. In London the book was praised for its "sheer immediacy", "its intimacy and precision", "the annihilation of distance between writer and reader",[21] but its reception in New Zealand was marred by concerns that bore little relation to its quality. There was fear that Janet Frame might be upset by her link to Cecelia Skyways. It was considered inappropriate to characterise James K. Baxter as too drunk to walk unaided to a podium to read his poetry. The novel has Baxter carried into a reading by Ron Mason and Rex Fairburn. Stead's account "is true except that the people who really carried him were Curnow and Fairburn. But the fact of the raincoat, the galoshes, and the feet not touching the floor, that happened at the Auckland University Hall. I shifted it to a house in the novel."[22] Today, connections and disparities between fact and fiction assume historic significance, while the novel's quality is evidenced by its publication by both Harvill and Collins in

1984, by Picador in 1986, Godwit in 1995, by Nakladni Zavod Matice Hrvatske (Croatia) in 1997, and by Harvill again in 2002.

All Visitors Ashore recreates some aspects of Stead's year in Takapuna. There are similarities between the central character Curl Skidmore and Karl Stead, but the novel provides very little information about Stead's personal life. It does, however, reflect matters of a more public nature that would have engaged Stead in the early fifties. Curl Skidmore confronts difficulties of his own making and difficulties arising from the era in which he lives. The waterside workers' strike of 1951 forms a backdrop against which the novel's events are played out. A number of literary figures were, at that time, known to be in favour of socialism. Sargeson and Ron Mason had, in earlier years, belonged to the Communist Party.[23] Although they drifted away after the Depression, their socialist sympathies endured.

In response to Labour's position, neither for nor against the waterside workers, Stead took a more radical position than his father, who was then secretary of the Auckland Labour Party. While the father was a cautious pragmatist, the son scorned Labour's failure to oppose Government policy and was indignant at regulations that undermined civil liberties. It was, Stead recalls, "a disillusioning time because it taught me ... how shallowly rooted our democracy is and how easily we give it away, because the legislation of that time ... just sold out all normal democratic rights and people accepted it and then re-elected the government which had done this."[24] Curl takes a stance similar to Stead's, challenging his father, a Labour Member of Parliament, and complaining that "the Opposition is sitting on the fence as usual."[25] The irony of the "closure of halls and the proscription of marches and meetings in the name of free speech" (p. 87) contributes to Stead's satire. At a public poetry reading, with Curl Skidmore presenting his "Takapuna Piece", the event is suddenly halted by a police raid. Emergency regulations "limited the freedom of assembly and curtailed the right of any person, whoever he may be, to publish lies and promote disorder". (p. 35) No one is permitted to support striking workers with food or money. The existence of pamphlets at the poetry reading, protesting against these measures, represents an offence. Curl's distribution of the same pamphlet at work brings his employment as a machine moulder to an end.

> And the boss says, 'Are you responsible for these pamphlets?'

> And Curl Skidmore says, 'Yes,' and the boss says, 'Do you know they're illegal?' and Curl Skidmore says, 'Yes,' and the boss says, 'Do you know you're the slowest machine moulder in the factory?' and Curl Skidmore says, 'Yes.' So the boss says, 'Yes. Yes. Yes. Three right answers, and you're fired,' and Curl Skidmore says, 'Thank God.' 'Don't thank Him, thank me,' says the boss. (p. 69)[26]

The 1950s are satirised, not for the purpose of effecting social change, since many features of the 1950s had improved by the 1980s, but because the fifties' pretentiousness and narrow-mindedness invite humorous treatment. The watersiders' strike was grim at the time. In retrospect, its protracted 151-day progress was tragic, but also ridiculous. Stead chooses "the old man in the Vicks advertisement" (p. 25) to report the words of a union official: "If they want us to work eighty hours that's our duty under the law and if we refuse it's a strike. If you keel over that's probably a strike too. I'm not sure what happens if they want us to work more hours than there are in the week." (p. 25) Stead wrests comedy from the unexpectedness of draconian government measures, certainly unexpected to those living in the 1980s or later.

The early 1950s were years in which Victorian attitudes and mores were preserved in something of a time warp. In the novel, Pat Bennett and Curl Skidmore live together in a Takapuna flat. Stead chooses to recreate for this purpose the flat in which he and Kay lived in 1955. The difference is that Pat and Curl are unmarried. Their cohabitation would have been scandalous, at a time when mixed flatting and people living together as partners were virtually unknown. Pat and Curl share accommodation "quite unacceptably and against all odds and in the teeth of family protests". (p. 42) Pat's parents terminate her student allowance.

Curl's mother and father, also disapproving, assume cartoon proportions. Having carefully arranged his sleeping bag on the divan for their visit, Curl tries to convince them that the relationship is innocent. "'We find we can study better together.' And, 'Don't be so old-fashioned.' And, 'Everything isn't what it seems' (it isn't of course – it's worse)." (pp. 42-3) The Momma's failure to acknowledge Pat's existence is replaced by her refusal to accept Pat's name. "But now Pat is being embraced too, the Momma is embarking on a new policy, it not having been possible in the past to embrace something which she did not recognize existed, calling her Dear and My dear and Patty-dear and Patricia (she doesn't believe anyone was ever called Patagonia – that is just one of Curl's stories)." (p. 43) Pat Bennett is Patagonia de Thierry Aorewa Bennett. Also called Cleopatra by Curl, she eventually establishes herself as an artist, Aorewa de Thierry.

A range of names bestowed on several characters adds wit, but also betrays a lack of secure identity. The variations of Skidmore's name all help to caricature him: Scamper, Skinflint, Skillsaw; his first names, Urlich Ambrose, become "Early (though he's usually late) ... Curl (though his hair is as waveless as a dam in summer)" (p. 20), Gurr-l, Earlybird, Curlyboy, Oilrich, Ambrosia. The many names emphasise a condition of mind to which he pays attention on one occasion: "I didn't know who I was ... I had crumbled to pieces inside myself and was nothing at all. ... No 'I' existed, there was only nothingness and fear." (p. 31)

Cecelia Skyways

In the novel, the birth name of Cecelia Skyways is Dawn Clegg. She bears traces of Janet Frame, but transcends Frame, emerging as a convincing and witty character in her own right. In a 1984 interview, Stead insisted that the conduct and character of Cecelia "must be judged as a piece of fiction".[27] By claiming to have been a nun who has forsaken her order, and by changing her name, Cecelia places a distance between her earlier life and her new life as a writer, a calling she pursues in Melior Farbro's garden hut. The situation and setting parallel that of Janet Frame as Sargeson's guest. According to Takapuna's policeman, Cecelia has not escaped from a nunnery, but from a mental institution. Melior aids and abets her concealment and secures her a passage on a ship to London.

Electric shock treatment in high dosage for the mentally ill indicates another dismal aspect of New Zealand life in the fifties. Critics of *All Visitors Ashore* have expressed dismay that Cecelia speaks of her "electrified head" and makes jokes about the merits of electric shock treatment: "I used to be known as Floodgates. Only had to think about crying and out it came. Probably the electricity that fixed it. Wonderful drying stuff. Dehydration of the tear ducts. Just what the doctor ordered." (p. 83) This dark humour did not disturb Janet Frame, who emphasised her appreciation of the novel as fiction by describing it as a "masterpiece of creative writing".[28]

Belief in Zen Buddhism is a feature of Cecelia's personality and thought. It is Stead who has studied the subject, not Frame, to Stead's knowledge. Cecilia reassures herself with Zen teachings. Bodhidharma, the reincarnated Zen Master in the form of a spider, advises her from the web, saying, "Go forward Cecelia Skyways, look for no protection but become your fear." (p. 16) Her characterisation has warmth and charm, so that, when she is about to leave the North Shore to journey overseas, Melior laments that he "would miss her terribly, she was a darling". (p. 106)

Despite her angelic appearance, which includes ginger-gold hair shining like a halo, Cecelia confesses to the Blessed Virgin, "You know as well as I do this is a man's world and a woman has to tell some little lies and some bloody whoppers to get by." In an impious letter to 'B V' she describes the young man, Curl Skidmore, who has two complete novels in his head:

> I thought it was a nice head and that there might have been another novel or two tucked away inside his trousers as well. (I'm glad you enjoy a joke. I've always thought a woman in your position who lacked a sense of humour would be sunk.) (p. 15)

Within the novel, Stead recreates an event that did indeed occur in Sargeson's garden. According to Michael King's account in his biography of Frame, *Wrestling with the Angel*, Sargeson told Stead that "Frame would welcome his opinion on poems she was writing".[29] Stead visited the garden hut and commented on her work. He returns to the episode in the poem "Takapuna (Janet Frame 1924-2004)", which appeared after her death. One of its six verses is as follows:

> Remember the day of our disaster?
> We sat in the hut and I criticised your poem.
> Clumsy, literal, your junior in years and in pain
> I'd thought it was what you wanted.[30]

David Eggleton, reviewing all the poetry in *The Red Tram*, makes just one comment on "Takapuna". He hones in on Frame's need for encouragement. This is a poem, he says, that "evokes W. Somerset

Maugham's piercing observation: people ask you for criticism, but they only want praise."[31]

In the novel, Cecelia arranges to discuss her poetry with Curl, having asked "Melior to ask him if he would" (p. 76), in the hope that seduction might be the outcome. She tearfully shares her disappointment with Melior when "Nothing happened" (p. 86). The episode effectively illustrates the awkwardness of Curl, who is generally out of his depth, poised to skid, or in the process of skidding. A disconcerted Curl explains the non-seduction to Pat, who says he should have "gone right ahead" but had he done so, she would have "murdered" him; "don't try it." (p. 80) Despite the warning, an actual seduction is foreshadowed, part of which Pat witnesses. An erotic scene between Curl and a singer named Felice becomes increasingly comical, as simultaneous happenings give an impression of life's complex ebb and flow in many places at once. Curl's serious enjoyment is interspersed with an image of Cecelia at the rail of a departing ocean liner, scanning the coast for Curl's farewell wave, and a glimpse of Pat on board a ferry heading back to the North Shore. Curl's adventure is ironically inflated and deflated: "perhaps it's as well that in a comic strip world where so much is ghastly and so much more is less than the heart desires, there should be, even if only for a short space, a capsule within which the illusion (or perhaps it is not an illusion) of perfection has been attained." (p. 114) The consequences of Curl's lapse are severe. He is an anti-hero for whom one disaster follows another.

When Pat finds herself pregnant, she demands an abortion. A shocked Curl speaks of his "fear of the law, horror at the possibilities, because this was 1951, and abortion figured in the news only when a back-street practitioner was brought to the courts, or when the body of some unfortunate girl for whom the operation had gone disastrously wrong was found dumped under Grafton Bridge or among trees on the lower slopes of the Domain". (p. 120) Though it is not a topic that lends itself readily to humour, Curl is caricatured. Having arrived at the premises of an abortionist, Pat is stoical, but Curl is cold and ill with fear. "No father-to-be, let it be said, paces the floor more anxiously than a father-not-to-be." (p. 131) The progress of the young couple to the secret venue is bizarre, with a series of nameless women, car journeys, passwords, an alleyway and a blindfold, and, finally, recourse to the services of National Women's Hospital.

Melior Farbro and Professor Skidmore

In shaping Melior, Stead exaggerates the most benevolent facets of Sargeson, who was generous, but not invariably benign. Melior is tolerant of Cecelia's eccentricity, and non-judgemental of Curl. When Curl tells him of his escapade with Felice, and Pat's discovery of it, "Melior tut-tutted and smiled and winked, and shook his head and frowned and laughed, and told you you were a double-deceiver and a rotten swine and guffawed so hard he fell off his stool." (p. 124)

Melior Farbro, formerly Melvin Heap, has changed his name, "partly because he didn't like the idea of a painting of his ... being referred to as 'a Heap', and partly because he'd wanted a foreign-sounding and slightly preposterous name to match the avant garde paintings he was doing in those days". (p. 127-8) The specific reason for Melior's choice is that Eliot's "The Waste Land" has a dedication: "For Ezra Pound, *il miglior fabbro*."[32] Pronounced 'melior farbro', the words mean 'the better artist' or 'the superior craftsman'. The name subtly adds prestige to Melior's status as an artist.

Frank Sargeson's name change, from Norris Davey, followed a conviction for a homosexual offence. Melior, too, is gay, in an era in which gay men needed to be discreet and vigilant. There was far greater tolerance toward homosexuality by the 1980s. The Homosexual Law Reform Act, decriminalising male homosexuality, was passed in 1986. In the constraining atmosphere of the 1950s, Melior is anxious for his former partner Kenny. Given that members of the Watersiders' Union are being targeted by the Government, he warns Kenny, who has been elected to the union executive, to be careful: "– they'll be hot on your tail if they can, this Government, so don't go taking any of your old risks. Look after yourself, Kenny, because ... your old friend still loves you, boy." (p. 11) The "old risks" allude, not to union activities, but to "cruising the loos and the docks for gentlemen partners". (p. 3)

Like Curl, Melior sympathises with the waterside workers. Melior paints a series of cartoons representing the political situation of the time. The exhibition of his work is not well received. "The next day's art critic headed his column, 'Not the New Zealand we all Know and Love'." (p. 141)

Empathy is required when an actual person is the origin of imaginary characterisation. Stead explains that the writer must be "really interested in the person, must observe and feel the way into being that person. You forget yourself, then pretend you are that person. But you're partly yourself."[33] In creating Melior Farbro, a Sargeson-type framework "into which you put some aspect of yourself"[34] was needed. Stead notes that, "the peculiarity of fiction ... is that every character draws life from its author and is by that altered, however subtly, from the original."[35] He writes, "I've come to realise that *every* character in fiction is more the author than anybody else."[36]

The names Skidmore and Stead suggest two extremes; Curl is frequently off-balance, while steadiness and steadfastness are associated with the author, who remains in secure control of his narrative from start to finish. Despite his ineptitude, however, Curl shares a number of characteristics with Stead. He is transported by music of the kind Stead favoured at that age.[37] Curl is keen to become a writer. Like Curl, Stead resented the time he was required to work during university vacations to sustain his student life. Curl's complaint as a metal worker voices a frustration Stead felt when he experienced the very job that Curl describes.

> So instead of arriving home in the afternoon in time to make a start on getting one of his novels down on paper, here he is all day, the sacred scrolls of fiction so shaken and jolted by the machine that there are times when, going over them as he cycles wearily down to the ferry wharf in the evening, he finds them mixed and blurred, one spool running into the other and both fading into an obscurity from which only sleep and the cold early light of morning over the Gulf can rescue them. (pp. 62-3)

In the 1980s, Professor Urlich Ambrose Skidmore, the narrator, observes with self-irony Curl's shortcomings. When the novel was reissued in 1996, British reviewer Richard Francis noted that it "suggests that the ambitions and frustrations of youth can be identified with those of a country, while it also demonstrates that the naïvety of young artists can be effectively and affectionately portrayed by a mature one."[38] Its literary merit acknowledged, *All Visitors Ashore* can be appreciated also for its recreation of the values and mores of the early 1950s, seen through the eyes of C. K. Stead, who, at that time, was involved in political discussion, in artistic and literary events, and in the struggle to survive as a student and writer.

The novel is punctuated with farewells as characters head overseas, leaving a repressive country, narrow in its outlook and opportunities. Travel abroad in the 1950s is described by Melior Farbro as what "most people who are worth anything in this place do". (p. 112) If talents were to find opportunities to flourish, experience elsewhere was essential. *All Visitors Ashore* highlights this 1950s' awareness among young people, the Steads included.

1 C. K. Stead, "While Down the Fleeces of our Sky", *Whether the Will Is Free: Poems 1954-62*, Auckland, Paul's Book Arcade, 1964, p. 18.
2 C. K. Stead, "A New Zealand Elegy", *Five for the Symbol*, Auckland, Longman Paul, 1981, p. 159.
3 C. K. Stead, "The Clodian Songbook/ 15", *Geographies*, Auckland, University of Auckland Press/ Oxford University Press, 1982, p. 73.
4 C. K. Stead, e-mail correspondence with author, 3 March 2006.
5 C. K. Stead, *In the Glass Case*, Auckland, Auckland University Press/ Oxford University Press, 1981, p. 262.
6 Kamala Jackson, "C. K. Stead: Poet, Novelist, Academic, Activist and Aucklander on his Origins", *Metro*, February 1985, p. 124.
7 Stead, "Letter (to R. R. D.)", *Whether the Will Is Free*, p. 20.
8 Jackson, *Metro*, February 1985, p. 124.
9 C. K. Stead, *The Writer at Work: Essays*, Dunedin, University of Otago Press, 2000, p. 215.
10 Jackson, "C. K. Stead, Poet, Novelist, Academic…", *Metro*, February 1985, p. 126.
11 Steve Braunias, "C. K., 70", *New Zealand Listener*, 11 January 2003, p. 60.
12 C. K. Stead, "Remembering the Fifties", *Landfall* Volume 185 (2), April 1993, p. 10.
13 ibid, p. 9.
14 C. K. Stead, *Kin of Place: Essays on 20 New Zealand Writers*, Auckland, Auckland University Press, 2002, p. 52.
15 Stead, *The Writer at Work*, p. 235.
16 ibid, p. 18.
17 Janet Frame, *An Angel at My Table: An Autobiography*, Auckland, Hutchinson, pp. 150-51.
18 Jackson, "C. K. Stead, Poet, Novelist, Academic…", *Metro*, February 1985, p. 126.
19 Stead, *The Writer at Work*, p. 24.
20 ibid, pp. 24-5.
21 Norman Shrapnell, cited by Bernard Orsman, "Critics Flatter NZ Novelist", *New Zealand News UK*, 19 September 1984, p. 6.
22 Stead, *The Writer at Work*, pp. 227-28.
23 Michael King, *The Penguin History of New Zealand*, Auckland, Penguin Books, 2003, p. 351.
24 David Young, "Tenants of Fiction", *New Zealand Listener*, 13 October 1984, p. 32.
25 C. K. Stead, *All Visitors Ashore*, London, Harvill Press, 1984, p. 44. Page numbers in brackets refer to this edition.
26 One of the many holiday jobs undertaken by Stead as a student was machine moulder at MacEwans Machinery.
27 Young "Tenants of Fiction", *New Zealand Listener*, 13 October 1984, p. 33.

28 ibid. These were Janet Frame's words in the course of an interview with David Young. They have often been quoted by Stead.

29 Michael King, *Wrestling with the Angel*, Auckland, Viking, 2000, p. 127.

30 C. K. Stead, "Takapuna (Janet Frame 1924-1994)", *The Red Tram*, Auckland University Press, 2004, pp. 54-5.

31 David Eggleton, "The Things that Matter", *New Zealand Listener*, 19 February 2005, p.38.

32 T. S. Eliot, "The Waste Land", *The Waste Land and Other Poems*, London, Faber and Faber, p. 25.

33 Stead, interview with author, 29 August 2005.

34 Stead, *The Writer at Work*, p. 237.

35 C. K. Stead, *Answering to the Language: Essays on Modern Writers*, Auckland University Press, 1989, p. 203.

36 Stead, *The Writer at Work*, p. 237.

37 Stead, *All Visitors Ashore*, p. 142: "those old 78s of Beniamino Gigli singing 'La Donna e Mobile' and 'Salve Dimora casta e pura', and the 'Eine Kleine Nacht' music on four sides of 45s, one side for each movement, and some Beethoven piano sonatas on 78s that had done heavy duty, and of course the Wagnermusic..."

38 Richard Francis, "Artist As a Young Man", *Times Literary Supplement*, 26 January 1996, p. 21.

CHAPTER THREE

"Cradled in the Great Cup of London"[1]

From Auckland to Armidale

Once examinations were over in November 1955, Stead became a postman. In theory, a man could deliver mail in the mornings and write in the afternoons. In reality, the job involved long hours especially since it included daily bus and ferry journeys between Takapuna and the Auckland mail centre.

After a day of torrential rain in early February, Stead returned to the verandah flat soaked to the skin. There he found a letter offering a lecturing position at the University of New England in Armidale, Australia. He had sought a scholarship to study in Britain, but few were available at the time, and had also expressed interest in a junior lectureship at either Victoria University or the University of Auckland. Victoria's Professor Ian Gordon had mentioned him to New England's Professor Piper as a promising academic and poet. The job offer was accepted and the Steads moved without delay to be in time for the new term at the beginning of March, 1956.

As well as providing courses for internal students, the University of New England conducted the state's distance education. Stead gave lectures and took tutorials internally, but most of his work was with extramural students. He set and marked assignments, sent out study guides on prescribed texts and was often required to travel to remote areas to hold weekend schools or workshops. These he enjoyed. In one of his letters to Sargeson, he described a visit to De La Salle seminary in Sydney with Catholic brothers enrolled to study English. The Saturday programme included "two one-hour lectures, and three hours of personal interviewing. Talked and drank wine till one am, and then the same programme on Sunday! Exhausting, but fun. The Catholic brothers fed us (lecturers) at midday, and we sat in high-backed chairs among tapestries and virgins, waited on by the lower brethren – wine, fruit, nuts, roast meats etc. ... Nice to taste the ascetic life now and then!"[2]

Stead's review of Keneally's *Woman of an Inner Sea* refers to a journey to teach students in Dubbo.

> There had been heavy rains, direct rail links were cut, so to give a few classes to a few students I had to travel 350 miles to Sydney, then a further 250 to Dubbo – all of it through an unvarying bluegum landscape. The rains continued and the Macquarie River rose twenty-four feet in the twenty-four hours I was in the town.[3]

A letter to Allen Curnow, five months after his arrival, mentioned that he had by then –

> ... travelled 3120 miles on NSW railways; been hotter and also colder than I've ever been in my life before; seen flood and snow for the first time in my life; got the feeling of a city of two million people (Sydney is terrific and I spend as much time there as I can – unfortunately not enough); learned a lot about the Australian countryside and character; and learned that Aussies and New Zealanders are, with a few minor adjustments, inter-changeable, but the Englishmen are foreigners.[4]

Some of the poetry published in *Whether the Will Is Free* was written in Armidale. Friends are mentioned by name in the poem "Four Harmonics of Regret", as they are in the later poem "Walking Westward". They hail from several different countries: "André the Pole", "Otto from Vienna", "Al from California", "Aussie M", "Izzy G German Jew". "Walking Westward" characterises each member of the group through a particular action. Izzy G, for example, is given to "sawing dangerously at the wheel (one of the first Holdens) because he insisted on turning to look at his passengers while he talked."[5] Once the Steads became settled in a furnished flat, they found that Izzy (Israel Getzler) was one of their neighbours. He lectured in the History Department and often drove them to and from the university.

Despite the friends, with whom they shared suppers and discussions on socialism, capitalism and marxism, in "the year of Suez and of Hungary",[6] Stead's poetry reflects a failure to settle into Australian life. "Autumn Letter (to F. S.)" recreates the bakery smells on the way to Sargeson's home, and, on arrival there, impressions of "Green, garlic, Bach, new bread, a stroking sea"[7]. Letters indicate how much he and Kay missed Sargeson and Takapuna. Kay describes Armidale as "dull, brutish",[8] and Stead calls it a "spiritual desert". The place has, he confesses, "been getting me down more than usual over the last few weeks – and that means pretty depressing. We both hate it, but fortunately we manage to take turns at the really lowest ebbs. Nostalgia for Takapuna and the visits to Esmonde Road becomes quite overwhelming at times."[9]

When Australian author Kylie Tennant presented a lecture at the university, Stead wrote to Sargeson of his immediate identification with her writer-unable-to-write:

> ... a writer who can't get anything down. She described the feeling of guilt, and said the writer who wasn't writing was the most miserable character alive. With nothing done for the last two months I comprehended more acutely than usual. The terrible thing about this place is that I have no identity at all as the person I want to be. ... The value of Takapuna, I realise now, is that there are the Smithymans, the Duggans ... with whom one has an identity as a writer. Here my writing is a kind of secret vice.[10]

The same letter speaks of satisfaction with a poem written half a year earlier.

> I'm quite sure the best thing I have ever done is one called "Whether the Will Is Free" – I wrote it in midwinter here, and sent a copy to Curnow. He is putting it in the Penguin, so my feeling that it is the kind of thing I <u>want</u> to write seems justified. ... But it was one of the rare things that are quite unpremeditated, which came entirely out of the subconscious without apparent cause. ... It's very strange though – for example the first snow hadn't fallen when the poem was written.

The setting is a "harsh and gum-grey"[11] winter landscape, with snow on the ground. Armidale is located on the New England Tableland at 3,300 feet, with very cold winter nights. The poem is positive in mood, despite the narrator's awareness that he is trapped in an "iron time", a winter in his life: "Under its ice my small life crawls/ Pecking and snuffing at grey walls."[12] There is slow progress in the broad scheme of things, but a close-up view provides forward momentum – a dog leaping across a snowy landscape "Spring-full as hope". Streams pursue their courses, reaching their inevitable destinations, flowing "even under ice, to sea". At the same time, music, to which the "doved hand" of a girl "Dances",[13] brings a physical surrender, beyond the governance of the narrator's will. The hand moves to the rhythm with dove-like grace. The old Germanic word "doved" can suggest, in addition, a suspension of the senses. On a winter's day, the music is able to transport and bring together the girl with the "doved hand" and the narrator "doved in snow".

> Whether the will is free or seems
> I would be music, doved in snow.[14]

The poem proposes patience, allowing events their own time. It simultaneously conceals a lack of patience. The line, "Willing to get to where I'm sent", can also imply urgency, with an effort of will producing action. This poised and equivocal poem seemed to Stead "as though it were someone else's"; there is "more there than I could ever put into a conscious piece".[15]

Throughout the Armidale experience, Stead anticipated further study in Britain. Kay's salary, as a University of New England librarian, met the couple's living expenses, while Stead's was saved for the UK. "Last Poem in Australia" refers to "that hovel town", Armidale, which "has weathered me". The poem anticipates departure, offering "That grace which nothing earns except in loss". In this place, the narrator admits to a sense of dislocation, of being "(Neither here nor there, neither alive nor dying)".[16]

The Steads left Armidale after a year and a half. "Walking Westward" records their farewell by Otto, "with Izzy, Iain Lonie, a dozen others". At Central Station in Sydney, Otto is there, having "driven all night/ to greet us at the other end".[17]

Stead was offered two scholarships in 1957. One was to Cambridge and the other was the Michael Hiatt Baker Scholarship to Bristol. At the time, study at Cambridge would have required the completion of a further undergraduate degree. In Bristol, Stead had the opportunity to work toward a PhD under the supervision of Professor L. C. Knights, a leading academic who subsequently attained the King Edward VII Chair of English Literature at Cambridge.

Bristol and London

In Bristol the Steads bought a Ford Popular which features in *The Secret History of Modernism*, the story "Figures of Speech", and in "Walking Westward". Its cost in 1958, the poem reveals, was 450 pounds "and you could drive it around Piccadilly Circus".[18] *The Secret History of Modernism* provides a description:

> ... it was tall-and-small, battleship-grey, narrow, basic inside, with a long gear-lever like a knob-topped walking stick, small bucket seats at the front, cramped double seat behind, and a boot which held the spare wheel with space for not more than one modest suitcase. Its tyres were narrow, its springs were not supple, it roared and shuddered if pushed much above fifty and felt unstable at that speed, as if it might topple cornering, or when the wind blew too hard. But a redoubtable car.[19]

The couple's accommodation at Westbury-on-Trym on the edge of Bristol was a comfortable flat. Stead seemed delighted to find himself in England. "The snow road leads/ to Westbury" he wrote in "Winter Song"; "you and I/ lie calm, lie deep,/ nightlong in intertwining sleep."[20] In this personal poem, he and Kay enjoy a sense of wellbeing. "Walking Westward" also refers to Westbury, where "a strange brilliance on the ceiling" is a reflection from snow. To a poet used to Auckland's colours, the contrast between the whiteness of "first snow"[21] and the blackness of bare trees was dramatic. A letter to Sargeson conveyed his unreserved pleasure.

> We have a beautiful little village to shop in here, very old, all heaped up on itself in stone, with a trickle of water which we take to be the Trym running under innumerable stone bridges. There are woods, a castle, a very ancient church, and I have my hair cut in a building that was a priory back in 715. ...

> Our flat is very large by our standards, kitchen, lounge, two bedrooms, bathroom – all our own.[22]

Stead's appreciation is clear in his depiction of Bristol University, Wills Castle, and the church of St Mary Redcliffe in "Walking Westward".

> St Mary Redcliffe spire
> dockside survivor
> sky-spear flying
> repeated in water[23]

Exploration of the countryside and towns in England and Wales in the Ford provided impressions that Stead later included in "A Race Apart". The story appeared in *Landfall*[24] in 1960, and, much later, in Stead's book of stories *Five for the Symbol*. In addition, it was published in 1961 as one of a collection of contemporary stories put out in England by Hutchinson, the first of their New Authors series.

A central character is Andrew Nicholson. Some of his qualities derive from Stead's friend Don Smith, whom the couple visited in Oxford. Stead shared the experience with Sargeson:

> We were in Oxford a week or so ago, the day after Don Smith won a big international half-mile at White City (beating the European champion Svengali in the process). He is now socially desirable and pursued everywhere by unfamiliar paws which clasp at him familiarly – congratulations, smiles and waves all up and down the Broad. We basked in reflected glory … . The sports writers are comparing him to Lovelock and referring to him as a Rhodes Scholar (which he isn't) to make the parallel complete. He is headlined as "Tall Handsome N.Zer", "Curly-Headed N.Zer" etc. Girls write to him and say they saw him in a coffee shop and would like to meet him. (He tears the letters up.) He is enormously impressive sitting in his digs making the kind of intelligent conversation athletes are supposed to be incapable of. … He is a member of a terribly exclusive Club – Vincents.[25]

Don Smith is later described by Stead as "having a brilliant season as a half-miler in Europe, and the following year ran for New Zealand at the Olympic Games in Rome".[26] "A Race Apart" explores what might happen if a capable New Zealander, an athlete who can offer lucid in-depth comments on *The Turn of the Screw* by Henry James for example, were to be employed as chauffeur for a landed English family. The story allows two different sets of expectations and assumptions (British upper class and New Zealand egalitarian) to interact, thereby creating amusing situations and dialogue.

Andrew Nicholson seeks the post as chauffeur so that he can use the estate's grassy parkland to maintain his training as a runner. The story is remarkable for its characterisation of the narrator Mrs Summerscroft, mother of three daughters and lady of the manor. She is affected by the young chauffeur, though she seems unaware of the attraction. Andrew Nicholson, like Don Smith, preserves his physical strength for his sport. Although Nicholson's mystique dissipates quite suddenly in the eyes of Mrs Summerscroft, her senses seem to have been awakened. She comes to address Nicholson's American friend Herman Parker by his first name, while he calls her Emily, a surprising breach of upper class protocol.

The idea of a chauffeuring role for his character may have come to Stead as he motored through the countryside, observing narrow lanes, villages, country churches and churchyards. Often he drove between Bristol and the town of Bath, a mere twenty miles to the south-east, where the Steads could attend festival performances:

> Menuhins (Y & H), Isaac Stern, Cherkassky, Rosalyn Tureck, Gielgud, Danish Royal Ballet, Elisabeth Schwarzkopf, London Philharmonic, London Mozart players, London Symphony Orchestra, Goldsborough Orchestra, Jennifer Vyvyan – etc. Bath is beautiful at this time of the year. We drove down there Saturday afternoon for a concert in the Abbey – with Barbara Mackay, an Auckland friend of Kay's who was staying with us, and two post-graduate students. Wonderful to sit under all that vaulting stone and stained glass listening to Bach and Mozart.[27]

After this outing, the five were about to begin their meal in Westbury-on-Trym when Hubert and Louise Henderson arrived.

> We hadn't seen them for two years – Hubert had just finished

> a term as UNESCO education advisor in Baghdad. Kay did some swift reshuffling of portions and we all sat down to what turned out to be a very gay meal. Hubert loses all the attributes of the public man when he gets with younger people (except his loud voice, which is a real roof-lifter). ... Louise and Hubert are going to France for a month and have said we can have their London flat while they are away – a real windfall for us as it is in Kensington and has a phone.[28]

Later Stead wrote to Sargeson from London. Settled at a desk in the North Library of the British Museum, he reported that he and Kay had spent most of June in the flat in Kensington, "a quite fantastic street of Embassies and expensive houses, noisy all night with the roar of expensive sports cars and the squeals of debutantes being pursued from wild parties by ex-public school boys".[29]

Although the couple enjoyed Bristol, they stayed there for one year only. London became their base from December 1958 until mid-1959, so that Stead could work in the British Museum and occasionally at the National Newspaper Library at Colindale. They rented a bed-sit in Phillimore Gardens, Kensington, which provides one of the settings for *The Secret History of Modernism*, with its "gas by shilling in the meter",[30] and toilet and bathroom shared with other tenants in the building. Mr Spiteri from Malta lived in the bed-sit next door. He is the very Mr Spiteri who appears in the novel, renamed Mr Spitfire by the character Samantha.

Kay found work in London assisting Canon John Collins, Dean of St Pauls and head of Christian Action. This organisation campaigned against apartheid in South Africa. London at the time was a centre for "all the good causes". The Steads attended protest rallies to combat apartheid, supported those involved with "South Africa Defence and Aid",[31] and were involved with the Campaign for Nuclear Disarmament. The excitement of the city animates the London sections of "Walking Westward", parts of *The Secret History of Modernism* and "Pictures in a Gallery Undersea". This poem, which appeared in 1959, "was voted by *Landfall* readers the best poem from the magazine's first fifteen years of publication".[32]

"I shall never go back" and "You too must stay."[33] These words from the poem are spoken by a woman who brings into focus a dilemma keenly debated by New Zealanders in London at the time, an on-going debate that exercises New Zealanders in London to this day. Professor Knights advised Stead against a return to his homeland; he "warned me delicately that, like Eric [McCormick], I too might vanish into obscurity in the South Pacific rather than fulfil my promise in a place able to appreciate and reward it."[34] Stead was offered a post at the University of Bristol that would have provided a smooth passage into an academic career in the UK.

"A tension exists somewhere in the mind of every New Zealander between 'here' and 'there'. ... For a writer it may be directly acknowledged in the form of a choice between staying and leaving." Stead's comment was originally expressed in a 1960 University of Auckland Winter Lecture. The talk identified disadvantages associated with life in New Zealand. "It is the combination of remoteness and *insignificance* which New Zealand writers feel. And to the insignificance of New Zealand I should add the thinness and uniformity of its society, its dependence on Europe and America, and a certain sourness that underlies its achievements."[35] He does not explain the "sourness", but it may arise from a resentment that follows from the limited range of opportunity for advancement or acknowledgement, which tended to favour relatively few.

"Pictures in a Gallery Undersea"

This long and challenging poem celebrates the abundant opportunities and the impressions of history that are "cradled in the great cup of London". Viewed as a geographical unit, the city is compact and densely populated, while New Zealand is long and narrow and sparsely populated. Historically, London is one of the cradles of European culture and literary heritage. The poem has falling snow cast a great mantle over bare trees, gutters, buildings, statues and monuments, extending beyond the winter in which the poem is set, to many winters, through which past monarchs, scholars and poets, and those whom they loved have lived. The "great cup" contains an august company. The poem sets in motion images of long-dead poets who appear and vanish – Wilde, Yeats, Pound and Eliot (here called "old Possum").

> And Ezra in billiard cloth trousers across the street
> Wearing an ear-ring of aquamarine,
> And old Possum hackneying past in a bowler to his funeral at
> the bank,

Turned
turned, and watching, faded from sight.[36]

The poem has a dream-like quality, as the narrator experiences the city during the hours of sleep, "on that long haul, midnight to dawn".[37] Locating the gallery "undersea" has a distancing effect. In a strange, freshly imagined setting, the famous city can be viewed as if for the first time. Images of London materialise and fade in the gallery, in which pictures have been turned to the wall, signalling the end of an earlier phase, to make way for a new development – a different manner of composition for a New Zealand poet. It is a modernist work[38] that allows readers to assemble, compare and contrast words, rhythms, echoes and allusions, discovering relationships for themselves.

> ... when I wrote a long poem called 'Pictures in a Gallery Undersea' in London in 1958 I was at least half conscious of doing something that hadn't been done in New Zealand poetry before, tapping sources that hadn't been tapped, and that the special effects were musical .... I knew that though there were some echoes of Eliot for particular effect, technically the poem owed everything to Ezra Pound's innovations in 'Hugh Selwyn Mauberley' and the Cantos. ... And I think I could have said that the musical structure of my poem was built up partly by putting contrasting things alongside each other – bits of literary history alongside obvious fictions, a passage of long lines after one in short lines, resonant romantic statements after curt ironic ones."[39]

Stead's poem includes allusions to "The Waste Land". The banks of Eliot's Thames are desolate; a rat creeps through vegetation. Though Stead is aware of London's polluted air and "the rubbish drifting at the water's edge" into which swans thrust their beaks, he relishes the city's distinctive atmosphere.

The River swans nor sang for the dead day
Nor proudly departed; but each hooked
One leg across its back, displaying a dirty web.[40]

Despite centuries of deaths, despite the suffering of Oscar Wilde and the horrors of the Tower, blood still pulses through a living city. A train is poised to move forward. There is movement among the characters. The ring of goldsmiths' hammers can be heard, a princess escapes from a ballroom, individuals shout, mouth a question, ask directions. Stead projects himself into a series of personae. A version of himself encounters his Swedish grandfather, before he journeys south, bearing part of Stead's origin "with him in his northern potency".[41] Stead plays the role of a boy selling a newspaper to Yeats "(I only a few feet tall, in cloth cap and boots/ Three sizes too large. ...)". Having purchased a paper, Yeats makes the familiar complaint that "there's nothing in it"[42] and demands his money back. There is energy and humour in Stead's poem, expressing his delight at the diversity and vitality of London.

Throughout the poem music creates a mood that is optimistic, yet mysterious. Initially Mozart, heard from a gramophone record, seems to be played by a girl "on her sun-bleached hair".[43] The poem concludes with an old man whose "unsheathed fingers struggled to revive/ The dead years on a battered violin".[44] Music and the echo of "sun-bleached" in the word "unsheathed" link the two individuals. Images suggest that music, "which took off gladly across the deserted Square",[45] is true freedom. Allen Phillipson draws attention to its significance in the poem.

> In "Pictures in a Gallery", where almost everything seems to be "falling ... descending ... dissolving," and "running away in drains," music is one of the few things that rises. In section I, the notes "beat" wings and "took off" like birds, moving "up through the watery air/ Of London." Later in the poem, "songs on the night" rise "above a quarrel of barrow wheels." (Phillipson's emphases added)[46]

Songs are associated with the work of the many poets who have spent time in London, their poetry recalled by its buildings, squares, parks, monuments, and even its stones. Phillipson suggests that "Stead feels the 'Stones of the sunken city' come to life and speak to him. In his excited eyes, the marble buildings of London are aquiver with ghostly presences ('*Où tant de marbre est tremblant sur tant d'ombres*')".[47] The epigraph to the final section, "*Chanterez-vous quand vous serez vaporeuse?...*",[48] anticipates an affirmative answer; poets are remembered and their work continues to sing. The song that is Stead's poem communicates excitement, energy, wonderment, regret.

Departure and the PhD

The Steads often attended performances at the Lyric Hammersmith, where Patrick McGoohan was outstanding as Robespierre in *Danton's Death* and in the title role of Ibsen's *Brandt*. At the Doves, a charming pub on the river at Hammersmith, the couple liked to drink with New Zealand friends who had a flat nearby. All too soon, the Doves and the first-rate drama productions were left behind. After only seven months in London, the Steads set sail for New Zealand. Regret associated with imminent departure is clear in "Walking Westward", published two decades later; "sweet Thames" and its swans are not simply allusions to "The Waste Land", and to Spenser's "Prothalamion", but an expression of affection for a river Stead was loath to leave.

> sweet Thames
>   numbering our days at the Doves
> last hours of our indifference –
> London
>   not style
> but sanity
> light on leaves falling over the towpath
> a red bus crossing Brunel's bridge
> the swans turning with the turning tide[49]

In London, there was an ease of mind Stead terms "indifference" and "sanity" as opposed to the burden implicit in commitments back home. The "swans turning" foreshadow his own "turning" homeward. There is melancholy in the falling leaves at the end of a season, and inevitability in the movement of the "red bus crossing Brunel's bridge".

Stead intended from the outset to return to New Zealand,[50] but he expected to spend at least two years in England. He was there only twenty-two months, returning home with his doctoral thesis incomplete. He wrote to Sargeson in November 1958 saying, "Have accepted a lectureship at Auckland to begin in June '59."[51] In the event, it was August before he arrived back in New Zealand, but it later became clear that the time in Bristol and London could have been extended. Instead the thesis was finished in Auckland while lectures were being newly prepared and presented, a cumulative workload that proved exhausting. Before leaving Britain Stead had taken his Viva at Nottingham, with external examiner Professor V. de Sola Pinto, on the basis of six completed chapters and an outline of what was to follow.

Stead wrote to Sargeson late in 1960 telling him that "The PhD is through – will be official in January. Knights says that Pinto 'entirely endorses the laudatory report I wrote on your dissertation before I left England' – he's now in the States. He goes on 'It is a first class piece of work; a pleasure to read; a real contribution to literary history and to critical thinking'."[52]

The outcome was the publication of the thesis as *The New Poetic*. It appeared first in 1964. By the late 1980s, it had sold more than 100,000 copies. "It had been prescribed, cited, quoted, especially in discussions of Eliot. Bits had been reprinted in four different Macmillan *Casebooks* and in several collections of essays on Yeats."[53] The acclaim was the result of a scholarly, yet readable, analysis of the poet's function and of the relationship between poets and their readers. Stead accounts for impoverishment in the quality of English popular poetry between 1909 and 1916, in the years when the likes of Henry Newbolt praised Empire, the public school and the glory of England. Against this unpromising background, Stead shows the emergence to full strength of Yeats and then Eliot.

Stead's argument offers a triangle image, to make visible the link between poet, audience and the truth or reality embodied in a poem. Distances between the three points are variable: "At one time we may find the poet and his audience close together, and 'Reality' a great distance from them. This elongation of the triangle stifles the poem, and to a later age it will seem merely the product of an agreement between the poet and his audience to deceive themselves. At another time we will find the poet close to the point 'Reality', but the audience a great distance from them both."[54] Stead claims that Yeats, in writing "Easter 1916", shows his "ability to assimilate a complex political event into the framework of a poem without distortion of the event or loss of its human character in abstraction".[55] Yeats achieves what could be considered an equal distance between the points of a theoretical triangle, an ideal distance, therefore, between himself and his audience.

Stead's analysis of Eliot's work pays less attention to the adjustable shape of the triangle and more to Eliot's own critical premises to explain his key concepts, especially the "dark embryo"[56] and the "Three Voices of Poetry".[57] *The New Poetic* provides fresh insight into Eliot's major work, expressing admiration for "The Waste Land", while taking issue with those parts of "The Four Quartets" that involve discourse and abstraction.

In 1964 Roy Fuller of *The London Magazine* judged *The New Poetic* to be "among the best Eliot criticism extant, right on the ball with every move it makes, truly appreciative, discriminating and interpretive".[58] Victoria University's Professor Ian Gordon challenged Stead's negative assessment of "The Four Quartets", but nevertheless found the book "first-rate ... by an acute and sensitive critic who can read poetry, not just talk about it".[59]

Although *The New Poetic* came close to going out of print in England in 1989, it remained readily available in the US. The English edition was subsequently reissued in 1997, "with a substantial quotation on its back cover from Seamus Heaney's discussion (in *The Government of the Tongue*) of the effect the book had on his own and others' reading and understanding of T. S. Eliot".[60] There was yet another reissue in 2005, by Continuum, with the name STEAD in large white letters on the cover and *The New Poetic* in rather small letters underneath.

1 C. K. Stead, "Pictures in a Gallery Undersea", *Whether the Will Is Free: Poems 1954-62*, Hamilton, Paul's Book Arcade, 1964, p. 52.
2 C. K. Stead, letter to Frank Sargeson, 1 May 1956, Turnbull Library Papers.
3 C. K. Stead, *The Writer at Work*, Dunedin, University of Otago Press, 2000, p. 166.
4 C. K. Stead, letter to Allen Curnow, 10 July 1956, Turnbull Library Papers.
5 C. K. Stead, "Walking Westward", *Walking Westward*, Auckland, The Shed, 1979, pp. 33-4.
6 Stead, "Walking Westward", *Walking Westward*, p. 34. The "year of Suez and Hungary" was the year in which the Egyptians reclaimed control of the Suez Canal, and the Hungarians revolted against Soviet control, a situation that led to the entry into Hungary of Soviet troops and the deaths of up to 50,000 people.
7 Stead, "Autumn Letter (to F. S.), "*Whether the Will Is Free*, p. 25.
8 C. K. Stead and Kay Stead, letter to Sargeson, 1 May 1956, Turnbull Library Papers.
9 C. K. Stead, letter to Sargeson, 5 October 1956, Turnbull Library Papers.
10 ibid.
11 Stead, "Whether the Will Is Free", *Whether the Will Is Free*, p. 34.
12 ibid, p. 35.
13 ibid, p. 34.
14 ibid, p. 35.
15 C. K. Stead, letter to Sargeson, 5 October 1956, Turnbull Library Papers.
16 Stead, "Last Poem in Australia", *Whether the Will Is Free*, p. 36.
17 Stead, "Walking Westward", *Walking Westward*, p. 42.
18 ibid, p. 47.

19 C. K. Stead, *The Secret History of Modernism*, London, Vintage, 2003, pp. 73-4.

20 Stead, "Winter Song", *Whether the Will Is Free*, p. 47.

21 Stead, "Walking Westward", *Walking Westward*, p. 43.

22 C. K. Stead, letter to Sargeson, 18 October 1957, Turnbull Library Papers.

23 Stead, "Walking Westward", *Walking Westward*, p. 43.

24 C. K. Stead, "A Race Apart", first published in *Landfall* 54, June 1960, pp. 120-157.

25 C. K. Stead, letter to Sargeson, 3 June 1958, Turnbull Library Papers.

26 Stead, *The Writer at Work*, p. 19, footnote.

27 Stead, letter to Sargeson, 3 June 1958, Turnbull.

28 ibid.

29 C. K. Stead, letter to Sargeson, 18 August 1958, Turnbull Library Papers.

30 Stead, *The Secret History of Modernism*, p. 24.

31 Stead, "Walking Westward", *Walking Westward*, p. 48.

32 The poem was first published by *Landfall* in June 1959. *The Oxford Companion to New Zealand Literature*, edited by Roger Robinson and Nelson Wattie, 1998, records the 1960 recognition received by Stead, p. 513.

33 Stead, "Pictures in a Gallery Undersea", *Whether the Will Is Free*, p. 52.

34 Stead, *The Writer at Work*, p. 67.

35 C. K. Stead, *In the Glass Case*, Auckland, Auckland University Press/ Oxford University Press, 1981, p. 248, and pp. 246-7. The essay's conclusion suggests that remoteness, if acknowledged, can be turned to advantage and may be "exploited as an analogue for the immovable tensions which are universal in human experience." p. 258.

36 Stead, "Pictures in a Gallery Undersea", *Whether the Will Is Free*, p. 55.

37 ibid, p. 52.

38 Stead describes Modernism as follows': "... we have now as elements in Modernist practice first the lack of logical or narrative structures, and in their place the aggregation of radioactive fragments within a 'Field'; second, the scoring of speech patterns to create a music which must predominate over any externally imposed form; and third, the use of suggestion, approximation, a carefully judged incompleteness as a way of engaging the reader in the action of poetry itself – all these combining ideally to increase the sense of an achieved reality." Stead, *In the Glass Case*, p. 153.

39 Stead, *In the Glass Case*, p. 266-267.

40 Stead, "Pictures in a Gallery Undersea", *Whether the Will Is Free*, p. 55.

41 ibid, p. 53.

42 ibid, p. 55.

43 ibid, p. 52.

44 ibid, p. 56.

45 ibid, p. 52.

46 Allan Phillipson, *C. K. Stead and Three Modes of New Zealand Poetry*, The University of British Columbia, July, 1997. Thesis submitted in partial fulfilment of requirements for Doctor of Philosophy. Electronic resource retrieved May 2006 from http://www.collectionscanada.gc.ca/obj/s4/f2/dsk3/ftp04/nq25137.pdf, p.82

47 ibid, p. 115. The French line which forms the epigraph to section ii can be translated, 'Where so much marble is trembling above so many shadows.'

48 Stead, "Pictures in a Gallery Undersea", *Whether the Will Is Free*, p. 55. The line which is the epigraph to section vii can be translated, 'Will you sing when you become a spirit?'

49 Stead, "Walking Westward", *Walking Westward*, pp. 48-9.

50 C. K. Stead, letter to Sargeson, 9 June 1957, Turnbull Library Papers. Furthermore, "Dialogue on a Northern Shore" is informed by Stead's commitment to New Zealand.

Written in the UK, this poetic dialogue presents a Young Man from "Ithaca", comparable to New Zealand, who visits the Old World. The second speaker, an Old Man, finds fault with the way the Young Man walks: "... walking as you do with your chin hooked over your shoulder/ And eyes blind to things about you." Stead, "Dialogue on a Northern Shore", *Whether the Will Is Free*, p. 41. The Young Man intends "To find some golden thing to lay at the feet of Ithaca", "Dialogue on a Northern Shore", p. 42, the inference being that he will return home, bringing with him the fruits of his experience and his gift of creativity.

51 C. K. Stead, letter to Sargeson, 7 November 1958, Turnbull Library Papers.

52 C. K. Stead, letter to Sargeson, no date, Turnbull Library Papers.

53 Stead, *The Writer at Work*, p. 184.

54 C. K. Stead, *The New Poetic*, London, Hutchinson & Co, 1964, p. 12.

55 ibid, p. 39.

56 ibid, p. 136.

57 ibid, p. 142.

58 Roy Fuller, "Special Notices", *The London Magazine*, July, 1964, p. 92.

59 Ian Gordon, "Poet and Audience", *New Zealand Listener*, 14 August 1964, p. 18.

60 Stead, *The Writer at Work*, p. 188.

CHAPTER FOUR

The Literary Nationalist

"In at the Beginning"[1]

Stead accepted the offer of a position at the University of Auckland, believing he could best contribute to New Zealand's literature from an Auckland base, interacting with other writers. "It was really this sort of idealism attached to my image of Frank and Allen that brought me back to New Zealand," he told reporter Janet McAllister in 2005. She was able to add, "He's curious about what might have been but doesn't regret the decision."[2]

Dan Davin offered an example of a New Zealander working and writing in Oxford, "trying to hold onto his subject as it slipped away from him". His desk was "covered with New Zealand maps, reference books and newspaper clippings".[3] It seemed to Stead that Davin was "running on dwindling resources".[4] Fleur Adcock observed that Stead was "in at the beginning. It's like having been in there with Shakespeare and Marlowe, with New Zealand literature having begun when it did. And if I had grown up in those circumstances I might have felt the same. *Of course* it would have been a romantic choice".[5] Nearly twenty years after taking up his university position, he told Michael Harlow that "living the kind of traditional family life I have led (and enjoyed, I should add), I've had to earn money one way or another and it's pretty hard to think of a mode of earning that would be better."[6]

Intent on succeeding professionally, Stead prepared his lectures meticulously. "It's certainly true that in my first years as an academic I really found it terribly hard work. I couldn't take it lightly. I couldn't do things off the cuff. Everything had to be prepared and over-prepared. I really ground the stuffing out of myself and couldn't write poetry."[7] His stage one English lectures in the Lower Lecture Theatre are remembered by students from the sixties. "Karl Stead used to make his entrance through the high doors at the back of the lecture theatre.

With his narrow beaked face and his black academic gown flapping as he made his descent, he looked not unlike a large bird of prey."[8] Students recall his passion for literature.

Warwick Roger, writing for *North and South*, asked Stead what the University of Auckland was like in 1960, prompting him to recall some of the remarkable colleagues of the day. He described the university as small, and staffed by quite distinguished people, including John Reid, Mike Joseph, Bill Pearson and Allen Curnow. Head of the English Department was Sydney Musgrove, characterised by Stead as "a great theatre man".[9] Keith Sinclair was in the History Department. Older and more gregarious than Stead, he found it hard to understand why Stead avoided gatherings of colleagues for lunch in the common room. Nevertheless, he and his wife invited the Steads to stay with them in their Coromandel bach, which led to the young couple's purchase of a nearby section that they owned until 1973. Coromandel settings, well known to Stead, became significant in his first novel, *Smith's Dream*.

Asked about students at Auckland University in the sixties, Stead judged them to be little different from students elsewhere.

> The good ones, the top students, are all the same. Good students are good students wherever they are, whether it's Auckland or Oxford. But there was always quite a tail because in those days law and commerce students had to do one unit of English whether they had any talent for English or not. It used to be that the tail in English was law and commerce students whereas now the brighter students go into law and commerce.[10]

Sargeson, Stead and "A Fitting Tribute"

The words "one Sargeson made a summer" allude to a golden time for the Steads in the regular company of Sargeson. They were among the "K. S.'s" harboured by the North Shore "Before the Fall",[11] a reference to their move from Takapuna to Armidale – comparable to an expulsion from Eden. Letters from Sargeson sustained both Steads during their time in Australia and England. Sargeson spoke with extraordinary honesty about all human inclinations and Stead was also very direct. Letters reveal their deep concern for each other. Sargeson suffered health problems and he worried about Janet Frame. Stead considered each situation thoughtfully. "I hope you won't stay depressed for long. I don't believe the years are piling up – what I always get with you is the feeling of no age at all (except the accumulation of experiences of various sorts) because you remain so completely open to everything new."[12] The stress and the difficulty of organising Janet Frame's departure for England, ensuring that she had sufficient funds and nursing her through the sickness that followed her inoculations prompted sympathy and encouragement from Stead:

> What a Hell of a time you've been having. And the way you write about it seems like a terrific revelation of the determination to survive. I'm sure you'll live to a ripe old age – and produce a lot more too – because no one could emerge so vigorously from so many landslides who wasn't strong as an ox and fundamentally determined to get on with the job. Your uncompromising attitude to everything (if you'll excuse the unsubtlety of direct praise) always leaves me gasping and ashamed. And if spiritual emanations help at all you should be constantly boosted by vibrations from K. – her attitude to you is almost grounds for divorce. I expect you will collapse to some extent when you finally get yourself clear of the rubble that seems to have descended on you, but you will be clear anyway, and then it's only a matter of rest to get you back to normal working again.[13]

Once Janet Frame was on her way to England, Sargeson suffered ongoing remorse at having launched her into the world. Stead consoled him: "I can imagine your reaction to Janet's departure – it's inevitable, but you should fight the sense of guilt because you've done more for her than anyone, and you have your own work to push on with."[14]

Stead considered Sargeson his "most exacting and sensitive critic".[15] Confidence in his protégé's talent came at the price of the mentor's reiterated misgivings. In his assessment, Stead's need to write was fundamental; it was something Sargeson understood from his own experience. Years earlier, when he believed he was being offered a partnership in his uncle's farm, he knew he must turn away from it.

> [I] now recognised in my love for the farm and all that the farm implied was a threat to the life I foresaw for myself as a writer. ... How could I have written at all if I had waited until

> evening, when I would have been exhausted by the work which had absorbed me ... ? Writing too was a mighty consumer of energy, besides a task one often went to with reluctance – not solely on account of its difficulty, but because every problem encountered had to be wrestled with in solitude.[16]

Stead's new job was demanding. In arguing the matter with Sargeson, he was also arguing with himself:

> I think where problems set in between Frank and me was when I came back from overseas and went into the university and for a while *was* virtually smothered. I was under tremendous pressure working very very hard trying to keep myself alive as a writer and at the same time trying to learn to be an academic, and I was rather irascible with Frank whenever he got on to this particular hobby-horse, because it didn't seem very helpful to tell me that I was making a mistake with my life and that I was ruining myself as a writer and that the university was a terrible place to be – even if he was right! ... But I would have a bit of a row with him and then I'd think Frank's company is too good to give away just because of one incident and so I'd let a little bit of time pass and then I'd go back.[17]

Sargeson's anxiety, which persisted for several years, eventually provoked a degree of annoyance. Stead retorted in November 1964,

> You should stop worrying about me. I chose my situation, and with only slight and occasional reservations about the university I'm very happy in it. Most important, I can't imagine another situation which is both better and possible. Anyway when I try to think of an ideal situation all that comes to mind is being in the university and having less work to do –

In fact, Stead's achievements as a writer at age thirty-two were considerable. In spite of the demands of his university position and the chronic shortage of free time to write, which had characterised each phase of his life as a young man, he had completed two lengthy and successful stories ("A Race Apart" and "A Fitting Tribute"), as well as several highly acclaimed poems. A book of poetry appeared in 1964.

His memorable Auckland University Winter Lecture "For the Hulk of the World's Between" was delivered in 1960 and significant essays on Allen Curnow and R. A. K. Mason appeared in *Landfall* and *Comment* in 1963. Stead's book, *The New Poetic*, was regarded by English critic John Press[18] as the best Eliot criticism since F. O. Matthiessen.

While teaching full-time, Stead found that ideas would accumulate but that he lacked the time to put them to the best use. Interviewed nearly twenty years later, Stead admitted, "The bad part is, I suppose, what's bad in having any form of employment at all – that it's simply draining. Energy that goes into your work doesn't go into your writing, and it's as simple as that."[19]

"A Fitting Tribute", written in 1964, was published the following year in *Landfall*. Reprinted in many collections, it appears in *Essential New Zealand Short Stories*, 2002, selected by Owen Marshall. The story is a fantasy, quite unlike Sargeson's realistic short fiction. A young mother is the narrator, partner to the hero, Julian Harp. Stead's good friend Barry Humphries provided inspiration for "the manic youth dancing in a 'teen club under the street where you could twist and stomp'." Humphries has described "A Fitting Tribute" as "An absolutely fabulous story!"[20] Julian Harp's comment, that "at night the timber houses of Auckland look like lanterns", was originally voiced by Humphries. Stead has always enjoyed his friend's outrageousness, his rebellion against "the sense of moral repression" and "the crushing weight of propriety"[21] that characterised both Australia and New Zealand in the 1960s.

Like "A Race Apart", the new story sprang from an idea, in this case the consequences of human flight, the flier propelled only by arm movement. Julian Harp plans and trains, and eventually rises skyward. The city of Auckland makes him a hero, transforming his appearance and history to fit a popular ideal: "the thing about him is that at the end he's become public property and if the public want to say that he had short hair and was clean-shaven and looked like an army officer then he damn well did, whatever the woman who knew him says."[22]

Acknowledgement of Stead's publications, originality and potential came in the form of a Nuffield Fellowship in 1965. A return to England allowed him to continue his research at the British Museum into "Poetry and Politics". Acclaim in the 1960s as an academic and as a creative writer saw him promoted to the rank of professor in 1967. "I was first appointed to this university at the bottom of the lecturer's scale when

I was about 27, and I think I went through the grades and had a chair at about 35; and I was fairly active and ambitious in every aspect of university life during that period."[23]

Hobson Bay and Oliver

In addition to progress as an academic and growing recognition as a writer, the 1960s saw changes in Stead's private life. In January 1963, two items of news were shared with Sargeson. The first was that the Steads were "buying a very cheap house":

> – it's a bach rather than a house – down near the Hobson Bay sewer pipe. (Do you know it? I'm not joking – it's a great concrete structure that runs right across the bay – makes an excellent pathway for walkers, and even cyclists.) The house is in Tohunga Crescent. It has a hut in the back yard I can fix up for writing in. I feel quite happy about the place because it's not worth much and consequently doesn't feel like an anchor or ball-and-chain. And it will save paying rent – though, of course, we don't much like the idea of leaving our present place.[24]

Prime real estate today, the bach with its sitting room, bedroom, kitchen and bathroom has been extended outwards and upwards over the years. In a leafy Parnell no-exit street that runs down to Hobson Bay, it overlooks mudflats at low tide and a seascape at high tide.

Stead's second news item was that Kay was pregnant. "We decided we were old enough and hardy enough to try even that! Can you imagine me pushing a pram? I'm quite looking forward to it."[25] Oliver William was born in August, 1963. He is next mentioned in a letter to Sargeson as an eighteen-month-old, when the family was in London. "Oliver is growing into a delightful chatterbox – a little of what he says is intelligible."[26] The boy features in "A Small Registry of Births and Deaths", published in *Landfall* in 1966. Its images form a hard-hitting political statement.

The poem begins with Oliver's birth – the impersonal nature of the hospital, then relief at hearing the new mother, albeit "Bloodshot and drugged", burbling about "our boy". The poet's imperative to safeguard his own child is juxtaposed against events in Vietnam, where forty-five children "were changed" when "a Free bomb fell on a school". America, espousing 'freedom', is responsible: "a sentimental nation/ That loves its cars/ As it loves its children." The poem, with controlled fury, proposes that President Lyndon Baines Johnson relate the bereavement suffered by scores of nameless Vietnamese families to imagined loss within his own family, "Bird" being the name Johnson used to address his wife, and the second name of his elder daughter.

> Lyndon
> If ever a missile
> Blows one of your Birds to bits
> Don't hate it, Lyndon –
> It was only misguided.[27]

Politics in Poetry

Stead justifies the presence of politics in his poetry. "Because poetry is one of my preoccupations I like to think that politics can get into the poems, but it has to happen on its own. And I think the only way it can happen is that the preoccupation, of whatever kind, has to become part of your whole emotional self. The longer you've had the preoccupation, and the more deeply embedded it is in your personality, the more likely it is to find ways to express itself."[28]

A poem that confronts America's policy of intervention and domination is cited by Stead and followed by his commentary in "A Poet's View" from *In the Glass Case*.

> Each day He dies to do me good,
> I sign a protest, join a march.
> What Wolf began, Eagle accomplishes.
>
> Minerva had a mouse in mind.
> It was a weasel, tore her beak.
> What Owl began, Eagle accomplishes.
>
> Eagle bears the Snake to die.
> Up there it twists about his throat.
> Out of the sun they fall like brass.
>
> I signed a protest, joined a march.
> Today he dies to do me good.

> What Eagle began, Serpent accomplishes.
> (C. K. Stead, 'April Notebook')

> Poetry is made with words; but during the middle and late sixties a very large *subject* forced its way into my poems. Ever since the Korean War, being angry at American foreign policy and at what I saw as our own slavish involvement in it had been a more or less continuing state of mind. But in 1965, when Lyndon Johnson began the bombardment of North Vietnam and simultaneously put half a million American soldiers into South Vietnam the ineptitude and brutality of that policy was all at once exposed and magnified. The movement of protest one had looked for for years developed and grew rapidly – first in America, then in Europe. By 1968 it had broadened to become something of a minor revolution in Western society.[29]

Stead employs symbols in "April Notebook" that place the situation in a long history of conflict, reaching back into mythology. Wolves prey on the industry of others, as did colonisers in South East Asia, before World War II. "Minerva", sometimes depicted as an owl, is the Roman Goddess of Wisdom and Warriors. Initially the Vietnamese sought unsuccessfully to regain their traditional territory. "Owl" is replaced by the more subtle machinations of "Snake", an allusion, perhaps, to Vietnamese guerillas. When "Eagle" battles against "Snake", both suffer injury. "Eagle" signifies America, but "Snake", strengthened to the tenacity and ingenuity of "Serpent", wins through eventually. In an essay, Stead has made his position clear: "K. attacked me at a party for presenting exclusively arguments in favour of North Viet Nam and the National Liberation Front. He did not see – still does not see – that that is the side I support."[30]

Stead's increasing anxiety at America's foreign policy came to be related, not just to one child, but to three. Oliver's arrival was followed by that of Charlotte in 1966 and Margaret early in 1970.

> One personal fact that deepened my feelings about these events was that by now I had children. My family and the war seemed to grow larger together. That made the war seem more real. The deaths weren't abstract, as they had seemed to be when I was a child. They were a dark stain over

> everything; and correspondingly the political commitment I felt was deeper and more implacable. I learned from that how people must have felt in the thirties, and in fact during any time when a great wrong seems about to precipitate radical change. Because as well as horror there was a compensating excitement. So much was going on at the emotional level one was very largely relieved of the burden of reason; and however dangerous such a state may be it has, as well as force, its own kind of purity.
>
> All this strong feeling got into the poems I wrote during those years, which are domestic poems, suburban New Zealand poems, clouded by world events, and they're printed in the first section of my book *Crossing the Bar*.[31]

Photographs from the late 1960s and early 1970s show Stead addressing protest rallies. He told Steve Braunias, "It was an obsession for almost five years, and it felt great! I enjoyed it! I was passionate about it, and spent a lot of time being angry, but the sense of being able to be with a group and express that anger was exhilarating".[32] Those were the hippie years, with young people in sandals, flowered shirts and long skirts. Men grew their hair long. Stead sported a bushy beard and wore corduroy trousers. The mood of the era is recreated in his 1992 novel, *The End of the Century at the End of the World*, in which a group of radicals share an old house. They use a car painted with red and purple swirls, pass round the dope bag and enjoy marijuana joints in a time of sexual freedom. Of major concern to them is the war in Vietnam. The novel's male narrator claims the war to be "a true expression of American foreign policy" and "the atrocities ... a true expression of the war".[33]

The novel includes one of the huge protest marches of the time, capturing its mood and intensity. Stead was among the marchers on several occasions. Protesters throughout New Zealand hoped that the country might withdraw from its involvement in Vietnam.

> The student group set off from Princes Street, the trade unionists and others from the bottom of Queen Street, and the two columns converged on the Town Hall. No one could remember a protest march in Auckland that had drawn so many thousands of people. ... At first it was solemn, almost

> funereal. Then from far off, as they moved down towards Queen Street, came the chants and shouts of the other column. The noise got louder, the two seeming to call and answer one another. ... As the two groups flowed together, filling the street, there was a feeling of exhilaration and of power ...[34]

Smith's Dream and the Inside of a Cell

A relatively small section of *The End of the Century at the End of the World* is focused on the war in Vietnam, whereas Stead's first novel, *Smith's Dream*, arose out of the protest movement against that war. "The idea was to try to imagine a Vietnam situation here in New Zealand. Some people saw it as a prophecy for the future. I saw it as an exercise in imagination."[35]

Despite the demands of the university and family life, Stead embarked on *Smith's Dream* in 1967, a project he could not continue in term-time. Vacations, though, were too short. To Sargeson he explained the problem.

> The whole subject of *Smith's Dream* is frightfully confused for me. When the idea first came to me it was blindingly clear and simple from beginning to end (when Smith was to be killed by Jesperson). I dashed down two chapters and then, because of work, had to put it aside for about eight months. When I went back to it the original idea remained only as an intellectual thing – the feeling, the clarity, the glitter had gone. I simply laboured the thing into being and it exists now as a cross between Graham Greene and John Mulgan, probably falling between the two stools.[36]

Stead was convinced that consistency of tone could not be achieved if time for writing was fragmented. "I don't think [*Smith's Dream*] is successful, really. I get the impression it's a readable book, and I think to some extent it does what it set out to do, but I can't imagine it being an experiment I'd want to repeat."[37]

Stead's reservations were not borne out by the book's sales, which number tens of thousands. A second edition has been followed by many reprints, with the novel extensively studied in schools, both as a literary text and as the source of the film *Sleeping Dogs*. Stead had no involvement in making the film, which Roger Donaldson directed. "I was about to go overseas when Roger came to me to ask if he could make a movie of the book. I said, 'Sure, just give me the papers you want signed.' I came back nine months later just in time for the first showing."[38] Stead was paid $5000, a very small sum considering the film's repeated screenings and its on-going use in the Film Studies syllabus in many secondary schools and universities.

Having addressed the philosophical question as to whether to emphasise a man's political responsibility or whether to permit Smith to live on his wits and his personal resources, like the 'man alone' of New Zealand legend, the author chose initially to allow Smith to survive. After the first edition, however, the ending was revised.

> Briefly, my first idea was that Smith should be killed at the end of the novel, and it was not until I reached the final chapter that I felt compelled by what I took to be a very strong 'artistic impulse' (not, I was sure, a sentimental one, or the wish for a 'happy ending') to have him survive. When the novel was first published some readers liked it but complained of the nebulous ending. And I had myself begun to see why it was that Smith ought to have been killed. The novel offered a fairly simple moral proposition. That you can escape political and social responsibility by getting away and being a 'man alone' in the bush is the old New Zealand dream – Smith's dream – and it is false. There is no escape. Smith tries it but life catches up with him in the form of Volkner's Special X. To have him drift off alone at the end of the book was to contradict its whole moral point. So now my original intention seemed undoubtedly right; and when a paper-back was planned for 1973 I changed the end. From that time on, through a large number of reprints, Smith has died on the last page.[39]

Smith's Dream recalls the draconian government measures of 1951, designed to discipline and constrain striking waterside workers. Those measures are extended and exaggerated in Stead's novel. At the same time, *Smith's Dream* foreshadows 1981 events, in which police with long batons and shields, a visible feature of *Sleeping Dogs*, confronted opponents to the Springbok Rugby Tour. Stead, whose career as a left-wing radical resurfaced in 1981, was involved in the protest movement against the tour. "That got me off my chair and even showed me the inside of a cell for the first time in my life."[40] Journalist Michelle Hewitson writes:

> There is a photograph of Stead standing on the field at Hamilton, facing the riot squad during the 1981 Springbok Tour, which recently appeared in the *Listener*.
>
> It was strange to see it after all this time, showing a side of the writer that many people have forgotten, or chosen to forget.
>
> The real story behind the picture, says Stead, "is that there was a little Maori girl standing behind me and she was just sort of holding herself up. And I turned around and said, 'I think I'm going to faint.' Not at all heroic."[41]

Stead had clambered through the boundary wire with the protesters: "The assault was exhilarating, the attainment of mid-field together with so many was ecstatic, and the long wait, threatened with being beaten to death by riot police and by the anger of the crowd, terrifying".[42] He was arrested and driven away in a police van, together with Tim Shadbolt, who remarked, "You scripted the whole thing, didn't you!"[43] In the course of a night spent in police custody, Stead wrote on the cell wall, "C. K. Stead, author of *Smith's Dream*, was here."[44] A prosecution was the outcome. He was convicted of 'disorderly behaviour' and fined $250 plus costs.

In Stead's novel *The Death of the Body*, his central character, Professor Harry Butler, has one conviction, deemed some years later by a police investigator to be "respectable". In Butler's case, it followed from an anti-Vietnam protest, opposing Spiro Agnew's mission to secure more New Zealand troops to support America's forces in Vietnam. Stead considers his own conviction not just to be "respectable", but he "likens the black mark against his name to a badge of honour".[45]

Nigel Cox noted in an article for *Quote/Unquote*[46] that *Smith's Dream* has often been viewed as a warning against Robert Muldoon's potential to act like a dictator. There was an occasion when the Steads met Muldoon, who mused with a certain pride that people thought of him as the model for Volkner, the dictator in the novel. Stead replied diplomatically.

> I thought it was my job to be polite, as he was a guest of

> the university. So I reassured him and said: 'You were a fairly junior Cabinet minister when I wrote that book.' And my wife said: 'Yes, you've just grown into the role.'[47]

Although the novel was finished in 1968, it took Stead some time to find the right publisher. A reader from Hutchinsons in London admired the book in 1969, but the company hesitated to commit to it. *Smith's Dream* finally appeared in 1971, put out by Longman Paul in Auckland. A publishing grant had been refused by the State Literary Fund, but, nevertheless, Longman Paul's publishing director Phoebe Meikle decided to take the risk and the publication went ahead.

Pressure of work at the university, the completion of a novel, and his on-going involvement in Vietnam protests must have made inroads into time for family life. Nevertheless, Stead's daughter Charlotte recalls the games her father played with her when she was very young.

> I have always got on extremely well with my father, from as far back as I can remember. All of us kids had a good relationship with both our parents. Dad has a very antic quality – nothing is ever dull or prosaic with him, and there were always these verbal jokes and games. When we, as small children played our imaginary games he would pick up on them and enlarge them, encouraging us to go further. He's a great parent – really fun and easy to get on with.
>
> When I was very little I played a game where Dad was my son, named Castle, and I was his terribly punitive mother. I would order him about, terrifying him, and the ultimate punishment was to hit him with the wooden spoon. If he was particularly naughty he would be 'spooned to death'. There was never any actual wooden spoon, nor any hitting. I would just stamp my feet and order him around. I'd be fierce and he'd pretend to be frightened and run away.[48]

Stead recalls the early imaginative games just as clearly.

> Charlotte used to play these pretend games with me. It started when she was a pre-schooler, and she had outrageous names for everything. There were additional characters like the boy next door and then his mother. I was her little boy, called Castle

ABOVE LEFT: Robert Flatt, son of John Flatt and father of Caroline Karlson, the greatgrand-father of Karlson (Karl) Stead.

ABOVE RIGHT: Karl's mother, Olive Karlson, aged sixteen.

BELOW: Christian and Caroline Karlson, parents of Olive and grandparents of Karl.

Above left: Karl's father, James (Jim) Walter Ambrose Stead, as a young man.

Above right: Karl's mother, Olive Karlson, as a young woman.

Below: Norma Stead aged three and her brother, Karl, aged eighteen months.

Above left: Karl aged two with Bill Bowmar at the Kaiwaka farm. “The old wooden verandah” is mentioned in *The Singing Whakapapa*.

Above right: Karl aged five or six with his mother.

Below: The Kaiwaka homestead today, home to Bowmar descendants. The brick chimney from the original homestead is still standing.

ABOVE: The crater of Maungawhau, Mt Eden, part of Karl's boyhood neighbourhood and the place where his characters from *The Singing Whakapapa*, "broke an arm each doing daring sledge runs down into the crater". (p.66)

RIGHT: Karl receives the chess champion prize in his final year at Mt Albert Grammar, 1950.

BELOW: The school's senior athletic team, 1950. Karl is second from the right, middle row.

ABOVE: With fellow University of Auckland students, eating lunch in Albert Park, April 1951: Barry Rodewald, Karl, Ian Hart, Steve Mannins.

RIGHT: Compulsory military training. Karl and a fellow cadet at the Ardmore rifle range, 1952.

BELOW: Auckland University Revue, "The Plotters", May 1953, with Karl fourth from left at back.

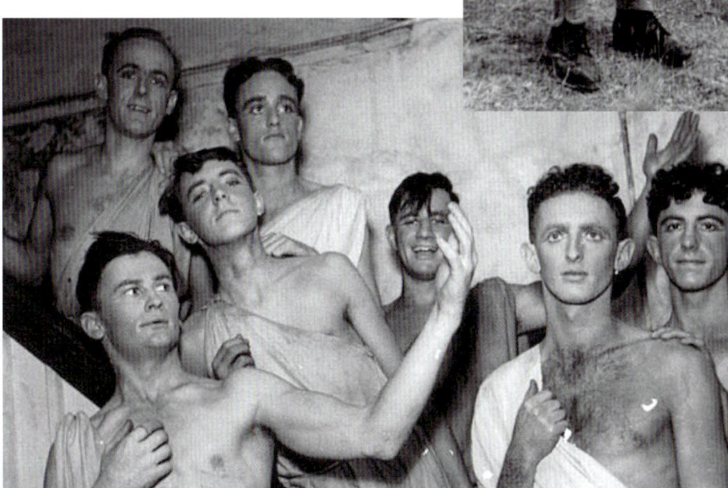

Top: Karl and Kay on their wedding day, January, 1955.
Above left: Graduates M.A. first-class honours.
Above right: Kay with Oliver aged three, 1966. Charlotte is expected.
Photo: Marti Friedlander

and that was a play on my full name, which is Karlson.

His account of Charlotte as a child discloses home experiences that would have ensured her imaginative capacity and her facility with language could flourish. He describes himself and Kay as "literary parents".

> Kay is a tremendous reader as well, and she read to all the children from a very early age, when they were hardly more than one year old. So they learned that books contain stuff they wanted to hear, then later stuff they could read. As they grew up books and literature would be discussed all the time, especially around the dinner table. Also, I carried around in my head a huge stock of poems, so when we were driving along in my car I would quote poetry to them.[49]

Stirrings of Disquiet

Stead has always been buoyed and supported by his own family. However, ill-will toward him stirred among members of the literary community from the 1960s. Spats between Stead and Maurice Shadbolt date back even further, with Stead deploring the quality of Shadbolt's prose, and Shadbolt defending poets Charles Doyle and Alistair Campbell against Stead's criticism of their work. Disquiet did not become significant, though, until Stead reviewed, for a 1967 *Landfall*, Fairburn's posthumous *Collected Poems*. The tenor of Stead's appraisal is described by James McNeish: "He lines the poems up one by one in rows and with insight tells us the composition of their parts. It is largely a destructive insight however."[50] Ian Hamilton's extended response to Stead's review finds fault with his failure to place Fairburn's work within its social and historical context. While agreeing with a number of points, conceding for example that Fairburn uses "faded language" in his early work, he considers Stead to have been "unnecessarily harsh",[51] failing, for example, to give credit for some fine poetry within the longer poems.

Indignation at Stead's criticism was spurred by popular regard for Fairburn. He was a favourite, "more widely admired," in Stead's opinion, "than any other of our poets".[52] To his credit, Stead calls his essay, reprinted in *In the Glass Case*, "The Argument Against", and draws attention to Ian Hamilton's "argument *for*", describing it as a "vigorous counter-statement, or counter-blast to my review".[53]

Misgivings in regard to Stead lay dormant in the literary world until 1979, through a decade in which he spent two extended periods out of the country and held a powerful position among writers, as chair of the Literary Fund from 1972 till 1975. The first of a series of letters, articles or reviews that found fault with Lauris Edmond's critical position or literary work appeared in 1979. This piece of criticism took the form of a carefully argued letter to the *Listener* for her review of books by Elizabeth Smither, Brian Turner and Kendrick Smithyman. Stead found her "uninformed" about Smithyman's work, and her tone to be generally "condescending".[54] In the years to come, his response to her work would cause resentment and anger among her supporters. Like Fairburn, Edmond was seen by Stead to be a favourite, and he considered the esteem that attended her work to be excessive.

1 C. K. Stead, *The Writer at Work*, Dunedin, University of Otago Press, 2000, p. 248.

2 Janet McAllister, "Friends and Foes", *NZ Herald*, 9 July 2005, Supplement p. 23.

3 Stead, *The Writer at Work*, p. 9. In the same opening paragraph of his Introduction, Stead states plainly that he had returned to New Zealand "because I was a literary nationalist".

4 Greg O'Brien (text), Robert Cross (photographs), "C. K. Stead: The Pigeon and the Clock", *Moments of Invention*, Heinemann Reed, 1988, p.77.

5 Stead, *The Writer at Work*, p. 248.

6 Michael Harlow, "Craft Interview with C. K. Stead", *Landfall* Volume 37 (4), December 1983, p. 457.

7 Kamala Jackson, "C. K. Stead: Poet, Novelist, Academic, Activist and Aucklander on his Origins", *Metro*, February 1985, p. 127.

8 ibid, p. 122.

9 Warwick Roger, "Face to Face: C. K. Stead", *North and South*, May 2004, p. 70.

10 ibid, p. 70.

11 C. K. Stead, "Sonnet 8", *Walking Westward*, Auckland, The Shed, 1979, p. 20. At a literal level, Sargeson is the author of "That Summer".

12 Michael King, *Frank Sargeson: A Life*, Auckland, NZ Viking, p. 329.

13 C. K. Stead, letter to Sargeson, 27 July 1956, Turnbull Library Papers.

14 C. K. Stead, letter to Sargeson, 8 August 1956, Turnbull Library Papers.

15 C. K. Stead, letter to Sargeson, 13 June 1972, Turnbull Library Papers.

16 King, *Frank Sargeson: A Life*, p. 110.

17 Stead, *The Writer at Work*, pp. 235-6.

18 C. K. Stead, letter to Sargeson, 16 November 1964.

19 Harlow, "Craft Interview with C. K. Stead", *Landfall*, December 1983, p. 457.

20 Steve Braunias, "In for the High Jump", *New Zealand Listener*, 30 July 1994, p. 35.

21 Stead, *The Writer at Work*, p. 131.

22 ibid, p. 242.

23 Harlow, "Craft Interview with C. K. Stead", *Landfall*, December 1983, p. 457.

24 C. K. Stead, letter to Sargeson, 23 January 1963, Turnbull Library Papers.
25 ibid.
26 C. K. Stead, letter to Sargeson, 28 March 1965, Turnbull Library Papers.
27 C. K. Stead, "A Small Registry of Births and Deaths", *Crossing the Bar*, Auckland University Press/ Oxford University Press, 1972, p. 17 and p. 18.
28 Stead, *The Writer at Work*, p. 230.
29 C. K. Stead, *In the Glass Case: Essays on New Zealand Literature*, Auckland, Auckland University Press/Oxford University Press, 1981, pp. 267-8.
30 C. K. Stead, "The Conference on Peace, Power and Politics in Asia", *Landfall* Volume 22 (2), June 1968, p. 145.
31 Stead, *In the Glass Case*, p. 268.
32 Braunias, "In for the High Jump", *New Zealand Listener*, 30 July 1994, p. 35.
33 C. K. Stead, *The End of the Century at the End of the World*, Auckland, HarperCollins, 1992, p. 65.
34 ibid, p. 78.
35 Roger, "Face to Face: C. K. Stead", *North & South*, May 2004, p. 71.
36 C. K. Stead, letter to Sargeson, 21 December 1972, Turnbull Library Papers.
37 Stephen Chan, "No Stainless Steel Poet", *New Argot*, May 1974, p. 15.
38 Roger, "Face to Face: C. K. Stead", *North & South*, May 2004, p. 71.
39 Stead, *In the Glass Case*, pp. 87-8.
40 Nigel Cox, "Leading with his Chin", *Quote/Unquote*, July 1994, p. 15.
41 Michele Hewitson, "Swimming Against the Tide", *Canvas*, 24 April 2004, p. 20.
42 C. K. Stead, letter to Allen Curnow, 27 July 1981, Turnbull Library Papers.
43 Braunias, "In for the High Jump", *New Zealand Listener*, 30 July 1994, p.35.
44 Brian Edwards, from an interview with C. K. Stead, *National Radio*, 3 December 1994.
45 Maggie Blake, "Stead's Dream a Nightmare", *Auckland Star*, 17 October 1983, p. B 1.
46 Cox, *Quote/Unquote*, July 1884, p. 14.
47 Blake, "Stead's Dream a Nightmare", *Auckland Star*, 17 October 1983, p. B 1.
48 Deborah Coddington, "Family Ties: In Good Stead", *North & South*, July 1999, p. 28.
49 ibid, p. 29.
50 James McNeish, "Letter to the Editor", *Landfall* Volume 21 (2), June 1967, p. 216.
51 Ian Hamilton, "Fairburn and Dr Stead", *Comment*, September 1967, p. 38.
52 Stead, *In the Glass Case*, p. 161.
53 ibid, p. 160.
54 C. K. Stead, "Letter to the Editor: Life, Literature and Poetry", *NZ Listener*, May 19 1979, p. 7.

CHAPTER FIVE

The Menton Legacy

"On the Stone Stairway"[1]

A Winn-Manson Mansfield Fellowship in 1972 provided Stead with seven months abroad in Menton. Research time in London followed. The children were two, five and eight when the family left New Zealand. Menton is the French Riviera town closest to the Italian border. An olive grove alongside the family's apartment is recalled in *Five for the Symbol*'s dedication: "To Oliver, Charlotte and Margaret/ in the olive grove/ and in the future". For Sargeson, Stead described his situation in Menton.

> I keep finding myself committing visual things to memory here. Today it was pigeons flying through the olive grove (<u>the</u> olive grove because we live beside it); yesterday it was a red-brick bumble bee. And everywhere you look there are 'views'. From our front balcony we look straight ahead to the sea; right to the old town; left to the grey/pink/orange rocks of the Maritime Alps and the headland beyond which is Italy. The garden is full of date palms, phoenix palms, mimosa. At the edge of the olive grove there are cypresses. There is a little lane runs down to the school the children go to and the houses are all pink and orange plaster peppered with bullet holes. Isola Bella is two minutes away with the same views. There is the villa which belongs to a larger Pension that looks down on it; a terrace in front of the villa, and below the terrace the little room, opening on to a garden, which the town bought as a memorial to KM. There are bronze plaques on either side of the door. Now that it's spring a lizard – not the ordinary kind of lizard of which there are thousands but a prehistoric looking affair like a small dragon – likes to come and sun itself

> on the plaque. ... The town has done very little to fit the KM room up for a writer. I had to buy a kerosene heater for cold days. But I like to have a room to go to.[2]

A stairway with stone steps hollowed by the feet of many generations leads to the heart of the town – a square surrounded by medieval buildings and churches. People from past centuries seem to be present still, in the form of shades and shadows watching over the ancient town square, according to Stead's poem "Walking Westward".

> On the stone stairway
> to the square of the churches
> oil lamps flare at a breath from the sea
> and across the water flicker
> lights of San Remo.
>
> The windows look upon the square
> the square looks over the water
> the town is still listening to music from the square
> at a light salt breath
> black smoke flaps from the oil flares
> dark heads look down
> shadows
> shades of shades
> *Sunt manes*
> and the ghosts live for ever [3]

Though written in 1978, "Walking Westward" is one of several works owing part of its detail and atmosphere to Stead's stay in Menton and his travels along the Mediterranean coast and into Italy.

The fellowship allowed Stead to devote himself to his own writing and to the work of Katherine Mansfield, which he re-read in its entirety. He explained to Sargeson that the Mansfield room, which was his workplace, attracted visitors.

> ... the Memorial draws even in winter a surprising number of visitors – almost all of them French. I ignore them and they are always surprised and usually scuttle off when they take a peep through the window and see someone at work. ... But one

> day the sun was shining and I opened the door to catch more of it and a middle-aged couple simply walked in. I tried to make it clear without being rude that the room wasn't 'open' to the public but the old lady, finding that I was a writer, had to tell me that her husband (who meanwhile was patrolling the edges of the room) had wanted to be a writer when he was young and had taken many notes for a projected work. But unfortunately, and incredibly, and even tragically, whenever he tried to begin to write he was overcome with tiredness – he became exhausted – and so the great work was never written. I was about to say Madame, I'm exhausted all the time, but then I thought it probably kinder to let her go on thinking that something strange and out of the ordinary had stemmed her dear husband's creative flow.[4]

Over the years, exhaustion has been mentioned intermittently in Stead's letters. His prodigious work output would have contributed to a condition that becomes an aspect of his conception of hell on earth in "Walking Westward". In addition to his teaching and administration as a university professor, his creative writing and critical essays, he edited and introduced *New Zealand Short Stories, Second Series* (1966) and *Shakespeare: Measure for Measure: a Casebook* (1971). The decade following the Mansfield Fellowship produced an even more extraordinary publishing record, with the release of *The Letters and Journals of Katherine Mansfield: A Selection* (1977), and the on-going publication of reviews and literary essays. His large work, *Pound, Yeats, Eliot and the Modernist Movement* was completed, a collection of stories was assembled, and volumes of poetry appeared in 1972, 1975, 1979 and 1982.

"Under the Sun"

Crossing the Bar, the 1972 poetry volume, includes work from the 1960s. Stead arrived in Menton after three years in which he had written no poetry. The shock of a "near disaster"[5] is credited with spurring him to produce a long poem sustained through ten sections called "Under the Sun". The family was driving near Nîmes, heading for Spain, when their van's steering failed and the vehicle slewed into a ditch. Kay spent a night in hospital under observation. Stead reported the event to Sargeson:

> We bought a van, ex of the Gloucester Constabulary, for our expeditions and for going to London with all our baggages, and had a wonderful time riding through wide France. But one morning it was possessed by an ancient and malevolent field spirit and simply leapt into a ditch. ... But it was a nasty moment. Kay spent a night in hospital being X-rayed (no damage) and stitched (just three stitches near her left eye). The rest of us bruised and shaken and the van abandoned in a wrecker's yard.[6]

"Under the Sun" provides an account of the accident.

> Would Provence have noticed had we all died in that ditch
> Blood filling your eyes and the children screaming?
> In that rush of bright green foliage
> That flood of grey earth pouring through the windscreen[7]

The crash is viewed as one more violent event in the violent history of the French countryside, where "Every stone had a blood stain./ Every rock had thrown back a human cry". On a solitary drive to revisit the accident site to hunt for lost items, including his spectacles, the poet empathises with MacDuff's feeling of desolation at having lost all his "pretty ones",[8] a tragedy that might well have befallen Stead himself.

Part of the poem's tapestry is provided by the town of Menton, with its "Indolent cafes", "stone benches", its "balconies that are hung with vines".[9] Pigeons, bright light, lizards and olive trees all seem to anticipate the impact of the crash.

Reflections on experiences in Italy and France in 1972 also found expression as sonnets. One, dedicated to Kay, recalls a visit by the Stead family to the Uffizi Gallery in Florence. Botticelli's "lines of cold melodic fire" are recorded in Stead's lines celebrating the painting of Venus, "who'd been waiting half a thousand years/ / To ride for us on her scallop shell out of those wavelets/Flowers falling around her, zephyrs breathing about her".[10] (p. 21) He describes to Sargeson his delight in the visit:

> Our trip to Florence, Pisa and the Coast of Tuscany was hardly less of a knock-out than the earlier one to Venice. Florence is an extraordinary city and the Uffizi Gallery where we'd

> designated Botticelli's 'Birth of Venus' as official 'summit' for the expedition (in the same way that the Piazza San Marco had been designated for the earlier one) proved to have so many 'summits' it left us panting for oxygen.[11]

The Scarf and Stead Families

Stead's story "The Town" has a setting derived from Menton, though Stead calls his fictional town Garavan, which is the name of the relatively modern port and adjacent district at the eastern end of Menton, where he and his family lived. Houses in Menton and in "The Town" are scarred with bullet holes, reminders of Italian occupation during World War II. The phenomenon is explained in Stead's story.

> I noticed bullet holes in the building directly below us. ... The next villa and the next, the apartment block below, they were all peppered. I hadn't noticed it before and I pointed it out to Fabrice. ...
>
> He pulled one of those pouting French faces. 'That was our Fascisti friends from along the coast. They waited till France had fallen, then they came to claim the town.'[12]

Stead makes the most of the exotic setting. Above Menton are "hill villages perched on impossible crags, medieval villages with tiny twisted buildings and twisted cobbled streets and passages and stairways – all still inhabited. There's nothing comparable in England."[13] New Zealanders travelling in England find familiar scenes, through their exposure to English literature, but the ancient villages in southern France and the medieval town centres of Menton, Monaco and Nice are different and unexpected. Even photographs do not prepare the visitor for the use of every square metre, the extraordinary angles and the narrowness of lanes between buildings.

Stead's story "The Town" has five major parts, named like separate chapters, each of which is divided into smaller sections. Episodes are juxtaposed in the way Stead likes to juxtapose sections within his long poems, allowing readers to make connections. The story is surprisingly complex, moving back and forth in time, and in and out of a range of settings derived from Menton, Monte Carlo, the neighbouring countryside and the coastal roads.

"The Town" includes a greater number of characters than is usual in a short story. Members of the Scarf family play central roles: parents and three children. The Scarfs have a son "getting on for nine years old"[14] and two girls aged five and "almost three".[15] Like Kay Stead, Toni Scarf is an attractive woman with black hair. The narrator, though, is not the father of the family, but a divorced New Zealander called Rod Millar, who finds himself fascinated by Toni Scarf. It is as if Stead has replaced himself with a different father/husband and then stepped back to recreate and appreciate characters who bear a likeness to his wife and children. The youngest character is Hermi, a reminder that Stead's youngest is Margaret Hermione. The five-year-old character Arlene watches President Pompidou on television at an event involving speeches, bands and a military parade. Her comment could have been made by Charlotte Stead, who was clever with humorous word-play from an early age: "'And there was a scream from the crowd,' she shouted, 'as Pumpy-do went *farting* down the street'."[16]

The Stead family would have experienced at least one major storm in Menton, like that which blows apartment windows open in "The Town" and causes a warship out in the bay to haul on its anchor chain. A comparable storm features in "Walking Westward".

> Menton   soixante-douze
> storm in the olives
> shutters banging
> woke to a strange light
> wind assaulting hillslope
> running at rockface
> driving home rainspears
> paper torn from hoardings on the Moyenne Corniche
> branches down in the garden of Blasco Ibanez
> frigate anchored off
>   in orange turbulence
> listing.[17]

The garden referred to in the poem is located in Menton's Avenue Blasco Ibanez, where a pool is surrounded by tiles depicting scenes from *Don Quixote* and busts of past novelists. It also features in "The Town" and is visited by Luke Scarf on his way home from school. "'It's creepy,' he said. And he added, 'That's why I come here.'"[18] Stead knew at first hand what would interest a boy of that age and how he would speak. Oliver and Charlotte attended school in Menton, acquiring a degree of competence in French. Their father told Sargeson that, after seven months, the children were keen to return to the company of children with whom they could converse in English, but that Charlotte's French accent was perfect.

For Stead, Menton was an ideal location. Even today, he might not retract his 1974 judgement that the Menton Fellowship provided him "with the most rewarding seven months I have spent outside New Zealand".[19] As a writer, he made new discoveries. "I feel as a result of my stay in Menton that I greatly enlarged my understanding of the art of fiction, both by the reading I did, and by the experiments I made in writing it."[20] Stead mentioned to Curnow, in March 1974, that he had just finished a novel set in France. Part of this work appeared in *Islands* that year as "Voiture d'Occasion", followed by the note, "C. K. Stead is close to finishing a novel of which the above is an extract."[21] The novel did not materialise, but sections from it were reshaped into "The Town", forty-five pages in length and dated 1974 in the story collection *Five for the Symbol*, where it was published for the first time in 1981. It has not received the acclaim of "A Race Apart" and "A Fitting Tribute".

Mansfield Research

Following the Menton fellowship, Stead and his family travelled to London where they spent five months while the writer made a study of the work of Katherine Mansfield, having in mind the publication of a selection of her letters and journals which, "set side by side, often illuminated one another. (...) In London I put the idea to Allen Lane and Penguin. It was accepted, and a contract drawn up."[22] Research took Stead to the Reading Room and Manuscript Section of the British Museum, which holds a number of Mansfield papers. He chose passages for their excellence.

> In selecting from the great mass of correspondence and journals available, I have been guided principally by the wish to represent Katherine Mansfield's writing at its best rather than to give a balanced biographical portrait. ... she is at her best when the writing is least deliberate, when it flows easily and naturally, governed by feeling and observation rather than by any apparent calculation of its effect.[23]

Stead was able to interview Mansfield's friend Ida Baker in 1972, though an account of the visit was not published until the year 2000 when it appeared as a chapter in *The Writer at Work*. He found her, aged 84, at home in a small thatched cottage in the countryside near Salisbury: "One can see that she was worthy of being Mansfield's friend – that the impression of her as a nonentity, an insignificant hanger-on, is quite wrong."[24] She appreciated the strengths of Mansfield's husband, John Middleton Murry, while being aware of his weaknesses. She was in no doubt that there was "great love" between Murry and Mansfield. The visit "made many things vivid. When she spoke with sudden emphasis of Lawrence striding up and down the room, impatient, on the verge of anger (he was waiting for lunch, which poor L.M. was making) she somehow conveyed an impression of his energy and urgency."[25] Stead's plan for *Mansfield: Letters and Journals* was to divide the book "into chapters according to where Katherine Mansfield was at the time of writing; and to provide an introduction, notes, and linking commentary".[26]

The book appeared in 1977, after delays in obtaining release of copyright material. Through his research, Stead increased his insight into Mansfield's thought as a writer, developing an understanding that would inform his successful 2004 novel, *Mansfield*.

Juan Quesada

Another legacy of the 1972 fellowship is a long poem, reminiscent of France in particular, written late in 1973 and into January 1974. It is the eight-page "Quesada". While it carries echoes of New Zealand's landscape and shoreline – flax, dunes and cicadas – it evokes a medieval Mediterranean atmosphere, with French phrases, black olives in the grass, grapes and a knightly central character. "Across the plain at nightfall a bonfire blazed for his coming."[27] The bonfire recalls guiding bonfires of old, while implying the passion of a woman who waits and expects his arrival.

The characterisation of Juan Quesada marks a new development for Stead. First-person poetry, which featured in "Under the Sun", is replaced in "Quesada" by a character viewed from an objective distance. Juan Quesada emerges as Everyman in his prime, a passionate dreamer who gains wisdom through suffering and who gives voice to it grandly. His name echoes and alludes to Don Quixote, the unsuccessful lover, a "*hero/fool*" who seeks or quests endlessly. "He is like Quixote but not Quixote. Like Quixote he has a mistress (real or imaginary) called Dulcinea."[28] The idealised object of his hopes is beautiful, but unpredictable.

Most of the lines in this clever and sensuous poem carry at least two levels of significance.

> Odysseus under wet snapping sheets
> Quesada in the saddle – all men are travellers
> Astride, under sheets, travellers and lovers, they go
> To prize the world apart, to learn the spaces
> In Circe's cave, on couches of blue satin
> In brown grass under summer olives.
> As long as seasons change don't look for stillness
> Dulcinea, don't ask for kindness or rest –
> Only the long reach of the mind always in love.[29]

The poem flaunts linguistic playfulness, which renders "Don Quichotte and Le Petit Prince" as "Donkey Shot and Liberty Prance", continuing, "Off with your pants and on with the dance".[30] In some of its musical, flowing lines, it balances philosophical truths. The "opaque equities of our world" are contrasted with the "translucent hyperboles of art".[31] The hero "had seen rainshine, he had seen sunfall".[32]

Walking Westward and University College London, 1977

The volume *Quesada*, published in 1975, includes a sequence of twelve poems using the open sonnet form, offering Stead's personal reactions to events that affected him, with tributes to his mother and to Norman Kirk, both of whom had died, and also to Maurice Duggan who was dying of cancer. These sonnets reappear together with nine more in *Walking Westward*. The most significant work in this 1979 volume is the long, complex title poem. Its twenty-five sections traverse parts of the world that had been significant in Stead's life – a western beach in New Zealand, an imaginary paradise inspired by Ngongotaha beside Lake Rotorua, Wellington, Kaiwaka, Auckland's Hobson Bay, Sydney, Armidale, London and the Mediterranean coast of France.

"Walking Westward" restates a problem identified twenty years earlier in "Pictures in a Gallery Undersea". The old tension between 'here' and 'there', New Zealand and Europe, is revisited. Stead's ongoing debate as to where he should locate himself lies at the heart of "Walking Westward", finished in June 1978, with memory of his recent experiences as an honoured guest in France and England fresh in his mind.

Stead had enjoyed another extended stay in Europe four years after the Menton fellowship. He spent a term lecturing on Modern Literature as an honorary research fellow at University College, London, from December 1976 until the end of June 1977. Through the offices of his friend and colleague Professor Karl Miller, Stead felt himself to be generously treated in London in ways that reinforced his confidence as a writer and academic. After leaving New Zealand with Kay and the children on December 11, Stead delivered his first lecture on the subject of "The Waste Land" at University College on December 17. Every lecture in the series on modernism in English poetry encompassed a large subject, and each was followed up with a two-hour seminar. The lectures would eventually be developed to form the chapters of Stead's book on Pound and the Modernist Movement.

At the end of June, the family headed for Menton, travelling through France in a VW van and staying in a flat they had booked. They were there for the month of July, before returning to London early in August. While in Menton, Stead wrote a further chapter for the Modernism book. His final assignment in Britain was the delivery of a lecture on Auden at the Scottish Universities' Summer School, prior to the family's return to New Zealand at the end of the month.

"Walking Westward" was written in the first half of the following year. Despondency at being in New Zealand may have contributed to the gloom of the poem's opening. More significantly, the poem begins with images of death and a void, reflecting the narrator's awareness of his own mortality.

> Out there is the world
> is nothing but the sun bleeding
>   cloud cerements[33]

"Walking Westward" plays on the universal concept of life as a westward journey toward the setting sun and death. The title is repeated on the book's cover in Chinese characters, calling to mind a famous Chinese legend of similar but not identical title – *Hsi Yii Chi* – *Journey to the West* or *Travelling West*, in which a pilgrim visits Paradise in search of scriptures containing 'wisdom'. He discovers paradise and hell to be states of mind revealed in life, not after death. This proposition finds expression in Stead's poem. Some sections celebrate natural beauty or art or friendship or love. Even a love affair that ended disastrously leaves a poignant memory.

> he had explored with her
> the caves of generation and the terraces of the stars[34]

Joyous impressions and memories are contrasted with impressions of a hell on earth, for which Stead uses the image "the smoky athletes/ longing for rest"[35] to represent the misery suffered by humans who are exhausted as they whirl through life without respite. Sportsmen in a Wellington pub are cut off from the natural world: "downstairs were the smoky athletes in the mirror".[36] Reminiscent of 'shades' in an underworld, they breathe polluted air. Lovers from Dante's *Inferno*, Paolo and Francesca, enter the poem "longing for rest" as they spin endlessly through the Upper Hell, where those guilty of the sins of the flesh are punished. In Dante's hell, the wind allows "no silence", a condition comparable to a landscape on earth that is swept by storm.

> Guessed what K. M. felt at Bandol
> death-drive
>   barrenness of that wind
> grains out of Africa
> breath of testaments
> for 3 days no silence among the tombs
> an old wind that knows no need but its own
> unloving wind that drives the lovers in hell
> Francesca recalling the tributary rivers
> longing for rest
> sulla marina dove il Po discende[37]

The final quoted line is from Dante's *Inferno* Book 5.

The Moon is personified as a thin "cold warrior/ wasted", who mounts stone steps and moves "between boards" on an ancient floor, the lines of which can be likened to an empty page waiting for words. The Moon seems exhausted, "spent", as it announces the poetic works Stead plans to write in the future: "PARIS/ SCORIA/ the WARS",[38] a projection of Stead's state of mind, perhaps, as he contemplates the intense effort required.

Stead and the Emperor Henshu

On the western beach at the beginning of "Walking Westward", the narrator is figuratively blind in comparison with Emperor Henshu of the third section who "walked into Paradise". An imaginary character, he is a poet at work. For him, the natural world is a source of creative energy. Quietude and focus allow him to see beneath surfaces. In his diary he records,

> "Green hair of girls
> lives under blue water
> combed by currents.
> Rain that picks at water
> hides hair from eyes,
> sun restores it to view."[39]

Henshu, "emperor among the poets," embodies an ideal; his "Paradise"[40] is where the poet can become one with a poem's shape and sound and fabric. Stead expresses this thought in "How It Came About" from the *Walking Westward* volume.

> For just a moment she thought she was truly herself
> And far, far from herself. She was the bones of a poem.[41]

The words "she" and "herself" have been amended to "he" and "himself" in Stead's recent edition of collected poems.[42] The significance of the lines, though, is unchanged. Whether through his own voice or that of a persona, there is joy in discovering that a work has developed its own life, drawing from the poet's personality and creativity to achieve quality. The poet is then in harmony with the person he aspires to be.

As he crafts the long "Walking Westward", Stead seems to seek the degree of composure that Henshu has gained. In the poem's final section, the poet-narrator is "rested". Observing sparrows in the pear tree making their exits and entrances, he suggests that life is a series of departures and arrivals. Equilibrium is implied at the poem's final section: "still at heart/ soothed as if by fingers/ that know a need".

nowhere to jet to but
gone tomorrow
walking westward
the green doors
the runnels of water.[43]

The "doors" open into gardens, the bush, imagination. Rivulets or "runnels of water" flow with energy and direction, unlike the formless "ocean/ darkness enfolding"[44] at the poem's opening. The positive mood of the conclusion is, however, undermined by the restlessness of "nowhere to jet to but/ gone tomorrow", betraying a readiness to be gone, should an opportunity arise. Alternatively, anyone may be "gone tomorrow"; there is no escape, by jet or other means, from life's progress toward death.

While in Menton in 1972, Stead observed his personal need to leave New Zealand regularly, to view it from a distance.

> I'm not a European, I'm a good keen kiwi and what is good for me being here is something to do with being shaken free of my own place for a bit – long enough to see it again freshly. And also being an academic I look down and find my feet set in concrete every few years and this is a way of breaking out. I like being here and I'm aware all the time that what is going on out there is of no intrinsic importance unless something is going on in here.[45]

Ambivalence and restlessness would have been more keenly felt back in New Zealand under pressure of the university routine. Stead's reputation as an academic and author led to an invitation to apply for the Robert Wallace Chair of English at the University of Melbourne, even though applications had closed three months earlier. He did not apply. Fortunately, Stead's remarkable publication record was rewarded with a three-year Senior Research Fellowship from the University of Auckland, which freed him from regular duties, allowing him to focus on research and writing in the years 1979, 1980 and 1981.

1 C. K. Stead, "Walking Westward", *Walking Westward*, Auckland, The Shed, 1979, p. 32.

2 C. K. Stead, letter to Sargeson, 27 March 1972, begun 22 March, Turnbull Library Papers.

3 Stead, "Walking Westward", *Walking Westward*, pp. 32-3.
4 Stead, letter to Frank Sargeson, 22 March 1972, Turnbull Library Papers.
5 C. K. Stead, *In the Glass Case*, Auckland University Press/Oxford University Press, 1981, p. 272.
6 Stead, letter to Frank Sargeson, 22 July 1972, Turnbull Library Papers.
7 C. K. Stead, "Under the Sun", *Quesada*, Auckland, The Shed, 1975, p. 11.
8 ibid, p. 11.
9 ibid, p. 10.
10 Stead, "10 (for Kay)", *Walking Westward*, p. 21.
11 C. K. Stead, letter to Frank Sargeson, 13 June 1972, Turnbull Library Papers.
12 C. K. Stead, "The Town", *Five for the Symbol*, Auckland, Longman Paul, 1981, p. 87.
13 C. K. Stead, letter to Frank Sargeson, 22 March 1972, Turnbull Library Papers.
14 Stead, "The Town", *Five for the Symbol*, p. 79.
15 ibid, p. 89.
16 ibid, p. 79.
17 Stead, "Walking Westward", *Walking Westward*, p. 46.
18 Stead, "The Town", *Five for the Symbol*, p. 79.
19 C. K. Stead, "A Room Much Maligned", *New Zealand Listener*, 18 May 1974, p. 29.
20 C. K. Stead, "Professor Stead's Work in Menton and London", *Ariel*, June 1973, p. 12.
21 C. K. Stead, "Voiture d'Occasion, *Islands* Vol. 3 (1), Autumn 1974, p. 62.
The narrator in "Voiture d'Occasion" is an unnamed American, whose feeling for Toni Scarf is developed more fully than Rod Millar's in the later story. Expansiveness is a feature of original episode from "Voiture d'Occasion":

> Toni was racing along under a transparent umbrella with a red scarf over her black hair. The pavement is so narrow there you have to step into the street to let people pass; and the street is so narrow when you step into it you hold up the crawling cars.
>
> Toni and I, heads down, ran straight into one another. For me it was a surprise because she'd been on my mind since that morning Bergen had brought them. I hadn't been able to stop thinking about her – I didn't know why – and now here she was.
>
> She said hullo and we both stepped into the roadway. Then we both laughed.
>
> 'We're holding up the traffic,' she said, and we stepped back on to the pavement.
>
> (Stead, "Voiture d'Occasion", p. 62)

The scene has been cut back for "The Town".

> I met Toni Scarf in pouring rain hurrying along under a transparent umbrella with a square of red silk over her black hair. The pavement is so narrow there you have to step into the street to let people pass; and the street is so narrow when you step into it you hold up the crawling cars.
>
> Toni and I ran into one another. She said hullo and we both stepped into the roadway.
>
> 'We're holding up the traffic,' she said, and we stepped back on to the pavement.
>
> (Stead, "The Town", *Five for the Symbol*, p. 68.)

22 C. K. Stead, *The Writer at Work: Essays*, Dunedin, University of Otago Press, 2000, p. 68.
23 C. K. Stead ed., *The Letters and Journals of Katherine Mansfield*, London, Allen Lane, 1977, p. 15.
24 Stead, *The Writer at Work*, p. 74.
25 Stead, *The Writer at Work*, p. 75. "L.M." is one of the names by which Ida Baker was known.

"To Katherine, Ida (who has written 'If your man fails *I am your trump card*') was 'Aida', 'the Albatross', 'the Rhodesian Mountain', 'the Dwarf', 'the FO (Faithful One). She was Jones. She was also 'LM' (Lesley Moore), the secret name Katherine had given her, echoing the brother's." (C. K. Stead, *Mansfield*, London, Vintage, 2004, p. 182.)

26 Stead, "Professor Stead's Work in Menton and London", *Ariel*, June 1973, p. 13.

27 Stead, "Quesada", *Quesada*, p. 19.

28 Stead, *In the Glass Case*, p. 275.

29 Stead, "Quesada", *Quesada*, pp. 20-21

30 ibid, p. 20.

31 ibid, p. 23.

32 ibid, p. 19.

33 Stead, "Walking Westward", *Walking Westward*, p. 32.

34 ibid, p. 45.

35 ibid, p. 47.

36 ibid, p. 46.

37 ibid, p. 47.

38 ibid, p. 47.

39 ibid, p. 33.

40 ibid, p. 33.

41 Stead, "How it Came About", *Walking Westward*, p. 12.

42 C. K. Stead, "How it Came About" from "Breaking the Neck: an Autumn Sketchbook", *C. K. Stead: Poems 1951-2008*, Auckland University Press, 2008, p. 88.

43 Stead, "Walking Westward", *Walking Westward*, p. 49.

44 ibid, p. 32.

45 C. K. Stead, letter to Frank Sargeson, 27 March 1972, begun 22 March, Turnbull Library Papers.

CHAPTER SIX

The Fellow and the Feminists

Senior Research Fellow

A remarkable number of new publications resulted from Stead's three-year senior research fellowship in arts. Projects which Stead anticipated while in receipt of the award included finishing the work on Pound and the Modernist Movement, assembling a volume of academic essays, and editing and introducing the stories of Maurice Duggan. These texts were completed. *In the Glass Case: Essays on New Zealand Literature*, 1981, acknowledges the support of the colleagues who endorsed Stead's nomination for a research fellowship. The book is a collection of articles written in the previous 20 years. Although *Pound, Yeats, Eliot and the Modernist Movement* was ready in 1981, publication was delayed through copyright issues until 1986. While on the fellowship Stead also completed a book of stories and wrote poetry that would appear in 1982 as *Geographies*. To conclude his astonishing three-year academic and creative output, Stead's second published novel, *All Visitors Ashore*, was written swiftly during the last six months of the fellowship. The novel was set aside before being shown to a publisher in 1983 and released in 1984.

In the Glass Case, to quote Ken Arvidson, contributes to "the biography of a culture".[1] Stead's essays on Mansfield through to poet David Mitchell give status and acknowledgement to all the writers selected. W. H. Oliver judged the work to be "the liveliest, sharpest, and most provocative book of New Zealand literary criticism that I have read".[2] He admires Stead's focus on texts as language, rather than conveyers of ideas. The inclusion of autobiographical elements in many of the commentaries surprised him, yet he concedes that they enliven the book.

Stead, the person and personality, present in every essay, speaks directly to the reader: "I made the point early on that Katherine

Mansfield worked largely by instinct. If I ask myself what it was an instinct *for*, I can only answer that it was for the real fiction, which comes from the exercise of imagination...".[3] The "Letter to Frank Sargeson" shows the involvement of the Steads in Sargeson's life. The Mulgan commentary begins with a dinner, which Stead attended, at the home of Mulgan's niece. He describes the Auckland environment that he and Mulgan both knew as children, and reflects on how much he and Mulgan have in common, before explaining the significance to him personally of reading *Man Alone* in 1949. This is followed by a perceptive critical analysis of the work. In conclusion, he reveals the result of his investigation into Mulgan's failure to win nomination for a Rhodes Scholarship in 1933.

The review of *In the Glass Case* by expatriate New Zealander Dan Davin gives greater attention to the Mulgan essay than to any other. He claims "facts as known to good and reliable narrators and friends of Mulgan"[4] to be the 'truth'. Stead's research called into question the popular belief that Mulgan had failed to win endorsement for his Rhodes Scholarship application, after falling foul of the university's Professorial Board, for the alleged reason that he had sympathised with the unemployed during riots in 1932 and supported the freedom of academics to speak out on such issues. After delving into archives, Stead concluded that Mulgan was passed over because his academic record was mediocre. To perpetuate the misinformation, Stead believed, was to denigrate others: "that mythology involved a slur on the names of other scholars (notably Haslam) who were supposed to have won the nomination unfairly."[5] Although academic excellence is only one of three major criteria on which candidature for the Rhodes depends, Stead exposed information that Mulgan supporters resented. University records show Mulgan's third year "average over eight papers was a fraction under sixty-two per cent. The academic case for him was therefore weak."[6]

Mulgan's sister asked Professor Keith Sinclair, who was writing a history of Auckland University, to prove Stead wrong. He was unable to do so. According to Vincent O'Sullivan's account in his biography of Mulgan, Sinclair heard from Willis Airey, present at the meeting of the professorial board, that "he did not believe that 'personal political prejudices' influenced the decision." Board member Professor Percy Burbridge, on the other hand, claimed that "'John Mulgan had shown radical sympathies during the year and a strongly conservative element on the board therefore opposed the nomination.'"[7] The rationale behind the decision-making cannot be finally proven, given that recollections and inferences differ. Stead concedes, "I don't think there can be any final answer to this question."[8]

Nevertheless Stead was vilified for demystifying the Mulgan myth. He was accused by Denis Glover of jealousy and of lacking the necessary qualifications to apply for a Rhodes Scholarship himself. To this remark, Stead replied facetiously: "of the 'necessary qualifications' I no doubt lacked the most crucial was celibacy. I had married while still an undergraduate, and the terms of the Rhodes Scholarship precluded not only those unnatural creatures women, but also men who had apparent and licensed commerce with them."[9] The ineligibility of married men prevented Stead from applying during his Masters year.

Most reviews of *In the Glass Case* are appreciative, with quibbles put forward in a professional manner. Dan Davin's appraisal is the exception, attacking Stead's work and his person with invective and caustic play on words.

> Lest the glass of the title give an impression of fragility, or of frailty, it must be said at once that Mr Stead ... feels that, in so far as he inhabits what must by now be the size of a greenhouse (or hothouse), he need not be inhibited from throwing stones or dropping bricks at its contents ...[10]

> There is a lack of magnanimity here which, for all Mr Stead's obvious ambition and indeed talent, suggests a complementary lack of magnitude. Nor is there space to demonstrate Mr Stead's political and polemical skills – he is the eel of New Zealand literary criticism.[11]

Davin also rejects Stead's assessment of Fairburn. W. H. Oliver, on the other hand, finds Stead's criticism of Fairburn justified by the poet's "pretentiousness, self-indulgence and attitude-striking", but expresses regret at what he regards as Stead's "self-exploration"[12] in the Mulgan essay. In answering this complaint, Stead cites Allen Tate's "insistence that the critic should identify personal elements in his relation to the writer and the work that were his subject".[13] The "self-exploration" is not gratuitous, but has relevance to a deeper appreciation of Mulgan's novel; in addition, Stead discusses its influence on his own novel,

Smith's Dream.

It was expected that *In the Glass Case* would be the outstanding entry in the 1982 Goodman Fielder Wattie Award for Non-Fiction. Instead, the prize went to a book of photographs with very little text, although literary excellence was specified as one of the criteria on which entries were to be judged. The panel's initial choice was the *Oxford History of New Zealand*, but this work was ineligible, as the rules required that the book be written by one author. Letters, voicing dismay or concern at Stead's failure to win, were sent to him by Allen Curnow, PEN and the Literary Fund.[14]

That year, the poetry collection *Geographies* also missed out on an award, though an adjudicator's report gave it high praise. The book opens with the long poem "SCORIA", set on the Auckland Isthmus, followed by "Yes T.S.", which takes readers round the world in imagination. A series of poems using Catullus as a persona forms the third section, and the concluding six poems are again located in the Auckland area. Of the concluding bracket, Stead wrote to Curnow, "I don't know whether the poems deserve it but they've certainly had me totally absorbed for days – especially last week when it seemed the top was going to come off my head I worked so hard".[15] While the earlier volume, *Walking Westward*, provoked a degree of negativity, *Geographies* received a much warmer reception.

"SCORIA" includes a series of contrasting sections, each with its own particular music that reflects sense and mood precisely: the terrifying force of a volcanic eruption – "night inflamed/ groaning under earth/ twittering in heaven/ trees tossing on windless slopes";[16] or an impression of a child sleeping – "those summer sundays late that drew you back/ to a dream of legs each fly a feather's point";[17] or a boy climbing into the ivy that covers a boundary wall, "you could walk on it lie down on it/ vanish in its broad top die in it/ breathing its scent like a dust that caught at the throat";[18] or the impression of high-jumping, using layout, capitals, spacing, to achieve emphasis and lightness.

driving
            DOWN
left foot shaking the earth
                        and out of that crouch
arms   shoulders   right leg gathering
the whole weight

UP
and over

'falling to foam'[19]

In addition to writing poetry and attending to major research projects during the fellowship years, Stead continued to write essays and articles, hand-delivering the first of a series to editor Karl Miller in London in 1980. Stead would supply the *London Review of Books* with material for the next fifteen years. From London, he travelled to Menton to finish and assemble *Five for the Symbol* – five stories written over twenty years – which appeared in 1981.

The three fellowship years involved frequent travel abroad. In April 1981 the League of Canadian Poets invited Stead to spend a fortnight in Toronto, Canada, where he gave readings from his work before flying to London, staying for three weeks to meet with publishers and colleagues, and returning home early in June. The following year, at the beginning of February, another all-expenses-paid invitation took him to Edmonton in Alberta, Canada. The visit to Edmonton led, eventually, to three stories, featuring an imaginary Canadian poet named Alban Ashtree.

Back at the university in 1982, Stead embarked on his final years of lecturing. His teaching programme included the University of Auckland's first creative writing course, which he designed and implemented. Among students who became well-known names in New Zealand literature were Greg O'Brien, Chris Price and Andrew Johnstone. Further focus on his own writing had to await sabbatical leave, which began in August 1984. Karl, Kay and their two daughters flew to London. The family rented a house there for a month, then spent several weeks travelling in a hired car through France for the most part, and also Italy, Switzerland and Germany. After Kay and the girls had returned home, Stead wrote a draft of *The Death of the Body*. London was his base, but he had conferences to attend in Milan and Copenhagen. The places and the journeys were integrated into the novel, with the author turning the disruption of travel to advantage. He drew on his visit to Rapallo and later trips to Turin and Kiel. While writing a story about events that take place in New Zealand, the narrator has a presence in London, Turin, Milan, Rapallo, Kiel and Copenhagen, from which distance he visualises the unfolding drama.

Cleverness in *The Death of the Body*

All Visitors Ashore had been described as 'very clever' by those who liked it and 'too clever', by those who didn't. Stead decided, therefore, to tell *The Death of the Body* as simply as possible. Despite this resolve, the *Listener* review found it "a work too clever for its own good".[20] Its cleverness has astonished Stead himself. In a 2004 interview, he told Warwick Roger that, "When I was in Sydney recently I was asked about *The Death of the Body* and so I set out to reread it as if it had been written by someone else and later I told the interviewer, 'This novel is cleverer than I am.' It's a hell of a clever novel. I doubt I could do it now."[21]

Stead has related the story of his initial difficulties with the work.

> I was writing in London, alone, away from my family. I had only three or four months in which to do it. I didn't care how long it might take revising and rewriting; but before I returned home to New Zealand I wanted a single unbroken draft from beginning to end. I wrote all day, every day. At the end of the first month I became depressed.
>
> I set out one morning from Mecklenburgh Square, along Oxford Street and across Hyde Park. By the time I got back I knew I had to scrap everything. I hadn't thought out what was wrong, or how I would do it differently. I just knew I had to make a new start. A whole month wasted! I ought to have been cast down, but I wasn't. I was elated. My depression was gone.
>
> So I began again with a description of my room in London. I adopted the voice of someone away from his home in Auckland, telling Harry Butler's story. That voice became the authority by which so much was known; and whose voice it was would be one of the questions a reader might hope to have answered by the end of the book.[22]

There is cleverness in the way an unnamed narrator engages with readers, encouraging them to assemble evidence and consider philosophical questions. He is friendly and disarming, taking readers into his confidence: "You know the signs, I'm sure. How to respond to them is up to you. You may be bored, irritated, disapproving, nostalgic, sympathetic, pleased, concerned. Any of these and half a dozen others is perfectly appropriate. What there can be no doubt about is what you're seeing."[23] The narrator even admits that his own account of events, or his theory of how things came together, "may not be right". (p. 140) He asks for understanding and patience. Only one piece of information can be released at a time, he explains, despite the fact that life proceeds on many fronts at once.

The traditional 'willing suspension of disbelief' and the privileged 'eye of God' perspective are replaced by a narrator who refuses to be omniscient. His admission that he does not always understand the motivation of the characters adds to his credibility. The identity of the narrator remains a puzzle until the book nears its conclusion.

Involving readers in finding answers is one means of catching attention and creating tension. Another is the suggestion, implicit in the title *The Death of the Body*, that the book is a thriller; the existence of a body is announced on the fourth page. On the second page, it is clear that three men are covertly observing a property. The reader wonders why this is necessary, how the body comes to be discovered, and how the victim met his fate.

Stead does not spell out the identity of a murderer, but provides enough information for readers to guess at the kind of criminals involved and the reason for the crime. The foreshadowing is masterly. As a new chapter often takes readers to a new setting, questions are carried forward, held over. The conclusion of Chapter 23 reads,

> 'Come and have a look at this.'
> They crouch side by side, staring down into the still pool twenty feet below. (p. 157)

This is a novel, Stead has explained, about "narrative and narrative frames. ... You can say it's a murder mystery; that's one frame. It's an academic novel, that's another. It's a domestic novel. The picture is there and you pick up one frame and you pick up another."[24] Within each frame there are scenes, like scenes in a play. The narrator is advised by the *Padrone* of the café where he likes to write: "Give me a scene ... Background. Foreground. I don't care. But a scene please Maestro." (p. 30) A series of scenes makes visible, for example, the nature of protagonist Harry Butler's first marriage and the way he becomes involved with his second wife, Claire. So that scene and situation will be easier to visualise, a film-like location is sometimes conjured up with wide shots, close-ups and vehicles or people moving through a defined space.

Venues on the far side of the world create a contrast with the New Zealand scenes that disclose the story's plot. In London or Rapallo or Copenhagen, the narrator engages in on-going debate as to how the novel should proceed. Stead dramatises the process of writing – the discipline, strategies and gamesmanship of the author – a component of the novel that is every bit as important, involving about the same number of pages, as the plot's situations and crises. A three-way tension is created between the narrator, a blue folder housing the Story, and the narrator's conversation partner named Uta: "a semi-comic figure, [she] is perhaps a muse, but she's also a moralist – probably more moralist than muse. So there's conflict between them."[25] Discussion between the narrator and Uta addresses difficulties a writer must overcome in being true to the integrity of the fiction, rather than providing outcomes that readers might hope for.

Comedy develops from Uta's misconception that the narrator and Harry Butler are the same person, causing her to be alternately angry and sympathetic. Despite the fact that her English is "pretty good", she makes errors, exclaiming that something is "the last hay". (p. 138) Indignantly, she describes Harry's sex life and his conduct as "wealthy" (p. 141) instead of 'rich', and guesses that "those four women ... are only the tip of his iceberg". (p. 141)

The novel's entertaining crime story is to some extent a smoke screen, as matters of greater moment are pursued. The philosophical relationship between Mind and Body resonates through the novel, its implications broadening as the work unfolds. As a professor of philosophy, Harry Butler is much preoccupied with a fundamental conundrum: "how did this thing which was so-and-so become *not* so-and-so?" (p. 10) At an opposite extreme, there is concern for the soul as well as pursuit of "*the* Reality" (p. 133) by Harry's Sufi wife and her tutor. Reviewer John Mellors notes that the novel "invites our involvement as detectives one minute, philosophers the next".[26] This novel addresses "the big questions", (p.10) which in turn exercise the reader: "in human affairs there are no causes, only facts and circumstances. But we all – even Harry – look for causes. We all ask 'Why'?" (p. 76)

Finally, sexual politics feature in this novel. A traumatic 1984 event shocked university staff and especially the English Department in which Stead was a professor. It involved the abduction and humiliation of drama lecturer Mervyn Thompson.

"The Writhing of a Corpse"

In *The Death of the Body*, Stead explained to Terry Locke, "the Mervyn Thompson events are there in the background and it's clear that I take a position of sympathy towards the harassed male harasser."[27]

> [A] group of feminists assaulted Mervyn Thompson, playwright and lecturer in drama in the Auckland University English Department, tied him to a tree, threatened him with castration, daubed 'rapist' on his car, and ran off when disturbed. Notices were put about the campus declaring Thompson was a rapist; and his plays were subsequently picketed by students and boycotted by more than one theatre group. The action against him seemed to have been taken in imitation of a feminist play, *Setting the Table*, by Renée Taylor (as she then was – she later shed the patronymic and became Renée), where women take action against a man they believe to be a rapist. Thompson, a strong feminist sympathiser, had put on a second production of the play in the English Department, and I remember arguing with him that he should not have. The play was agitprop – weak dramatically ... Thompson thus became the victim of a propaganda he had given support to; and in all he has said and written about this subject since, I'm not sure that that is an irony he has fully apprehended.[28]

When he wrote *The Death of the Body* in 1984 and 1985, Stead was not to know that his colleague would die of cancer in 1992, aged 57, but he *did* know that Thompson had not recovered from the assault. The man felt that the event had destroyed his life. He remarked, "I sometimes think I died in 1984 and that all subsequent activity has been the writhing of a corpse."[29]

In a 1991 interview with Fleur Adcock, Stead admitted, "I've taken issue with feminists, and I've teased them in my novel *The Death of the Body*."[30] The book provoked angry reaction. In 1986, the feminists were well organised and aggressive. Stead has remarked that he intended the part played by the feminists in the novel to be witty and amusing, but it would have been difficult for him to achieve a light tone in creating his two members of the women's collective. They can be viewed as caricatures, being unattractive, spiky-haired, and dressed in overalls, but, given that theft and defamation of character are among their misdemeanours, they do not emerge as comic characters.

Michael Gifkins, reviewing the novel for the *Listener*, seems riled by it. The source of his irritation is clear in the opening paragraph: "What ... gives the author the right to savage roly-poly 'dykes' who comprise the women's collective in the philosophy department at Auckland University, where his hero Harry Butler holds a chair?" This is a strange question, given the creative freedom of the fiction writer. Gifkins may have thought Stead had overstepped the bounds of political correctness with the spiky-haired pair. The reviewer, though, has stepped outside the bounds of professionalism by including an attack on Stead, not as a writer, but in his role as professor: "his own tenure was distinguished by a reluctance ever to back down from a scrap".[31]

In *The Death of the Body*, Harry Butler's resourceful wife defeats the feminists. When no escape seemed possible, she provides an unexpected and clever resolution, in keeping with prior events. The feminists fail to dishonour Harry Butler. The novel's final irony is that Professor Butler becomes a chastened and more considerate man: "He will become a more disciplined academic, a more compliant husband, a more dutiful father, a more dependable person." The narrator asks wryly, "Is it also the death of the body?" (p. 187) The concession is in keeping with a widespread understanding following the Thompson affair, namely that men throughout the country, working with women or with women as students, will act more responsibly toward them in future. When the novel was first published, the conduct of Stead's feminist characters and their defeat at the hands of Claire Butler made a political statement. Today the issue can be seen to belong to a phase of New Zealand's social history, and as one strand of a plot concerned with the integration of truth and fiction and disparities between the two.

Most reviewers were not disturbed by the sexual politics. In London, Elaine Feinstein wrote, "I was amused by the insurgent bullying of campus women campaigning to have the student mistress join their battle against sexual harassment."[32] While Colleen Reilly in *The Dominion* sees the "depiction of women in a university setting" to be "a minor theme in the novel",[33] Reginald Berry in *Landfall* makes no reference at all to the feminist issue, but focuses on more significant aspects of the novel, such as the way active collaboration between reader and author is encouraged, maintaining a high level of reader involvement and a high level of interest in the story itself.[34]

Conflict between feminist activists and academic liberals was a reality in the mid-1980s, part of a widespread suspicion that academic liberals, holding positions in teaching institutions, may have been liberal in terms of sexual morality. Thompson strenuously denied that he was a rapist, but admitted to consensual affairs with students. Mark Williams claims that a relationship between a student and a man in a position of relative power falls within the radical feminists' "very generous definition" of rape.

> Rape was an act inseparable from power, the power held by men in society as it was presently constituted (the 'patriarchy'). Men in power who had sex with women over whom they exercised that power were rapists by definition and Thompson's notion that no rape occurred where both partners were 'willing' missed the point.[35]

The Feminists

The Thompson affair led to a strengthening of procedures to address and deal with sexual harassment in the workplace. Protocols to warn and counsel women became more widespread and laws on the subject became more specific in 1993. Departments of Women's Studies at universities flourished in the late 1980s and early 1990s, but, under pressure from commercially oriented policy decisions, most have now disappeared or amalgamated with other departments such as Sociology. The Ministry of Women's Affairs, established in 1986, continues however to exercise a significant role in social policy decisions, initiating and monitoring legislation affecting women. The feminist anger of the 1980s has dissipated. Changes intended to remove disadvantages faced by women have been enacted into law.[36]

For Stead, one aftermath of the Thompson affair was the rumour that he was to be next. "It was because I had taken such a strong stance against the radical feminists ... No, I didn't take the rumours seriously. I suppose I couldn't imagine being enticed out in the middle of the night to begin with."[37]

Labels such as 'misogynist', a term used by Cathy Dunsford to describe Stead, or 'sexist', a term given him by the feminists, run counter to the way he is regarded by his own wife and children. Stephen Stratford, in preparing a 1990 *Metro* article, met Stead's "close-knit loyal family". He reports that, when "Dale Spender was to give her 'C. K. Stead Memorial Lecture' at last year's women's book festival", daughters Charlotte and Margaret, then aged twenty-two and nineteen, "had to be dissuaded from going along to wave banners in support" of their father. Furthermore, Stead's "26-year-old son Oliver weighed in with a ringing defence of his dad, particularly on his alleged sexism. 'These days in the Stead family the women go out to work while the men stay at home to look after the children,' he wrote. 'To assert that my father is not sympathetic to these issues is absurd.'"[38]

The character Harry Butler alleges that "grammatical bullying by feminists is the most conspicuous form of sexual harassment in the university" (p. 131), a statement that Stead quotes in a subsequent critical essay, explaining exactly what he means by "grammatical bullying": "One thing you may not do is refer to a 'heroine'. There must be only heroes, female or male, just as there must be no actresses, only actors, female or male. So Cleopatra, or Juliet, or Brunhilde, is now a hero, to be played by an actor."[39]

1 Ken Arvidson, "The Biography of a Culture", *New Zealand Listener*, 27 February 1982, p. 74.
2 W. H. Oliver, *Comment 15*, April 1982, p. 33.
3 C. K. Stead, *In the Glass Case: Essays on New Zealand Literature*, Auckland University Press/Oxford University Press, 1981, p. 45.
4 Dan Davin, "Reviews", *Review of English Studies*, February 1984, p. 110.
5 Stead, *In the Glass Case*, p. 97.
6 ibid. p. 95. Mulgan's ability, however, was never in question. He later gained a First at Oxford. At the University of Auckland, his third year of study was combined with the editorship of the student newspaper *Craccum*, and a position on the student executive.
7 Vincent O'Sullivan, *Long Journey to the Border*, Auckland, Penguin Books, 2003, p. 77.
8 Stead, *In the Glass Case*, p. 97.
9 ibid. p. 98.
10 Davin, "Reviews", *Review of English Studies*, February 1984, p. 109.
11 ibid. p. 111.
12 Oliver, *Comment 15*, April 1982, p. 34.
13 C. K. Stead, *Kin of Place: Essays on 20 New Zealand Writers*, Auckland University Press, 2002, p. 195.
14 Allen Curnow, letter to Karl Stead, 5 August 1982, Turnbull Library Papers.
15 C. K. Stead, letter to Curnow, 26 March 1981, Turnbull Library Papers.
16 C. K. Stead, "SCORIA", *Geographies*, 1982, Auckland University Press/Oxford University Press, p. 15.
17 ibid. p. 16. (The word "sunday" has no capital.)

[18] ibid. p. 11.
[19] ibid. p. 17.
[20] Michael Gifkins, "I Am Not this Body", *New Zealand Listener*, 25 October 1986, p. 70.
[21] Warwick Roger, "Face to Face: C. K. Stead", *North and South*, May 2004, p. 72.
[22] C. K. Stead, *The Writer at Work*, Dunedin, University of Otago Press, 2000, p. 209.
[23] C. K. Stead, *The Death of the Body*, London, Collins, 1986, pp. 12-13. Numbers in brackets in this chapter refer to this edition.
[24] Stead, *The Writer at Work*, p. 237.
[25] ibid. p. 238.
[26] John Mellors, " His Master's Voice", *London Magazine*, November 1986, p. 102.
[27] Stead, *The Writer at Work*, p. 267.
[28] C. K. Stead, *Answering to the Language: Essays on Modern Writers*, Auckland University Press, 1989, pp. 279-280.
[29] Murray Edmond, "The Terror and the Pity of 1984: Mervyn Thompson's *Coaltown Blues*", *Landfall,* Autumn 2005, p. 19.
[30] Stead, "With Fleur Adcock, 1991", *The Writer at Work*, p. 254.
[31] Gifkins, "I Am Not this Body", *New Zealand Listener*, 25 October 1986, p. 70.
[32] Elaine Feinstein, "When Hearts Need to Be as Hard as Nuts", *London Times*, 28 August 1986.
[33] Colleen Reilly, "Keeping Us on Our Toes", *Dominion*, 5 October 1991, p.11.
[34] Reginald Berry, "Stead's Dream", *Landfall*, September 1987, p. 345.
[35] Mark Williams, *Leaving the Highway: Six Contemporary New Zealand Novelists*, Auckland University Press, 1990, p. 72.
[36] In addition to laws designed to offer greater protection to women, especially in the workplace and in teaching institutions, child-care facilities have improved in the past 20 years, extending the option for women to be both mothers and members of the paid workforce.
[37] Steve Braunias, "In for the High Jump", *New Zealand Listener*, 30 July 1994, p. 35.
[38] Stephen Stratford, "Blaspheming Against the Pieties: Why the Literati Hate C. K. Stead", *Metro*, April 1990, pages 76 and 78.
[39] Stead, *Answering to the Language*, p. 196.

CHAPTER SEVEN

"*The Masks of Catullus*"[1]

Catullus and Clodia

Stead's Catullus is speaker or listener in more than sixty poems published between 1979 and 2004. In creating Catullus, Stead employs again a strategy effective in the poem "Quesada". Distance is established between the poet's own reflections-opinions-emotions and those of the protagonist. The choice of Catullus suggests that Stead was attracted to the spontaneous and erotic poetry[2] of Roman poet Gaius Valerius Catullus, and to the personality and temperament reflected in his work.

The dates of the Roman poet's birth and death are uncertain, but it is known that he was alive between 84 and 54BC. In 1972 the Stead family visited Italy from their base in Menton, venturing as far as the Adriatic. On the return journey, Stead wrote to Sargeson that they camped beside Lake Garda, near Verona, birthplace of Catullus, "at Sirmione, for the sake of Tennyson and Catullus – no longer 'olive silvery Sirmio' (we run to much better olive groves around Menton) but the little town of Sirmione is still very beautiful".[3] At Sirmio by the lake, the family of Catullus owned a villa, to which he became heir after his brother's death.

In a 1991 interview with Fleur Adcock, Stead spoke of using poems by Catullus as a starting point, after which each poem "goes in its own direction", resolving a problem, which he defines as

> difficulty in creating male characters – the inhibition about anything that might seem to be making claims for oneself. So the speaker in the poem becomes a persona somewhere between myself and Catullus. That allows me a freedom to use personal experience, to invent experiences I've never had, and to adapt experience of Catullus's, in a mixture which is

> determined by the poem. The poem gets in control instead of either me or Catullus or facts.[4]

Stead gives vitality to a character/narrator that develops and gains substance in the course of twenty-five years.

There is irony and wit in the links and differences between the Roman and the contemporary work. Stead's first Catullus poem is "Caesar is still Caesar", published in *Walking Westward* in 1979. The year 1982 saw the publication of "The Clodian Songbook", a sequence of 15 poems in *Geographies*, spoken by Stead's Catullus. Every one has a number reference to the original Catullus poem,[5] providing an opportunity for the range of allusions to be broadened, should a reader choose to consult the Roman poems. A second Clodian sequence of 21 poems appears in *Between* (1988), most of which are reprinted in *Straw into Gold* (1997) under the heading "The Masks of Catullus", the ascribed dates being "the 1970s and '80s". There are Catullus poems later in the same volume and in *The Right Thing* (2000). *Dog* (2002) includes "Cat/ullus", meaning 'a cat by any name', in memory of Stead's cat. Its final line is mock-heroic – "Frater, ave (etc)"[6] from the elegy (Poem 101) written by Catullus to his brother. Also in *Dog*, "Catullus 65" springs from Poem 65 by Catullus. Written as if "by my older friend Catullus", it is hoped that this elegy addressed to Curnow will be revealed to the deceased poet mysteriously: "Let it come to you".[7] *The Red Tram* (2004) includes two love poems featuring Stead's Catullus.

Poems by the Roman Catullus address a number of female lovers, of whom "Lesbia" is just one. Eight poems are devoted to her. She is believed to be Clodia Metelli, a married woman, with whom he enjoyed and endured a love-hate relationship. Other Catullus poems concern his male partners, in a culture where bisexuality was the norm. Some of Stead's Catullus poems include homosexuals as friends. It is clear, for example, that the character Furius bears a trace of Frank Sargeson. In one poem, Furius returns from a Gay Rights Convention with his partner and, in another, a neighbour complains that his hedge encroaches on the footpath – which, in the case of Sargeson's hedge, it did.

Almost half of Stead's Catullus poems are addressed to just one composite woman, the many-faceted Clodia, representing the complex and mysterious female psyche. Inconstant and unpredictable, she is endlessly alluring – a muse, lover, combatant and source of frustration. The Clodia poems provide an opportunity for sensuousness. Stead often celebrates passion and sexuality. "Quesada" and a section like the following from "Walking Westward" offer examples from his earlier work:

> a blunt arrow-head of crisp hair
>   pointing the way
> down
>   into another dimension
> only perfect world
>   slippery sided
> inward-enclosing
>   welcome
> and welcome
>   and welcome
> "die when thou hast lived"[8]

Stead's Poem 20 from the first "Clodian Songbook" gives an impression of delight in consummation and its aftermath. His Catullus speaks with contentment; the event is compared ironically to a "natural/ disaster" and likened to the sinking of the Titanic or closing "at the Anemone".[9] The sequence of images forms a contrast to the originating piece by Catullus, also a poem of fulfillment. Lesbia has returned to him: "Who happier than I?" he asks.[10] At one level, Stead's writing seems innocent. In Poem 9, his Catullus invites Clodia to dinner, with the host promising "the big/things" and giving as examples, "(love/ ideas /bananas)".[11] Poem 10 from Stead's second Clodian sequence finds his Catullus with a "tree" in his "trousers", promising to be Clodia's "sure-fire brigade" to extinguish the "fire" in her "garden".[12] The originating Catullus poem lacks ambiguity and is bawdy rather than sensuous. Lovemaking with "sweet Ipsithilla" is anticipated: "stuffed with food/ I'm ripe for stuffing you."[13] By contrast, sensuality in Stead's work is offered with lightness and humour.

Stead's "Clodian Songbook" includes anger, bitterness and jealousy: Clodia is unfaithful to Catullus; she devotes more feeling and attention to her pet bird than to him; another suitor finds her interesting or wins her favour. In the cleverest of the angry poems, Stead's Catullus says he loves Clodia as "the lone lawn daisy/ loves/ the Masport mower". A witty taunt alleges that "she's known to her 300 loveless lovers/ as the scrum machine".[14] The source poem by Catullus finds Lesbia accused of having 300 lovers and of being blind to the love Catullus once had for her. He laments the destruction of his love, which is like a flower crushed by a plough-blade.

Stead's Catullus poems elevate the act of love and the state of being in love. They also dramatise the condition of being at odds with a lover. Asked by journalist Steve Braunias what reading experience might have led to erotica in his writing, Stead's reply was something of a non-sequitur: "That's just my own unfortunate temperament."[15] Erotica features in Stead's fiction as well as poetry; it is part of the fabric of *All Visitors Ashore*, *The Death of the Body*, *The Singing Whakapapa*, and the story "Sex in America".

When Stead was a young man, relationships between men and women were expected to lead to an enduring marriage.[16] In an era that lauded fidelity, covert affairs were commonplace. Stead's writing reflects the conventions and conduct of his time – the ideal of the stable marriage, and the tensions and intensity of the illicit affair. In all of Stead's novels apart from *My Name Was Judas*, extra-marital liaisons are significant. Notwithstanding, most marriages in his fiction show remarkable resilience.

Like his characters Harry Butler, Hugh Grady, Jesse Fischer, Donovan O'Dwyer and Friedrich Goldstein, Stead has enjoyed a stable marriage. These characters, however, from five different novels all involve themselves in extra-marital affairs. Kai Jensen, in *The Oxford Companion to New Zealand Literature*, discusses Stead's work, conjecturing that there is "an apparent extra-marital affair which recurs in various poems and two novels, and difficulties surrounding women and their claims: all these matters are presented to us under a veil of fiction that is at times alarmingly diaphanous."[17] Despite such an aspersion, Kay Stead's allegiance to her husband has never wavered. "I adore him," she says, referring to a marriage in which there has been "high romance from day one",[18] and Stead calls Kay his "second self".[19] He addresses her in the 2004 poem "You", recalling his unexpected arrival at a friend's wedding in 1954, after having secured leave from compulsory military training by calling it a funeral: "your blush of pleasure/ cheered me like a crowd." The poem concludes,

Forgive my trespasses.
Stay close. Hold my hand."[20]

Stead has often acknowledged Kay's contribution to his work as a writer. In *Pound, Yeats, Eliot and the Modernist Movement*, for instance, he writes, "Kay Stead, my first and best reader, read and commented on the chapters as they were written."[21] In his very latest publication, *Collected Poems 1951-2006*, he concludes his "Foreword" with – "the huge acknowledgement to Kay, which the poems themselves make in so many different ways, overt and oblique, from *Whether the Will Is Free* all the way through to *The Black River*."[22]

Nostalgia and Scorn

Some of Stead's Catullus poems are tender and sympathetic, while others are cutting and scornful. A nostalgic piece, addressed to Clodia but reminiscent of Kay, recalls the North Shore before the Harbour Bridge replaced the old ferries and brought new development. After recreating sights, smells, sounds and atmosphere, magical in retrospect – remembered from the year in Takapuna – Stead's Catullus concludes, "Clodia weeps for the days of our youth."[23] Another nostalgic poem recreates a shore, possibly of Lake Rotorua with its willows and fishermen, where Stead often spent holidays in his teen-age years. The Catullus poem, from which it originates, speaks of the excellence of a yacht which bore the young Roman through the Adriatic. Stead's Catullus lays his ear against the wooden prow of a beached yacht, recalling the urgent journeying of his youthful self, "under bellying moons"; huge Pacific moons can be associated with fullness of sail and an abundance of sexual energy in his "hot youth".[24]

A poem that is personal, offering Stead's own feeling, is Poem 15 from the first Clodian sequence, an elegiac address to his friend Ian Lamont, killed at eighteen, whom he calls Ianus. It takes as its starting point a poem written by Catullus on visiting the grave of his brother to offer a greeting and salute. At the beginning of *Talking About O'Dwyer*, Stead provides his own translation of this lament by Catullus, dedicating the poem to Parata Heta Thompson, the Maori soldier shot in Crete by his own captain, an event that assumes significance in the novel. Stead's translation concludes, "Brother for ever, for ever/ haere ra!"[25]

In a 1983 interview with Elizabeth Alley, Stead remarked that his sonnets were autobiographical, but, because his ego was suppressed or absent, they did not suit his temperament.[26] Ego is no longer suppressed in the Catullus poems, allowing Stead a personal freedom. If there are autobiographical elements, they have become invisible, as characters with Roman names engage in ancient pursuits. He has chosen the persona of a poet who wrote in an age that allowed individual freedom for men, not only in relation to sexuality, but in the way rivals were dealt to. Lampooning other poets, popular in Catullus's time, seems to have struck a chord with Stead. One third of Stead's Catullus poems concerns other writers and shows him at his most scornful. The same can be said for those poems by the Roman Catullus that refer to fellow poets. While Stead is not, of course, the narrator of these poems, their sentiments concur with essays and letters he has written, conveying impatience at the esteem enjoyed by favourites, when their work seems slack or second-rate.

Calvus and Ravidus are two characters who receive harsh treatment from Stead's Catullus and friends. Pages of poetry by Calvus are referred to as "arsepaper".[27] It is clear that Stead's Catullus considers himself the better poet. Between Calvus and Stead's Catullus there seem to be intermittent forays, as if they were sometimes sparring partners and sometimes allies. After one encounter with his rival, Calvus calls for an end to animosities: "Give over Catullus/ stop playing the lone wolf./ Living's our only offence./ We do it together."[28] Ravidus is a publisher who has become an editor and, in the opinion of Stead's Catullus, is a writer of "execrable prose".[29]

It is instructive to place Stead's cryptic four-lined address to Suffenia alongside the poem's ancient counterpart. Suffenia's shortcomings may be comparable to those of Catullus's Suffenus, "a poet/ who turns out verse by the yard". He is blind to his own limitations and "fancies himself/ in the role of a poet".[30] Stead's Suffenia "opens her legs to life" but she chooses to ride Pegasus "side-saddle",[31] implying constraint or limitation as a poet. Pegasus was tamed by Athena and placed at the service of poets.

At a reading of his work at the University of Alberta in Edmonton, Stead included the four-lined poem, explaining that it was "about a lady poet in New Zealand. Naughty. I feel ashamed of that, but once you've thought of it, it's irresistible."[32] The identity of the "lady poet" might have remained a mystery, had Stead not written two further poems in which she features. She and "Tullius Tuhoe" carry off literary prizes, while Catullus reflects with heavy irony that they "are truly the best/ among our writers/ as it is true to say/ Catullus is the worst."[33] The protest against positive discrimination toward women and Maori is in keeping with a consistent position advanced by Stead's essays. In this instance, whoever may have inspired the creation of Suffenia is of little relevance to the theme of the poem.

Stead has often found the matter of literary prizes irksome. He has complained not only of positive discrimination, but has called book awards "a reflection of commerce and popular taste".[34] The acclaimed *All Visitors Ashore* was not short-listed for the Wattie Award, and *The Secret History of Modernism* despite, Stead notes, "stunning overseas reviews" did not make the Montana shortlist. These remarks, in *Book Self* (2008), are followed by the claim that "someone, himself a novelist, often in the running for prizes, was a judge in both cases seventeen years apart."[35] When Stead remarks on his failure to make the shortlist for a literary award, he knows how those well-disposed toward him will react: "They will be shaking their heads and saying, 'There he goes again.'"[36] They would, no doubt, prefer the stoical stance adopted by his narrator in "Honours are Declined" from *The Black River* (2007), who renounces concern for acclaim or awards, anticipating that art will survive beyond the lifetime of the writer.

> You say there should be laurels.
> Let the page have them.
> This late summer
> I'll settle for the shade.[37]

Stead's third poem featuring Suffenia is not concerned with awards or recognition, but with integrity. "Suffenia the Poet", first published in 1998, offers physical details: "a neck-scarf hiding her wattles" and a "painted-on face". Stronger evidence that the poem is a thinly veiled travesty of one of Stead's contemporaries lies in the emphasis on truth: "Cassandra/ the truth-teller", "painfully honest", "her lying verses" and "'Believe me! Believe!'"[38] This poem has occasioned comment from two reviewers of *The Right Thing*, the Stead collection in which it first appeared. Ken Arvidson affects puzzlement and irritation. "If real, she could be one of a dozen poets, none of whom obviously deserves detraction. If not real, what is the point of such an unattractive fiction?"[39] Harry Ricketts regards the poem as "one of Stead's sharpest caricatures" and considers his other Catullus poems to have a "less excoriating effect".[40]

After an interval of time, from a 2009 perspective, Ricketts can view the range, the wit and the barbs of the Catullus poems with relish. "The persona of Catullus (with a nod to Pound's Propertius) allows Stead extra room to play. Here the voice is given free rein, not at all on best behaviour." Ricketts appreciates the stratagem of a mask that has allowed Stead to be "romantic", "*faux*-repining" or "elegiac".[41]

As to the "lady poet" who bears a relationship to Suffenia, Stead's literary criticism provides the clues. There is one writer whose integrity has been questioned by Stead time and again. *Book Self* describes Lauris Edmond as "an entertaining companion but a foolish and mendacious person".[42] He challenged the truthfulness of her poetry and the honesty of her autobiography. His review of her third volume of autobiography has the title, "Honest Lauris, Honest Iago", and includes the words, "Behind, or beyond, style lies the difficult question of truthfulness."[43]

For the *Sunday Star Times* to commission Stead to write this review was provocative, given that, by 1992, his attitude to Edmond's work was well documented. Long before the identity of Suffenia became obvious through the appearance of "Suffenia the Poet", his treatment of Edmond had polarised opinion, arousing indignation among some, and satisfaction among those who took the part of her estranged husband Trevor Edmond in the division of loyalty following publication of the autobiography.

Lauris Edmond had complained that women tend to be ignored by male critics. Stead, in 1989, countered the criticism, focusing on her poem "The Lecture", published in the *Listener*. Subsequently, Nigel Cox asks, "Did he have to slice Lauris Edmond's poem 'The Lecture' into such small pieces to 'prove' that women's poetry must be subjected to the same critical standards as men's?"[44] Stead's commentary finds fault with the poem, but his concluding paragraph concedes, "In this poem you can see Edmond's skills as a writer. She is sensitive. She uses language intelligently and economically. The cadences are beautiful, the fireflies finely observed." His final words, though, are dismissive: "But some kind of rigour is lacking and so the whole effect is poetic in the bad sense. 'Truth...courage...candour' are precisely what is lacking. This is what I would say of it if the poem were by a man. ... It seems to me the Women's Movement as it operates in the literary sphere has to decide which it wants – to be patronised, or to be treated as equals."[45]

In 2002, Stead's renewed discussion of Edmond's work finds fault with "Poem for a Marriage": "The whole poem has the feel of a single and very meagre idea intoned into an empty kerosene drum in order to make it resonate".[46] In that *Kin of Place* essay, Stead scorns Roger Robinson's championing of Edmond by saying, "He was just being nice about Lauris Edmond whom everyone else was being nice about. (...) Enough of this clubby stuff! It is time to look hard at the words on the page."[47] While some would be persuaded by Stead's arguments, supporters of Edmond have harboured resentment at the tenor and the personal nature of the criticism. Others may well ask whether disparagement (no doubt enjoyed in the time of Catullus the Roman) should enter literary discourse in our day and age.

In *Book Self*, Stead speaks of an essay –

> which I probably won't write, about a style I would call 'Wellington Pedestrian', with O'Sullivan, Lauris Edmond and Louis Johnson as the chief exponents. It would be partly about semi-*official* art; the art of a provincial capital – rather like a medieval European city state. Vince is the best brain of the three. None of them, I think, aspires to 'music'; and none is much interested in, or more than basically competent in, matters of poetic form.[48]

Such opinions of fellow writers will surely fuel antipathy in some quarters and hinder appreciation of the poet who has donned the masks of Catullus with such skill and flair.

By harking back to specific poems by Catullus, Stead transports him into the present; an ancient Roman poet and a contemporary New Zealand poet articulate comparable human concerns across the divide of twenty centuries and from opposite sides of the globe. Poems that call forth the work of Gaius Valerius Catullus attest to the enduring life of poetry.

1 C. K. Stead, *Straw into Gold*, Auckland University Press, 1997, pp. 59-78.

2 Betty Radice (ed.), *The Poems of Catullus*, Harmondsworth, Penguin Books, 1966. Radice describes Catullus as an erotic poet, capable of "colloquial grossness", p. 27.

3 C. K. Stead, letter to Sargeson, Menton, 4 May 1972, Turnbull Library Papers.

4 C. K. Stead, *The Writer at Work: Essays*, Dunedin, University of Otago Press, 2000, p. 257.

5 C. K. Stead, "Acknowledgements", *Geographies*, Auckland University Press/Oxford University Press, 1982, NP.

6 C. K. Stead, "Cat/ullus", *Dog*, Auckland University Press, 2002, p. 29.
7 Stead, "Catullus 65", *Dog*, p. 54.
8 C. K. Stead, "Walking Westward", *Walking Westward*, Auckland, The Shed, 1979, p, 37. The line "die when thou hast lived" is from *Antony and Cleopatra*; 'when' means 'where'.
9 C. K. Stead, "From the Clodian Songbook: 29", *Between*, Auckland University Press, 1988, p. 57.
10 Radice (ed.) "Poem 107", *The Poems of Catullus*, p. 219.
11 Stead, "The Clodian Songbook: 9", *Geographies*, p. 67.
12 Stead, "From the Clodian Songbook: 10", *Between*, p. 46.
13 Radice (ed.) "Poem 32", *The Poems of Catullus*, p. 89.
14 Stead, "The Clodian Songbook: 7", *Geographies*, p. 65.
15 Steve Braunias, "In for the High Jump", *New Zealand Listener*, 30 July 1994, p. 36.
16 The social pressure on young people to marry is portrayed with particular clarity in Christine Cole Catley's biography of Beatrice Hill Tinsley, born eight years later than Stead, when those mores held sway. (*Bright Star*, Auckland, Cape Catley, 2006.)
17 Kai Jensen, "Stead", *The Oxford Companion to New Zealand Literature*, Roger Robinson and Nelson Wattie (eds.), 1998, p. 514.
18 Margo White, "Mr Congeniality", *Metro*, August 2005, p. 61.
19 C. K. Stead, "Zagreb", *The Right Thing*, Auckland University Press, 2000, p. 60.
20 C. K. Stead, "You", *The Red Tram*, Auckland University Press, 2004, p. 22.
21 C. K. Stead, *Pound, Yeats, Eliot and the Modernist Movement*, Basingstoke Hampshire, MacMillan, 1986, p. vi.
22 C. K. Stead, *Collected Poems, 1951-2006*, Auckland University Press, 2008, p. xv.
23 Stead, "The Clodian Songbook: 12", *Geographies*, p. 70. The comparison of the North Shore with Eden "before the Fall", before the completion of the Harbour Bridge, appears in Poem 12 in the Clodian Songbook, and also in Sonnet 8, in *Walking Westward*, p. 20. "How many K. S.'s could the North Shore harbour/ /Before the Fall?"
24 Stead, "The Clodian Songbook: 3", *Geographies*, p. 61.
25 C. K. Stead, *Talking About O'Dwyer*, Auckland, Penguin Books, 1999, p.6.
26 Elizabeth Alley, interview with C.K. Stead on "SCORIA", *Concert Programme*, 15 October 1983.
27 Stead, "From the Clodian Songbook: 5", *Between*, p. 41.
28 Stead, "Dogs 2 (Calvus replies)", *Straw into Gold*, p. 154.
29 Stead, "Ravidus the Bookman", *The Right Thing*, 2000, p. 38.
30 Radice (ed.) "Poem 22", *The Poems of Catullus*, pp. 75-6.
31 Stead, "The Clodian Songbook: 14", *Geographies*, p. 72.
32 C. K. Stead, from an address delivered at the University of Alberta, Edmonton, Canada, 16 February 1982.
33 Stead, "From the Clodian Songbook: 16", *Between*, p. 53.
34 C. K. Stead, *Book Self*, Auckland University Press, 2008, p. 295.
35 ibid, p. 296. Stead offers quotations from *The Irish Times*: "as subtle as Jane Austen and as fatalistic as Thomas Hardy ... a minor miracle of a novel", and equally enthusiastic remarks from the *Daily Telegraph* and *The Spectator*.
36 ibid, p. 294.
37 C. K. Stead, "Remembering Anactoria: Honours Are Declined", *The Black River*, Auckland University Press, 2007, p. 33.
38 C. K. Stead, "Suffenia the Poet", in *New Writing* 7, Carmen Callil and Craig Raine (eds.) London, Vintage, in association with the British Council, 1998, p. 393.

[39] Ken Arvidson, "Stead Muses on Life's Experiences", *Waikato Times*, 18 March 2000, p. 16.

[40] Harry Ricketts, "Sylvia, Meet Horace", *New Zealand Listener*, 1 April 2000, p. 44.

[41] Harry Ricketts, "All in the Voice", *New Zealand Listener*, 7 February 2009, p. 37.

[42] Stead, *Book Self*, p. 237.

[43] Stead, "Honest Lauris, Honest Iago", *The Writer at Work*, p. 50. Stead alleges that the children of Edmond had called the truthfulness of an earlier volume of autobiography into question: in a letter to a Wellington newspaper "two of her daughters ... complain about reviewers who, ignorant of the facts, described the second volume of their mother's work as 'honest'."

[44] Nigel Cox, *Quote/Unquote*, July 1994, p. 15. Stead's analysis of "The Lecture" appears in C. K. Stead, "The New Victorians", *Answering to the Language*, Auckland University Press, 1989, p. 282.

[45] Stead, *Answering to the Language*, p. 283.

[46] C. K. Stead, *Kin of Place: Essays on 20 New Zealand Writers*, Auckland University Press, 2002, p. 299.

[47] ibid, p. 300.

[48] Stead, *Book Self*, p. 381.

CHAPTER EIGHT

To Hollywood

Controversy and Early Retirement

Having won the respect of New Zealand's left-wing liberals for his anti-Vietnam activities and his 1981 anti-Springbok tour stance, Stead was astonished to find himself described as right-wing, because of his attitudes to race relations and education.

In reviewing *the bone people* for *Ariel*, in October 1985, Stead questioned Keri Hulme's claim to 'Maoriness'. She identifies with fundamental Maori values, has immersed herself in the culture and is well-versed in her iwi heritage – matters of greater significance to Maori than the number of immediate forebears of that race. Stead's question represented an affront and its implications offended Hulme: "To say that I'm now claiming the one-eighth because it's trendy and fashionable to do it now – that's very insulting indeed."[1]

As for Ihimaera's *The Matriarch*, Stead found the novel problematic. His review can be read as a challenge to those who admire the work. Included in his commentary, though, are gratuitous inferences concerning the Maori attitude to land: "And though Maori insist that for them the land has spiritual value which the Pakeha does not understand, they go on selling it. Their sense of its spiritual value is always sharpest once the material value has been realised – and that has always been the case."[2] Maori find this remark ill-informed. Iwi and hapu have not entered lightly into those land sales they have authorised. Moreover, land has enduring spiritual value, which is retained whether or not it is sold.[3]

Also unpopular with Maori – and others as well – was Stead's criticism of editors Wedde and McQueen who included poetry in Maori language in *The Penguin Book of New Zealand Verse*. Wedde is accused of bowing to political correctness, given that he was unable to judge the merit of the Maori poetry. To Stead, the selection, in its

English translation, seems poor.

> It may be that the Maori behind these verses, and many like them, is fine, noble, striking, inventive or beautiful. If it is, the translations haven't done justice to the originals. On the other hand if the translations match the quality of the originals then they might be better left unexposed to comparison. Either way the loss is to the mana of Maori.[4]

The editors did, of course, take advice from speakers of the language. Michael King argues persuasively that, while the Maori poetry is excellent, it cannot be adequately expressed in English. He shows how much is lost through translation: resonance, repetition of sounds, onomatopoeia, a wealth of allusion and reference to whakatauki (proverbs). "Maori oral culture is extraordinarily dependent on the *sound* of words, Maori words, for the conveying of thought and feeling." King regrets that there have not been "more people by now [who] would have been exposed to our twin literary heritage and taken advantage of its richness – as writers and consumers; and as critics – not because it is politically correct, not because it will win Brownie points, but because they have experienced the depth and the awe and the resonance that both cultures have to offer."[5]

Even before his reviews of work by Maori, Stead was reputed to be unsympathetic to an emphasis on Maori literature in the new, revised secondary school English syllabus. After addressing the National Association of Teachers of English in 1982, he was shocked to find himself "cast in the role of savager of the poor, the semi-literate, the under-privileged, the Maori", observing, "I have never met such hostility from an audience."[6] He had alleged that the New English Syllabus lacked sufficient rigour in its English language and literature programme. Far from being deterred by the unpopularity of his stance, Stead was expressing the same ideas, more expansively, a decade later. He continued to complain that the secondary schools were failing to include the most significant literary works.

> Great literature is unsafe; it's subversive; the moralist has never been able to depend on it. It teaches that life is more complex than religions and ideologies would want us to believe. It mocks empires and scorns bureaucracies. It teaches

> scepticism. It sometimes sets beauty in competition with virtue, and lets beauty win. It excites the mind and imagination to reach beyond the limits of the ordinary and the good-orderly. It tells the hard truths. It shows life as it really is, not as we think it ought to be.[7]

Stead has argued consistently that the new policies would have the effect of dispensing with depth and breadth of education in European literary and intellectual traditions. Had he felt inclined to propose that New Zealand students needed to enter two realms of traditional knowledge concurrently – the European and that pertaining to Maori culture, mythology and oral traditions – he might have won a measure of support. He believed, though, that Maori culture was receiving undue attention, while the European heritage, "the broader cultural and historical framework",[8] was being neglected.

> I don't think that at the moment enough people are speaking out frankly and clearly on behalf of Pakeha culture ... all the voices are speaking for Maori culture. If no one was speaking for Maori culture, I'm the kind of perverse person who might be doing it, but at the moment the silence seems all to be on the side of Pakeha culture.[9]

Stead also took issue with the teaching of English in New Zealand universities. According to Mark Williams, the professor was "routinely condemned within the academy as a conservative",[10] reacting as he did against an undue focus on theory. Stead was convinced that "the fashion for literary theory has been damaging to the simple practice of reading books, and consequently bad for literature."[11] He discusses the positions of Barthes, Lacan, Derrida and Foucault in his essay "English in our Universities", which explains critical theory in a manner a layperson can follow, in contrast to theorist colleagues who were, Stead believed, "replacing civilised literary discourse with an occult language available only to the initiated, while, behind their back, Commerce, which 'in theory' they deplored, was quietly taking over the institution that employed them."[12] Twenty-five years later, many would agree that these concerns were justified. While the emphasis on theory has moderated, the acceptance by university administrators of a corporate, commercial model of governance can now be seen to have undermined fundamental principles of university education, according to *Crisis of Identity* (2007) by Wilf Malcolm, former Vice-Chancellor of the University of Waikato, and Nicholas Tarling, Emeritus Professor of History at the University of Auckland.[13]

Williams believes that Stead would have found "academia increasingly alien"[14] in the 1980s. Economic rationalisation began to affect university programmes and teaching, with a 'sinking lid' policy, staff redundancies, and reduction in the range of papers being offered, especially in Humanities. For Stead, the changes included a welcome opportunity to take early retirement. In a letter to Allen Curnow, he speaks of negotiation between the Association of University Teachers and the government. If an early retirement package were to be put into effect, he wrote, "I would settle down to some longer works I have in mind."[15] As the years passed, Stead's wish to focus primarily on writing had intensified. He admitted to "a conflict" between what his academic position required of him and what he "wanted most to be doing".[16] When the long-heralded scheme was implemented in 1986, Stead, after twenty-six years on the staff of Auckland University, accepted its provisions, which included for him the title Emeritus Professor. He was free from the beginning of August that year.

Stead and Professor Bill Harper

After lecturing at the Yeats Summer School in Sligo, immediately following retirement, Stead flew to America to prepare for *Sister Hollywood*, which called for careful on-site research. He stayed in Los Angeles with a friend and colleague, visiting film sets and studios, and delving into archives to find out how the movie world functioned in the 1940s and '50s. He checked out the long corridor of record files at Warner Studio, which was formerly the Sam Goldwyn Studio. Old films were available for viewing and Stead was able to read relevant letters, stories and novels. Recorded in the Turnbull Library are details of significant films, created in Hollywood in those years, which Stead investigated. The Turnbull also holds Stead's list of more than thirty novels and autobiographies set in Hollywood or about Hollywood personalities of the time, including *Letters from Hollywood* by Michael Moorcock, and Scott Fitzgerald's *Hollywood Years*. Stead explored the suburbs of Pacific Palisades, Westwood, Santa Monica and Sherman Oaks to provide credible home settings for his characters and accurate locations for film-making.

Several of Stead's novels include a character who resembles him. In *Sister Hollywood* this character is Bill Harper, who is the same age as Stead, grows up in Mt Eden, and becomes a professor of English literature. Stead tried to relegate Bill to the background, focusing on the fortunes and characterisation of Edith or Edie Harper, Bill's eldest sister, who becomes Arlene Tamworth.

> I always have a problem with characters who might be identified as myself, and particularly with showing them in a good light. Because the character of the brother in *Sister Hollywood* has so much in common with myself I was inhibited about building him out, so he remains rather insubstantial; whereas I always find it easy to develop women characters, partly because women have been the dominant presences in my life, far more than men, so I feel fairly confident writing about women, but also … nobody's going to think I'm writing about myself. So in terms of *personality* (as distinct from external facts) there is far more of me in the sister than there is in the brother.[17]

The way Stead's temperament has entered the character of Hollywood scriptwriter, Arlene, belongs to the mysterious process of creativity. The very obvious links between Stead and Bill Harper are of interest for the light they throw on some of Stead's boyhood experiences, especially those that prepared him to write a novel about Hollywood.

In the 1930s, '40s and '50s, the cinema offered weekly entertainment in a pre-television era for many New Zealand families. During his boyhood and adolescence, Stead, like his character Bill, saw the major films and many minor ones. These exercised a potent influence during primary school years, especially as he was bored by other aspects of his life. Boredom is a condition Stead has complained about in essays and interviews. Bill's report is that, "My life in those years consisted of degrees of boredom. Primary school was a form of slow torture from which I escaped into fantasy, and it's bizarre to reflect that probably more often than not the forms the fantasy took had been manufactured in the brains of Louis B. Mayer, or Jack Cohn, or Walt Disney, or Sam Goldwyn, or Darryl Zanuck."[18]

Reflecting on, reliving or remaking fantasies encountered at the cinema would have been part of Stead's experience, too. What Bill observes can be applied to Stead and to all those who saw films regularly in those years: "the great world out there existed in images, and for everyone, not just for children, one of the big image-forming forces, perhaps the biggest, was Hollywood. Sometimes we let the Hollywood cameras decide how we saw the world; at other times we resisted. But always as a force it was there." (p. 23) The writing of *Sister Hollywood*, with a scriptwriter as heroine, called for knowledge of the history and traditions of film, as past films provide the heritage a scriptwriter draws on and deviates from.

Stead's knowledge of the Hollywood scene was well developed long before he began research for *Sister Hollywood*. Grandmother Karlson was devoted to the cinema, her escapism reflecting a failure to come to terms with widowhood. She collected from the local stationery store weekly magazines that dramatised the glamour of Hollywood, disclosing the fortunes of the stars and starlets, their love affairs, triumphs and failures. In those days Hollywood offered a dream career, with special appeal to attractive or talented young women. Hollywood's standards of beauty and fashion were disseminated worldwide via magazines like those that entered the Stead household. The embarrassing grandmother in the novel reflects quite accurately the habits of Stead's grandmother. Bill reports that "late in the afternoon, she would set off hobbling towards town for a five o'clock session at the pictures. If she liked a movie she would go to it every night of the week." (p. 30)

Stead's interest in films would surely have developed his ability to visualise scenes. Many episodes in *Sister Hollywood* have a filmic quality. One example is a scene in which two small children (Bill and his sister Ellie) get out of bed late at night, reach up to handles to open doors and hurry to the source of disturbing sounds. "We burst out of darkness into very bright light. Our mother is in the corner of the room, pressed against dark panels of wood. She's yelling something. I've never seen her yell like that. And our father is hitting her." (p. 218) There is credibility in the responses and interaction of Stead's characters. The boy is shocked at seeing his father strike his mother: "she either screamed, or she subsided in a sobbing heap. I feared the screams. They were like the collapse of a whole civilization." (p. 55)

The parents in *Sister Hollywood*, *The Singing Whakapapa* and *All Visitors Ashore* all spring from the Stead parents, the author exaggerating different features or qualities and then developing the characters imaginatively. Jim Stead and his wife loved each other but were at odds with each other. The parents are caricatured with exuberance in *All Visitors Ashore* and with good humour in *The Singing Whakapapa*. *Sister Hollywood* exaggerates a darker side of their marriage. Stead has admitted that his parents were divided by differences of temperament, which sometimes led to violent arguments. Like Bill in *Sister Hollywood*, he would rush from room to room, closing windows to prevent the sound of disharmony from being heard throughout a neighbourhood of potential constituents. Both Mr Harper and Stead's father aspired to selection as the local Labour Party candidate.

Bill's teenage hobbies take him away from the tensions of home as often as possible, to play tennis, soccer and chess. So it was with Stead, who, at that age, enjoyed these very hobbies. Like Stead, Bill discovers poetry in those years. Bill also finds that he has within himself more than one character: "there were not just two characters. There were three, there were six, there were a great number." (p. 95) Stead, too, has an ability to gain access to many facets of his personality, allowing him to intuit his characters' range of feelings and reactions.

Parallels between Bill and Stead extend to their adult attitudes toward Europe, especially London. Although the following is Bill's statement, Stead has made similar remarks: "London especially felt like a second home. It was a place that welcomed me, that used and rewarded my talents, that gave me warm friends and clever colleagues. But it wasn't home. Home was Auckland city, and the little bungalow (getting bigger as we pushed out walls and built upstairs extensions) ..." (p. 153) The description of the bungalow fits Stead's home in Parnell, though the setting for Bill and wife Marion's home is Milford Beach.

Kay and Karl Stead have a bach at Karekare, which they built in 1975. A holiday home and writing retreat, its verandah is where the possums that feature in Stead's poem "St Francis at Karekare" were fed.[19] Such a place becomes Bill and Marion's bach "up the valley from Karekare Beach ... From our bach the land drops, all in thick bush, then rises until finally it comes out on a grassy headland, about a mile away as the crow flies. Marion and I sometimes follow the road around – it's about three miles that way – until we can stand on the grassy headland and look across at our bach buried among tall kauris and rimus." (p. 167) From that "grassy headland", Stead viewed the "great outreach" to the west, which begins "Walking Westward".

As a professor of English who attended conferences and speaking engagements abroad, Stead travelled regularly via Los Angeles. Bill, holding the same professional position, also passes through Los Angeles. Eventually he stays in the city with a colleague, gives lectures at UCLA and searches Hollywood for the sister who had left home some thirty years earlier.

History and Illusion

Whereas authorial options in shaping a novel are made visible in *The Death of the Body*, there is no attempt to expose the writing process in *Sister Hollywood*. The omniscient Bill is a narrator who knows far more than any brother could possibly have been told, even by the most forthright of sisters. A central chapter (Chapter 8) in the present tense depicts Arlene's past life in Hollywood, reinforcing the impression of an all-knowing narrator.

With Hollywood and the city of Auckland juxtaposed, the novel explores the way reality and illusion are linked and at variance with each other. Hollywood's illusory worlds are contrasted with historic details and the realities of life in Auckland during and immediately after the war. It is true that World War II ended when Stead was twelve years old and he was, like Bill Harper, called upon to ring the school bell in celebration. Both author and character experienced a certain anxiety: "I couldn't remember a time when there hadn't been, not just *a* war, but *the* war." (p. 26) The same feeling is expressed by Stead in "Walking Westward":

> Pemberton
> who told me to ring the bell
> because the War was over
> (50 million dead and half of Europe in ruins)
> and ringing the bell I was worried
> it had been War so long
> what would Peace be like?"[20]

Stead recreates a post-war conflict, historically accurate, which saw American society and, in particular, the Hollywood film industry, under siege from the House Un-American Activities Committee, as efforts were made to uncover communism at the end of the 1940s and into the 1950s. Hearings in Washington, credibly recreated by Stead, take on an aura of farce and fantasy.

> A screenwriter, Ayn Rand, suggested that an MGM movie called *Song of Russia* had been Communist propaganda because it showed Russians smiling, looking prosperous and happy; and Robert Taylor apologised for his part in it, saying that if there hadn't been a war going on in which Russia was America's ally, he would never have agreed to make it. (p. 84)

Bertolt Brecht cleverly convinced the Un-American Activities Committee of his innocence by saying that, "as a foreigner he couldn't claim the protection of the Constitution of the United States and so would answer all questions put to him." (p. 86) Ironically, the citizens of America had received no protection whatsoever from the Constitution. Brecht politely denied ever having been a communist, corrected what he said were mistranslations of his poems and, within a few days, flew from New York to Switzerland to East Berlin. Another historical event that impacts upon characters in the novel is the execution of the Jewish couple, Julius and Ethel Rosenberg, judged guilty of spying.

Stead details the differences between the dream of Hollywood and the reality of people trying to make a career or earn a living there. To Arlene and husband Rocky it seems that the "'real' Hollywood was somewhere else, as unreachable as ever". Its existence is "not a place; it was a state of mind". (p. 47) Stead's characters make difficult and truthful discoveries. A dream goal can blind a person to other avenues and opportunities.

In his review of *Sister Hollywood* Ian Wedde gives attention to Bill's adolescent fascination with a beautiful sister, seven years his senior, while devoting just one brief paragraph to Edie/Arlene in Hollywood. Although the book is focused on Hollywood and a female scriptwriter, Lydia Wevers remarks that she finds "the sensitive sexually tormented young New Zealand male growing into manhood wearisomely ubiquitous in New Zealand literature".[21] Wedde and Wevers were two of the book's unenthusiastic New Zealand reviewers.

Whereas Wevers sees Auckland and Hollywood forming "parallel clichés", John Mellors for the *London Magazine* appreciates Stead's searching look at Hollywood, "not exploring it for satire or farce. Stead does not make cheap fun of 'tinseltown'. People of talent, with creative skills and flair work in Stead's studios."[22] Toby Moore of the *Times Literary Supplement* admires the exploration of Hollywood "as a perception rather than a place"[23] and describes the work as a "considerable feat of construction". The novel's accomplishments seem to have eluded most New Zealand reviewers. Michael King is an exception, noting "marvellous evocations of an Auckland suburb in wartime, the vicissitudes of the New Zealand Labour Movement, the physical and cultural climate of Los Angeles, and the deliberations of the Congressional Un-American Activities Committee".[24] King's review implies a serious and original work of fiction.

Stead shows insight into the detail of life in Hollywood in the late 1940s and early 1950s – its complex commercial games, its vicious competitiveness, and its endless parties where people attempted to promote themselves. The thoroughness of Stead's research and the depth of his knowledge have led to a credible reconstruction of the Hollywood scene, an aspect of the novel appreciated by those with knowledge of the industry.

The End of the Eighties and Stead's "Negative Thrust"

Sister Hollywood provoked no controversy, but Stead's other 1989 publications did. His essay "The New Victorians" appeared in *Metro*, in February, acknowledging that "Feminism and anti-racism have hit us late, hard and together."[25] Its contentious views offended significant numbers of women, members of the literary community, academics, and Maori.

The controversial essay challenges the choice of Goodman Fielder Wattie Book Award winners and includes Stead's original unfavourable analysis of Lauris Edmond's poem, "The Lecture". In addition, the essay describes the rhetoric of the Women's Movement as "an unpleasant combination of moralist busy-bodying and political manipulation".[26] Stead claims never to have doubted the truth of the assertion that, for some women, "creativity was held back … by domestic responsibility," but wonders "about the husbands of those years whose creativity was not merely held back – it was crushed altogether – by the parallel necessity to earn a living and support a wife and family".[27] Economics, not gender, have, in Stead's opinion, made it difficult for women to write full-time.

"The New Victorians" suggests that the Treaty of Waitangi, when it was signed, took no account of New Zealanders who were neither English nor Maori – that those whom Keith Sinclair calls the 'native born' were not party to the Treaty. Stead believed that this view of the

Treaty, though "in the minds of many Pakehas", was voiced "only in private between (so to speak) consenting adults".[28] The essay concludes by noting "how far" he and his country "had drifted apart".[29] These words, in fact, conclude his book *Answering to the Language*, published late 1989, in which the essay is reprinted.

Answering to the Language also includes republication of Stead's reviews of *the bone people*, *The Matriarch*, and the Wedde/McQueen anthology. It is intriguing to look back at the immediate response to Stead's attitudes, and then at the further outcomes in the course of the following decade.

The initial *Metro* publication of "The New Victorians" led directly to Stead's failure to become chair of the National Library in 1989. Cabinet Minister Margaret Shields, having been briefed by the Ministry of Women's Affairs, vetoed his appointment. Her 'briefing' took the form of a copy of the essay.[30] Camille Guy summed up Stead's reputation at the time by saying, "A couple of book reviews and a provocative piece of social criticism have made Stead the bête noir of New Zealand's liberal intellectual community".[31] Stephen Stratford, writing a few months later, called Stead "the John McEnroe of New Zealand letters", attributing his reputation to a long history of "caustic reviews" and "public squabbles".[32] Mark Williams makes a comment that applies to the book as a whole and to the final essay, "The New Victorians" as well: "The negative thrust of Stead's polemical drive has overwhelmed the critical and historical interest that has always lain at the centre of his power as a critic."[33]

In Britain, the book seems to have been read with enjoyment. Tom Aitken of *The Times Literary Supplement* gives his review the title "Antipodean Dogfights". Having referred to Stead's "generally mild manner" and "moments when Stead's mildness becomes firm disapproval", he then remarks gleefully that "Stead can be irresistibly waspish."[34]

In New Zealand, negativity toward Stead impacted in unforeseen ways. Anger that had simmered throughout the 1980s erupted in the 1990s in response to Stead's being asked to fulfil three literary assignments, the first a poetry writing commission.

Hostility was the response to the discovery that Stead had been called upon, for a fee of $5,000, to write a poem or poems celebrating New Zealand's sesquicentenary. In 1990 Stephen Stratford explained how the commission came about.

> Two years ago [1988], Bryce Harland, our high commissioner in London, asked fellow-expatriate Robert Burchfield for ways to commemorate 1990. Burchfield had seen in the *London Review of Books* some poems of Stead's related to particular events, including the *Rainbow Warrior* bombing, and suggested he be commissioned to write a poem which could be published in the *Times* or *LRB*.
> Bassett [Minister of Culture] did consult some New Zealand residents – like Internal Affairs secretary Peter Boag – then in August 1988 asked Stead if he would accept the commission. "I said I wasn't sure if I could write a poem but I would try. If I could write a poem to my satisfaction, then I would accept."
> He could and did. Stead started work on March 10 last year, writing in longhand in a hard-backed notebook, and by September had written the 51 poems published as *Voices*.
> "I was commissioned to write a poem and I wrote a book," he says somewhat defensively. "I could have written a limerick and taken the money. A tremendous amount of technical work went into it – there're a lot of sonnets there, 18 or 19 with formal rhyme schemes ... That's hard work – it's like invisible mending."[35]

The poems in *Voices*, published in 1990, offer individual testimonies at particular moments of history, from "The Missionary" of 1820 to the voice of the secret agent involved in the sinking of the Rainbow Warrior in 1985, and the 1990 poem, "At the Grave of Governor Hobson". The poet invested research and care in creating the sequence.

> There's a lot of half-concealed rhyming, quite tight verse forms, and a basic regular five-stress line; so it's more conservative – there isn't the kind of technical excitement that there has been with other things I've written. I suppose I felt intuitively that to mix that sort of historical material with technical experimentation wouldn't have been quite fulfilling the commission.[36]

A Radio New Zealand recording of the work, with contrasting voices and sensitive musical backing, prompted spontaneous enthusiasm from radio listeners. Despite this outcome there were complaints:

"the commission should have been awarded through a competition or selection by PEN." Stead remarked that, had there been such a process, "either nothing would have come of it or something predictable would have".[37]

In his 2009 review of Stead's 2008 *Collected Poems 1951-2006*, Harry Ricketts finds that *Voices* "remains an underrated collection".[38] Melbourne academic Justin Clemens, also reviewing *Collected Poems*, features one extensive quotation; ten lines have been selected from *Voices*: "At the Grave of Governor Hobson".[39] This poem was described by Kevin Ireland, back in 1990, as the book's "outstanding concluding work ... assured, allusive, satisfying". Ireland's *Listener* review was virtually alone in paying serious critical attention to *Voices*. His account acknowledges "an agreeable, well-written and dignified work". Before addressing the quality of the poetry, though, Ireland devotes four paragraphs to circumstances attending Stead's "poetic patronage" and to his observation that the writer "has not had a good press lately."[40]

Other outbursts against Stead were prompted by his next official literary mission: a flight to Britain to choose a residence in London, where New Zealand writers could live and work for between one and five months. A third assignment to meet with disapproval would be Stead's editing of the *Faber Book of Contemporary South Pacific Stories*, an undertaking discussed in Chapter Ten.

1 Geoff Chapple, "Writer Charges Book Sabotaged", *Sunday Star Times*, 30 January 1994, p. A5.

2 C. K. Stead, *Answering to the Language: Essays on Modern Writers*, Auckland University Press, 1989, p. 190.

3 When compensation is sought from the Waitangi Tribunal for stolen or confiscated land, Maori do not seek financial recompense alone. An apology from the Crown, like that given to the Parihaka people, is a highly valued component of a Treaty Settlement.

4 Stead, *Answering to the Language*, p. 143.

5 Michael King, "Ethnic Cleansing", *Metro*, January 1993, p. 135.

6 Stead, *Answering to the Language*, pp. 277-8.

7 C. K. Stead, *The Writer at Work: Essays*, Dunedin, University of Otago Press, 2000, p. 112.

8 ibid, p. 113.

9 Stephen Stratford, "Blaspheming Against the Pieties: Why the Literati Hate C. K. Stead", *Metro*, April 1990, p. 81.

10 Mark Williams, "Asking the Hard Questions", *New Zealand Books*, March 2001, p. 13.

11 Stead, *The Writer at Work*, p. 122.

12 ibid, p. 11.

13. Wilf Malcolm and Nicholas Tarling, *Crisis of Identity? The Mission and Management of Universities in New Zealand*, Wellington, Dunmore Publishing Ltd, 2007.
14. Williams, "Asking the Hard Questions", *New Zealand Books*, March 2001, p. 12.
15. C. K. Stead, letter to Allen and Jeny Curnow, 24 May 1983.
16. Stead, *The Writer at Work*, p. 10.
17. ibid, p. 241.
18. C. K. Stead, *Sister Hollywood*, London, Collins, 1989, p. 22. Page numbers in brackets in this chapter refer to this edition.
19. C. K. Stead, "St Francis at Karekare", *Geographies*, Auckland University Press/Oxford University Press, 1982, pp. 83-4.
20. C. K. Stead, "Walking Westward", *Walking Westward*, Auckland, The Shed, 1979, p. 38.
21. Lydia Wevers, "Parallel Clichés of Tinsel Town", *Dominion Sunday Times*, 22 October 1989, p. 19.
22. John Mellors, "Obsessions and Illusions", *London Magazine*, Oct/Nov 1989, p. 134.
23. Toby Moore, "C. K. Stead: *Sister Hollywood*", *Times Literary Supplement*, 11 August 1989, p. 877.
24. Michael King, "High Accomplishments", *Metro*, December 1989, p. 190.
25. Stead, *Answering to the Language*, p. 285.
26. ibid, p. 278.
27. ibid, p. 281.
28. ibid, p. 285.
29. ibid, p. 287.
30. Stratford, "Blaspheming Against the Pieties", *Metro*, April 1990, p. 72.
31. Camille Guy, "A War of Words", *NZ Herald*, 14 December 1989, p. 8.
32. Stratford, "Blaspheming Against the Pieties", *Metro*, April 1990, p. 72.
33. Mark Williams, "Our Most Trenchant Critic", *The Dominion*, 4 November 1989, p. 9.
34. Tom Aitken, "Antipodean Dogfights", *Times Literary Supplement*, 22 February 1991, p. 10.
35. Stratford, "Blaspheming Against the Pieties", *Metro*, April 1990, p. 80.
36. Stead, *The Writer at Work*, pp. 243-4.
37. Stratford, "Blaspheming Against the Pieties", *Metro*, April 1990, p. 80.
38. Harry Ricketts, "All in the Voice", *New Zealand Listener*, 7 February 2009, p. 37.
39. Justin Clemens, "Kiwi Poet with his Eye on Here and Beyond", *The Australian*, 20 December 2008.
40. Kevin Ireland, "Polished Reflections", *New Zealand Listener*, 6 February 1990.

CHAPTER NINE

"Prose is the Necessary Donkey"[1]

Frontline and the London Flat

A 1990 television documentary, "How D'Ye Do, Mr Governor", examined a range of attitudes to the Treaty of Waitangi, with host and interviewer Ian Johnstone. Stead took his place among the speakers. According to a report for *Metro* by Stephen Stratford,

> Ian Johnstone asked Stead how he saw the Treaty. "For me the Treaty is a document which doesn't fit modern New Zealand," began Stead hesitantly.
> "Another view from…" interrupted Johnstone and the camera swung away. When eventually he got back to Stead many minutes later, he misquoted him as having said the Treaty wasn't relevant.[2]

Stead also took part in a televised public affairs programme, *Frontline*, which discussed the purchase of a London flat by the Ministry of Arts and Culture. The two television experiences contributed to his satirical treatment of *Frontline* in the novel *The End of the Century at the End of the World*, in which character Dan Cooper MP is interviewed. He finds his replies have been cut and placed in new contexts. The novel's *Frontline* includes fatuous interview questions tossed at Dan: "'I understand you're some kind of patron of the NZSO. But where does the Treaty of Waitangi fit in?' Cooper: 'I don't know. Does it have to fit in?'"[3] Dan is accused of having a "Eurocentric" attitude to New Zealand culture, an accusation that has also been levelled at Stead.

In 1989, Stead played a part in a government initiative that was widely condemned for being Eurocentric. He was asked to find a suitable London flat to provide residencies of one-to-two months and three-to-five months for writers. The Minister of Arts and Culture, Michael

Bassett, conceived of the scheme as a contribution to New Zealand's sesquicentennial celebrations. That Stead should have received a trip abroad, having already been called upon to write poetry for the sesquicentenary, prompted allegations of cronyism. Stead protested, claiming that he and Bassett had never visited each other's homes, nor even attended the same dinner party.[4]

Stead chose an apartment in Bloomsbury: "a 'spacious' one-bedroom flat, suitable for a writer and partner, within walking distance of Piccadilly Circus and major cultural attractions." There were some who questioned Stead's expertise in property acquisition. He replied by asking, "Do you want a real estate agent to buy a property for writers? What I've got is so brilliantly strategically placed you wouldn't believe it."[5]

Public response to the London flat was close to wholesale condemnation. Gordon Campbell began his *Listener* article, "At a time when 70,000 people in New Zealand are homeless, the government's decision to spend $342,849 on the 75-year lease of a one-bedroom flat in London for writers was bound to raise a rumpus." Long-term bitterness at under-funding of the arts affected the attitude of writers, with John Cranna, Auckland branch president for the Society of Authors (PEN), remarking that funding in New Zealand "was relatively far lower than in Australia or Canada, and was a pittance compared to the funds lavished on sport in general, and the Commonwealth Games in particular. More, he suspects, was spent on the Games than on the arts in New Zealand in the last 100 years."[6] Bassett was addressing a deficiency in arts funding, but in a way that stirred jealousies and resentment. University staff were considered by the general public to be advantaged, given their sabbatical leave entitlements. It was imagined that the flat would offer the greatest benefit to academics, becoming another perk for the already privileged.

There were murmurs that Stead could have expected to profit personally. He was indignant: "I was roundly angry with a lot of people in PEN, because I had undertaken something not in the spirit of self-interest at all but because I wanted other New Zealand writers to share the pleasures of London which I experience annually."[7] While he felt that he might reasonably take a turn as resident, having given a month of his time to the assignment, he already had a range of accommodation options available in London. For instance, in 1990 he stayed "upstairs in the Ladbroke Road house" of good friends.[8]

Michael Bassett's proposal was undermined by PEN in a letter of protest signed by 27 members. The idea was rejected on the grounds that not all branches had been fully consulted and that New Zealand's young writers were "no longer turning to Europe for inspiration".[9] Not generally known at the time was Bassett's intention to pass ownership of the London flat to PEN NZ. The property, purchased with Lottery Board funds set aside to mark 1990 celebrations, was sold by a new government the following year.[10]

Today it is hard to believe that such an opportunity was played away, given that residencies for New Zealand writers are now offered in Berlin, Beijing, Cork (Ireland), Hawai'i, Iowa, New Delhi, Menton – and even Antarctica. A place to stay in London would have been useful, not only for those carrying out historical or biographical research, but for those engaged in creative writing. Even without the need to delve into museums and libraries, London offers opportunities to join writing networks and to enjoy the stimulation of a rich cultural life. It is acknowledged that the cost of air travel is within the means of many New Zealanders in the 21st century, but the cost of accommodation in London is more likely to be a problem.

Some argued against the London flat in 1989 by saying that women in particular could not afford to fly to the other side of the world. One counter-proposal, the development of a writers' retreat on an island near Whakatane, involved a large house where twenty writers at once could enjoy space and privacy. In 1990, there was clear need for residencies in New Zealand – while at the same time there was need for writers' accommodation abroad. In 2009, New Zealand provides a dozen or more residences for writers. Whether located in New Zealand or overseas, they generally come with provision for property maintenance as well as support for the resident, the income varying according to the prestige of the award.[11]

The London flat controversy informs some of the attitudes and comments in *The End of the Century at the End of the World*. At issue in the novel is whether the North Shore cottage of fictional author Hilda Tapler should be bought and preserved as part of the country's literary heritage. Those behind a television current affairs programme sabotage the project. Dan Cooper, the character championing the cause, admits that the late Hilda Tapler was his aunt. A personal interest deemed inappropriate is disclosed. As he struggles to secure the cottage, Dan finds his support base disappearing. "A representative from PEN, a young man with spiky hair and an anxious face, agrees that his organisation supported the scheme. But he personally was not told that the writer in question was related to the Minister." (p. 202)

Significant fiction by Hilda Tapler has been published in England.

> INT: You see, Minister, a lot of people are going to think here we are spending public money on yet another Eurocentric icon when this is our sesquicentenary year, the year when we ought to feel we've come of age as a Pacific nation...
> COOPER: We'll have come of age as a Pacific nation when we stop going on about it. (p. 185)

In reviewing *The End of the Century at the End of the World*, Tom Aitken, writing for the *Times Literary Supplement*, quotes the above retort by Dan Cooper and sums up the argument: "Stead implies that for his country's ideologues to turn their backs on Europe is futile and perversely self-impoverishing, and he pointedly enriches his book with quotations from European texts."[12] The title of Stead's novel draws attention to New Zealand's location at the greatest possible distance from Europe, alluding to Curnow's line, "Here is the world's end where wonders cease." His poem is quoted in full, prior to the beginning of the novel.

Laura as Author

Stead's main female character in *The End of the Century at the End of the World* is Laura Barber, an aspiring novelist. She is conducting research at the university into the life and work of Hilda Tapler. Links between Stead and Professor Steve Casey, Laura's supervisor, tease readers. Steve and Laura were students together twenty years earlier. He went abroad on a scholarship, returned as a lecturer and rose rapidly to his professorial position. His name forms a light-hearted link to Stead's – Ca-sey = K. C. Read backwards, the result is C. K. Steve. In some respects he is Stead's opposite. Unlike Stead, he prefers "Post-Structuralist modes of thought". (p. 26) The professor has a minor role. He appears, recedes into the background, then resurfaces at the novel's conclusion. The echo of Casey in C. K. offers a foil, while some of Stead's predilections and opinions are embraced by other characters.

Laura's injunction to herself to "Turn off your mind machine, Laura. Get on with your word-work" (p. 29) is also Stead's policy in creating poetry or fiction.[13] Stead shares with Hilda Tapler the belief that a person laments at the end of a life what he or she has not attempted: "In old age it was the things not done that you regretted, more – far more – than the mistakes." (p. 115) Stead's poem "Takapuna" includes a comparable thought: "the thing that happens /dies when it happens./ The thing that doesn't happen lives for ever."[14]

Laura sees her own writing as "fiction in the service of what had once been fact". (p. 123) She observes that people rewrite and refashion their own histories, and even remake themselves. The novel has two first-person narrators, Laura Barber and Dan Cooper. Both mix fact and fiction, blurring the boundaries between them. For example, Dan remembers being taken as a child to a North Shore beach by his writer aunt and one of her friends, a man who, "in his bathing suit, found a stick he pretended was a musical pipe, and with seaweed wreathed in his hair did a Pan-dance in the shallows, prancing on his toes, lifting his knees high, bending forward as if playing on the pipe. And just at that moment the big guns on the headland went off". (p. 117) Stead has previously recounted such a story, in which Sargeson was the Pan dancer in company with Janet Frame and the Steads. The episode gives a touch of credibility to the aunt's association with an earlier generation of writers on the North Shore, and with Sargeson in particular.

Moravia and the Art of the Novelist

Another writer who becomes significant in *The End of the Century at the End of the World* is the Italian novelist Alberto Moravia. Dan Cooper describes Moravia's *Conjugal Love* to Laura: "Really I thought it was the most beautiful book I'd ever read. I suppose I was impressionable – but it was something to do with the style – like a cold, clear light. It gave me a new idea of what a novel could be." (p. 154) This reaction is very like Stead's on first reading the novel as a student in Auckland.

Conjugal Love explores an author's state of mind and mental processes before, during, and after the creation of a novel. Moravia's "psychology of authorship" (p. 199) is discussed by Laura and Dan. Characters who are writers, in both Stead's work and in Moravia's, agonise over their completed work, despairing that a novel which earlier appeared to be a masterpiece subsequently seems worthless. Stead's Laura and Moravia's Silvio find it difficult to read their own work after the first draft is finished, a state of mind Stead himself has experienced, with *All Visitors Ashore* a case in point.

Questions raised by Moravia are taken seriously by Stead: "What is the source of the story we are being told? Whose narrative is it, and what is its authority?" In an essay, Stead considers Moravia's contention that third-person narrative "had the effect of '[inhibiting] the illusion and delight of representation in the novel' – an interesting statement because it meant whatever steps he took to overcome the problem were taken still in the interests of mimesis".[15] A third-person narrator is at times introduced by Laura to allow certain events to be told dispassionately, as if they were fiction, but with the implication that they are fact. Stead experiments with alternatives to a third-person narrative by using a range of 'primary' sources – journal entries, letters, a television transcript, two first-person accounts, and part of a character's autobiographical novel.

This novel employs a range of means to encourage active engagement in the reading process. A narrator consults readers in weighing up how best to continue the story, and even suggests that they may like to recount an episode differently, as long as particular items of information are somehow included.[16] Each of the novel's seven chapters includes a dream. With their mystery and impression of irrelevance, dreams contribute to a modernist texture. Readers can contrast and connect memories, images and impressions. This, as Allan Phillipson points out, is the modernist way, which Stead often employs in his poetry. At the same time, it is a postmodern ploy for the author to be visible and working overtly with his material. Stead uses both approaches.

Phillipson describes Stead's account of Mansfield's "*Je ne parle pas français*", which establishes a central reference point, then moves "in circles about it, going back and forward in time. The result is a further thickening of texture".[17] He finds a similar centre or focus in Stead's novel, which also ranges back and forth in time. Whereas Phillipson appreciates Stead's modernist strategies in *The End of the Century at the End of the World*, and enjoys his freedom as a reader to arrange the fragments, interludes, letters and other such material, Owen Marshall complains of "Rather too much to-ing and fro-ing for my taste, with artifice rather than art supreme, but it gets there in the end".[18] Out of the circling and the accretions, a character named Maurice Scobie confronts his death. The novel concludes with his funeral, which brings the key players together.

A Vendetta?

A disagreement between Stead and Dick Scott is thought to have given rise to the creation of Maurice Scobie as a form of retaliation. Maurice certainly suffers a number of reversals, but the allegation is unconvincing. He is a man of charm and wit. "He's my favourite rel. I love him," says his granddaughter. (p. 128) At his funeral she speaks with clarity of a particular feature of his character; like a good many New Zealanders in the second half of the twentieth century, he progresses from belief in communism to renunciation of allegiance to it: "Once there was a man with a very big faith and very little doubt. Every year of his life the faith shrank and the doubt grew. In the end the doubt ate up the faith, and the man was free." (p. 211)

A connection between Maurice and Scott exists, but it has nothing to do with a vendetta. Quite simply, Stead could see fictional potential in a situation disclosed to him by Scott. Events patterned on an American woman's affair with Dick Scott are woven into Stead's novel. Maurice Scobie pursues an affair with an American woman, Lee Lomas. Her husband, Dick Lomas, eventually leaves Auckland for America with a new partner, soon to be followed by his distraught wife and their children. Such a sequence of events is related in Scott's 2004 autobiography, *Dick Scott: A Radical Writer's Life*,[19] in which he names the actual American woman and her husband.

Maurice Scobie is brought up on a Kaiwaka farm, a setting derived from the farm Stead visited as a boy. A pool Stead recalls as magical, below a waterfall, with small fish suspended in shafts of light, is Maurice's "favourite place" (p. 116), to which he takes Laura. She stays with him overnight in the old farmhouse. Though the house has fallen into disrepair, the big scrubbed table and the black wood range in the kitchen are like those Stead remembers.

Maurice proves to be a natural philosopher, refusing to feel guilt, dismissing it as egotism: "I'm just a fragment of the process, an insignificant speck, an aggregation of cells that have come together and are about to fly apart." (p. 179) The novel places lost personal opportunities within a vast time scale and in the context of terrestrial upheaval: "underground the plates advanced on one another and ground their teeth and checked their watches second by millennial second against the next eruption." (p. 35) For Maurice, music and poetry are redemptive and he has confidence that the work of great writers endures; their poetry is quoted, and details from their fiction recalled. Maurice shares with Stead a passion for music – Strauss's "Four Last Songs", for example.

Wilkins

It comes as a surprise to find critic Damien Wilkins maintaining that Stead was "chronically bored" by the requirements of writing *The End of the Century at the End of the World* and would rather have been writing poetry. His review is provocatively titled "The Self-loathing of a Stead Novel". He alleges "a deep-seated ambivalence and scepticism on the part of the writer about the whole business of the novelist".[20]

Such was the impact of the Wilkins review, that Stead integrates it into his 2001 novel, *The Secret History of Modernism*, changing the name of the reviewer to Mendel Hand, critic of novels written by Stead's character Laszlo Winter.

> The line Hand took was that my novels were full of poetry – quotations from the masters – and of a craving for poetry, and that every fiction I wrote hated itself for not being a poem. Further, he argued that because of this love of the concision and sharpness of poetry, I was bored by the necessity of having to body forth scenes, and so shirked my duties as a fiction writer.[21]

In conversation Stead has remarked he admired the Wilkins review, that he found it witty and intelligent,[22] appreciating, no doubt, an element of truth in the hyperbole: "to poetry's angel, prose is the necessary donkey."[23]

Nevertheless, Stead's 1985 interview with Harry Ricketts reflects his devotion to fiction as well as poetry.

> If I could have arranged my life to suit myself – which very few people are able to do – I would have written a lot more fiction. And I would still like to ... traditionally people talk about it as if you must be a poet or a fiction writer and think that if you try to be both you can't be serious about either. But Lawrence was serious at both. So was Hardy.[24]

The End of the Century at the End of the World was not a novel that flowed swiftly on to the page like *All Visitors Ashore*. Stead, like his character Laura, brings into the fiction part of a novel begun years earlier. He wrote *The Magic Bagwash* in 1970 and revisited it two years later in Menton. A four and a half page section sent to *Islands* in 1972 was published as "Horses", before *The Magic Bagwash* was relegated to a trunk, where it lay until 1990. The anecdote at the centre of "Horses" reappears as a crisp two-page account in *The End of the Century at the End of the World*.

A writer who has "learnt a great deal about fiction by doing it",[25] Stead has sought effective techniques for each new novel. In *The End of the Century at the End of the World*, he strategically arranges his material to heighten credibility. After his first novel, he became conscious of the need to ensure that the reader remains alert:

> there have to be strategies to trap and hold attention. If you get onto one conventional mode of fiction and you pedal along and never change then you're not exercising as well as you might the possibilities for prodding the reader awake, and one of those is to make frequent changes of tone and pace. One of the things about *Smith's Dream* as a novel, I thought after I'd done it, is that it's a long smooth surface and that the reader can just skate over the surface. Fast. You've somehow got to break up the surface; you've got to have cross-threads all the time.[26]

Within a decade, four contrasting works follow *The End of the Century at the End of the World*, all of which find different ways to "trap and hold attention", to "break up the surface" and to interweave "cross-threads": *The Singing Whakapapa*, 1994, an historical novel that required extensive research; *Villa Vittoria*, 1997, a thriller against a background of Italian politics; *Talking About O'Dwyer*, 1999, a war story and love story with a cleverly developed plot; and *The Secret History of Modernism*, 2001, concerned with relationships within a group of expatriate postgraduate students and their friends in London in the 1950s. All reflect Stead's increasing versatility in the genre.

1 Damien Wilkins, "The Self-loathing of a Stead Novel", *New Zealand Books*, 27 December 1992, p. 6.

2 Stephen Stratford, "Blaspheming Against the Pieties: Why the Literati Hate C. K. Stead", *Metro*, April 1990, p. 81.

3 C. K. Stead, *The End of the Century at the End of the World*, Auckland, HarperCollins, 1992, p. 166.
Page numbers in brackets refer to this edition.

4 Stratford, Blaspheming Against the Pieties", *Metro*, April 1990, p. 80.

5 Gordon Campbell, "Sword Fighting at PEN", *New Zealand Listener*, 5 March 1990, p. 35.

6 ibid, p. 34.

7 C. K. Stead, *The Writer at Work*, Dunedin, University of Otago Press, 2000, p. 243.

8 C. K. Stead, letter to Curnow, 29 September 1990, Turnbull Library Papers.

9 Campbell, "Sword Fighting at PEN", *New Zealand Listener*, 5 March 1990, p. 34.

10 C. K. Stead, *Book Self*, Auckland University Press, 2008, p. 327 and p. 328.

11 Some of the New Zealand residencies: Auckland (Buddle Findlay Sargeson Fellowship, and the Michael King Writers' Centre Residency); Wellington (Randell Cottage, and the National Library Fellowship); Foxton Beach; Great Barrier Island; Rotorua; Dunedin (Robert Lord Writers' Cottage).

12 Tom Aitken, "Auckland Affairs", *Times Literary Supplement*, 11 December 1992, p. 20.

13 Quoting Mallarmé, Stead has said that "Poetry is not made of ideas; or subjects, it's made of words." C. K. Stead, *In the Glass Case*, Auckland University Press/Oxford University Press, 1981, p. 267.

14 C. K. Stead, "Takapuna", *The Red Tram*, Auckland University Press, 2004, p. 55.

15 Stead, *The Writer* at Work, p. 86.

16 Stead, *The End of the Century at the End of the World*: see pages 185-6.

17 Allan Phillipson. *C. K. Stead and Three Modes of New Zealand Poetry*, The University of British Columbia, July, 1997. Thesis submitted in partial fulfilment of requirements for Doctor of Philosophy. Electronic resource retrieved May 2006 from http://www.collectionscanada.gc.ca/obj/s4/f2/dsk3/ftp04/ng25137.pdf, p. 377.

18 Owen Marshall, "Power of Language to Influence Beliefs", *Dominion*, 3 October 1992, p. 13.

19 Dick Scott, *Dick Scott: A Radical Writer's Life*, Auckland, Reed Publishing, 2004, p. 228.

20 Wilkins, "The Self-loathing of a Stead Novel", *New Zealand Books*, 27 December 1992, p. 6.

21 C. K. Stead, *The Secret History of Modernism*, London, The Harvill Press, 2001, p. 114.

22 C. K. Stead, interview with author, 28 August 2005.

23 Wilkins, "The Self-loathing of a Stead Novel", *New Zealand Books*, 27 December 1992, p. 6.

24 Stead, *The Writer at Work*, p. 231.

25 C. K. Stead, "One Thing Leads to Another", opening address in the Distinguished Alumni Series, Auckland, Maidment Theatre, 3 March 2008.

26 Stead, *The Writer at Work*, pp. 238-9.

CHAPTER TEN

The "Plume of Bees"

Questioning 'Whakapapa'

The Singing Whakapapa was not published in Britain. Nevertheless, it was judged "brilliant"[1] by John de Falbe, who chose to comment on *The Singing Whakapapa* while reviewing *Talking About O'Dwyer* for the *Spectator*. In New Zealand the use of the word 'Whakapapa' in the title was considered arrogant and inappropriate. Steve Braunias in the *Listener* records Geoff Chapple's statement that "people had told him, 'Stead has no right to use that word.'"[2] The people are not named, but Chapple and Braunias are giving expression to a muttered indignation. Behind that indignation lies Stead's lack of patience with political correctness and his irreverent attitude to the Treaty of Waitangi.

Stead exercised neither caution nor diplomacy in commenting on the Treaty of Waitangi in essays and in a *Metro* article, where he makes his point by alluding to the folk tale "The Emperor's New Clothes". Individuals comprising the story's foolish populace, who need a small child to inform them of the truth, are likened by Stead to historians, academics, the judiciary and other New Zealand professionals.

> This story makes me think of the discussions which have gone on in recent years about the Treaty of Waitangi. Like the emperor's officials, our politicians and bureaucrats, our educationalists, historians, intellectuals and literary persons, and finally and most surprisingly, our jurists, not least Mr Justice Cooke, President of the Court of Appeal, have seemed to trip over one another in their eagerness to see in that informal and expedient document, made to serve the needs of a time long gone and a situation no longer pertaining, a force and authority which a more candid appraisal might acknowledge it cannot possess. ... Our professional community, it seems to

> me, has been mesmerised by the murmured repetition of Delphic phrases – "principles of the Treaty", "founding document", "sacred compact", "partnership", "tangata whenua" – while the ordinary person in the street has looked on, unconvinced but silent."[3]

Stead has dared to express views shared by many "ordinary" persons, who would have been delighted with the satire. On the other hand, the "politicians and bureaucrats, our educationalists, historians ..." are unlikely to have been amused. In one of an authoritative series of essays edited by Sir Hugh Kawharu, Ranginui Walker describes the Treaty signing as "an historic muddle"[4] but regards the work of the Waitangi Tribunal as essential to "nation-building" and "a means of resolving conflicts over past injustices".[5] The English and Maori texts of the Treaty contradict each other, but, in the Epilogue of both versions, Crown and Maori accept "the full spirit" of the Treaty. Following from this degree of accord, the "principles of the Treaty" have been formulated by jurists and historians, contributing to a way forward.[6] Those working to achieve progress would not have taken kindly to finding "the principles of the Treaty" mocked as a sham.

The Singing Whakapapa reveals an author who is even-handed in depicting Maori characters. Stead's articles and interviews, however, have led to the view that there are gaps in his grasp of cultural concepts. An example is provided by a comment Stead made on the television programme *Frontline*. Asked if he felt himself to be tangata whenua, Stead replied, "I am tangata whenua. I have no other place than New Zealand. This is where I belong."[7] He is one of a good many Pakeha who would consider themselves tangata whenua by virtue of their New Zealand birth. The literal translation is 'people of the land', with tangata whenua commonly used among Maori to refer to those with ties to an area of land that is home through ownership or occupation by their family and forebears. The words also carry a more profound level of traditional meaning, forming a spiritual and genealogical concept. Having traced their lineage to an occupant of one of the Great Canoes, the tangata whenua then trace their genealogy mythically back to Rangi and Papa-tu-a-nuku, the Sky Father and Earth Mother. The view of Maori well-versed in their own language and culture would be that Stead belongs in New Zealand, not because he is tangata whenua, but because a Treaty was signed in 1840, granting his forebear John Flatt and his other European relatives the right to reside in this country. It was Maori Land Court Judge Eddie Durie who, in 1990, first described Pakeha as "tangata Tiriti – those who belong to the land by right of the Treaty".[8]

A fictional counterpart to Stead's relationship to Maori culture and language can be found at the end of his story "A Short History of New Zealand". The narrator dreams that imaginary writer Angela McIlroy speaks to him "in fluent Maori" and that he "strained to hear what it was she was telling him, certain that he did understand – that he was capable of it – but never quite making sense of it. It was like something just beyond reach ...". Without knowledge of the language, cultural understanding is "just beyond reach".[9] With an artist's insight, but surely without imagining that he could possibly share his narrator's difficulty, Stead shows his awareness that it is the language that carries a culture's concepts.

The Polynesian Cold Shoulder

In refusing to grant an interview concerning Stead in 1989, Albert Wendt told a reporter that he "detests Stead's views on biculturalism and no longer admires his literary criticism, but doesn't want to participate in any profile of the man".[10] This was an expression of the so-called 'Polynesian cold shoulder'. Among situations that may have contributed to Polynesian dismissiveness was Stead's description of Maori as "Stone Age" people during an *Insight* radio documentary. There were both Maori and Pakeha listeners who considered it insulting.

> The Maori culture has been an oral culture, a tribal culture and has been technologically primitive. I mean, it's a Stone Age culture. The other one is a written culture with a long historical tradition including cross-references of many languages in Europe and a long tradition going back to the Greeks and Romans. So in terms of quantity of product, so to speak, the literature and history of art that has been produced, the variety of it, the range of human experiences that is expressed in it, is enormously, incomparably and undeniably larger and richer than the Maori culture, which is the culture of one Polynesian group isolated in the South Pacific.[11]

No one would deny that the multi-cultural European heritage of literature and art is broader, more varied and more ancient than that of Maori. In this statement, which Stead would have considered mild-mannered and factual, his reference to a "Stone Age culture" tends to be remembered and cited. The reason for this may be that familiar connotations of "Stone Age" extend beyond the absence of metals. Unless a discussion pertains specifically to the use of stone implements, as opposed to metal implements,[12] the term is thought to have a pejorative ring. It is not generally applied to a culture as complex as that of the Maori, with their rich oral traditions reaching back to central Pacific origins, their skill in shaping tools of stone and volcanic glass, and their expertise in navigation, gardening, working with flax, carving and building in wood.

Stead has, from time to time, been ignored or rebuffed by Maori and Polynesians. Keri Hulme was one of four writers to withdraw her work from the *Faber Book of Contemporary South Pacific Stories*. For this collection, Stead had been invited by the publishing company to be the editor. For the third time within five years, a literary assignment he was asked to fulfil provoked public disfavour. By way of explanation to Faber, Hulme mentioned the "extensive history of insult and attack that surrounds Karl Stead's relations with Maori and Polynesian writers". The accusation astonished Stead; on reviewing the 'history' he "could find neither insult nor attack".[13] He was shocked by the withdrawal of Wendt, Hulme, Ihimaera and Grace from the Faber publication, after they had signed contracts agreeing to their stories' inclusion.

Stead, in "A Note on Absences" at the book's opening, infers that the authors in question may have been less than pleased with his critical judgement of Maori writing. He justifies his position, saying, "To give Maori or Pacific Island writers special exemption from all but favourable notice, which is what these four appear to want, and mostly get, would have seemed patronising".[14] Such a comment would have inflamed rather than appeased Polynesian indignation, as would the gratuitous remark (in this introduction to a book of stories) regarding two of Wendt's novels: "I very much regret the absences – particularly of Hulme, whose work has a stunning directness and force; and of Wendt, because his short stories, before his two novels *Ola* and *Black Rainbow*, which suggest some kind of collapse of his talent, represent some of the best of Pacific writing."[15] The statement's generosity is undermined by a side-swipe.

David Eggleton, reviewing the Faber collection for *Quote/Unquote*, considers the reasoning that might have motivated those who withdrew: "By implication their studied absence is intended as a vote of no-confidence in someone with a purported track record of cultural insensitivity being given the right to help shape cultural hegemony in the South Pacific."[16]

In 1994, Mark Williams noted "a profound shift in New Zealand cultural attitudes and directions, the implications of which are still being uneasily assimilated".

> Stead's left-liberal activism of the sixties and seventies did not anticipate, and could not accommodate, the radical and fundamental politics of the late eighties, which aimed at nothing less than the remaking of New Zealand as Aotearoa, a country no longer tied nostalgically or culturally to Europe but part of the Pacific, and to which the liberal conscience of the white academic male was merely the smokescreen of the oppressor.[17]

John Newton has placed Stead's readings of Maori literature in a social context, identifying his failure to accommodate or adjust to changes in the thinking of many New Zealanders. Not only have Maori writers offered a different cultural perspective and value system, but many Pakeha have become attuned to them – so finely attuned in the case of Baxter, for example, that Maori concepts and attitudes have been integrated into the "Jerusalem Sonnets". While observing Stead's acknowledgement that "Maori elements seem here to have become a deep and genuine part of Baxter's intellectual and emotional life",[18] Newton believes that the dimension lies outside Stead's experience or serious research, and alleges "a failure, not so much to notice this change as to *bring it into relation* not just with his reading of Baxter but with his narrative of New Zealand writing. The price of this neglect will duly be exacted in the loss of poise, and the loss of at least one portion of his audience."[19] Stead would probably have lost "one portion of his audience" fifteen or more years before John Newton's surmise in 2001. These potential readers would, in all likelihood, have shunned *The Singing Whakapapa*.

Stead's criticism of Maori fiction in the 1980s had led to an impression of condescension and provoked a defensiveness among Maori. He acknowledges that these essays in *Answering to the Language* have "negative overtones": "It will be said I am racist, or at least anti-Maori. I will have to live with that, although I know it to be untrue."[20]

In *The Singing Whakapapa*, Stead provides a view of Maori that is balanced, moderate and respectful. The novel is grounded in careful research.

The Singing Whakapapa: Maori and John Flatt

"There has always been a degree of accord between Maori and Pakeha – a fund of goodwill on both sides and the wish to resolve differences. There are also clear conflicts of interest. ... My proper function as I see it – as poet, fiction writer, essayist, reviewer – is to represent truthfully."[21] *The Singing Whakapapa* is as truthful as the author could make it to the nineteenth century Maori history he delved into, and to the nineteenth century history of his own family.

The novel involves the author's great-great-grandfather John Flatt, and recreates, in some detail, the lives of Stead's mother and her parents, Christian and Caroline Karlson, who are named Carl and Charlotte Christianson in the novel. *The Singing Whakapapa* interweaves three different stories – that of contemporary Hugh (Hugo Wolf) Grady and his immediate family, that of the Flatt family from January 1835, and that of Carl Christianson's family from about 1870.

Stead explained to reporter Kathryn Vivian, "I began my research into my family with the idea of taking the story, making some up, changing people's names and inventing history. What I discovered was much more interesting than the invention would ever have been." Two years of research and writing were required. Stead gives credit to Kay: she "works at a library and helped me enormously with a lot of the research for this book".[22] She investigated, for example, Church Missionary Society records.

Stead's place in the family tree is taken by Hugh Grady. Hugh's forebears are Stead's forebears and Hugh's childhood experiences are derived from the author's own life in the 1930s and '40s. Several factual experiences and situations from Stead's boyhood, which appear in Chapter Two of *Plume of Bees*, were gleaned from *The Singing Whakapapa*. The interaction and cooperation in the novel between sixty year-old librarian Hugh Grady and his young helper Jean-Anne Devantier parallel the teamwork of the two Steads. It was Kay and Karl who, on visiting Wairere Falls near Matamata, scene of a confrontation between John Flatt and Maori, arrived at an understanding of what must have taken place there in 1836. In the novel, Hugh and Jean-Anne visit the site and arrive at the same understanding.

John Flatt offers a Pakeha view of Maori in the 1830s and '40s. Information used in the novel derives from his personal journals and letters and his reports to the Church Missionary Society. Shortly after his arrival in the Bay of Islands, Flatt describes a canoe bearing a cloaked figure and two dozen Maori paddlers. The swift canoe and its occupants seem impressive and powerful. Nevertheless, to his superiors, Flatt describes the Maori as "poor ignorant heathens". He "reproaches himself for an insincerity he knew would persist because it was expected of him..."[23]

Flatt's diary and the novel indicate the willingness of Maori to sell land in the Tamaki Isthmus. It is not productive land. On the contrary, it is lying idle because ownership is disputed by enemy tribes. When two Maori warn Flatt that this land of uncertain Maori ownership has already been purchased by other Europeans, the Reverend Henry Williams does not want to know. Shrewdness characterises the buyers and the sellers. The Maori readily accept payment from yet another set of European buyers and hope to see their people employed in making the land productive. The purchase, arranged by Williams, is illicit. Land deals of this kind did, in fact, take place.

In the novel, as in history, Flatt is an agriculturalist. He expected to assist with the mission farm at Waimate in the Bay of Islands. Because the missionaries are keen to prevent news of their land purchases from reaching London, Flatt is sent three hundred kilometres to the south to assist Reverend Brown at a mission near Matamata, which has been established at the insistence of "the old warrior Te Waharoa". While claiming that he and his people are eager to "learn the Christian lesson of peace" (p. 57), Te Waharoa prepares for war. Flatt nevertheless finds that there is about the man "something gentle, thoughtful, wise and strong" (p. 73) and he respects the chief's reasoning ability. "Waharoa, having asked Mrs Brown what food he would eat in heaven, and having been told that a spirit needs none, pointed out that the Rev Brown had preached the resurrection of the body. Mrs B considers this a merry example of what she too calls the simple uncivilised mind, which has no notion of the spiritual body." Flatt adds wryly, "I have not much idea of it either... " (p. 61)

Both the novel and Flatt's records include accounts of murder, revenge, cannibalism and the capture of slaves. After a successful raid, warriors head for home carrying "the spoils of war including baskets of human flesh". (p. 71) The inter-tribal conflict seems to historian Hugh Grady to be "cold, cruel, duplicitous, heartless and violent, like the internecine wars of the Mafia, or the murders and revenges of the IRA and the UDA. But it was exciting; and much more interesting if it wasn't sentimentalised." (pp. 67-8) The novel's violence is not gratuitous. It is integral to the plot, at the heart of which is Flatt's love for the Maori girl Tarore. On a journey with Flatt and a party of her own people, she is murdered by Ngati Whakaue warriors. Historical accounts of this actual event are available.[24] Her copy of the Gospel of Luke is taken by an assailant, who is later converted to Christianity after studying the text. Tarore's death is believed to have led to peace among the tribes of the Rotorua and Tauranga regions. She is recalled in the inscription on a cross marking her grave near the township of Waharoa, on the site of Te Waharoa's pa. In 1977, the grave was rededicated by the Maori Queen: "TARORE, aged 12 years, whose Maori Gospel of St Luke brought peace to the tribes of Aotearoa..." (p. 272). Hugh Grady gives credit to Maori oral history: "Flatt had vanished into the dustiest corners of the Pakeha record; Tarore had survived in the word-of-mouth which is Maori history" (p. 273). Hugh believes, though, that her age was fifteen or sixteen, rather than twelve. The forgiveness of Tarore's murderer by her Christian father halts the cycle of retribution.

Stead's stance as a writer is a-religious. Nevertheless, he shows familiarity with the texts and beliefs that would have been important to his characters. A biblical text quoted by John Flatt has particular significance: "Beware ye the leaven of the Pharisees which is hypocrisy." Fortunes are shaped by liaisons between men and women, which often occur out of wedlock. Those who accuse their fellows of misdemeanour are likely to be as guilty as the accused. The novel includes information filed in Church Missionary Society records to this day: several missionaries in New Zealand in 1836 fell from grace through alcohol, accepting sexual favours from Maori women, and involvement in homosexual practices. The Society's response was to recall single men to England to find themselves wives.

It is on record that Flatt returned to England, where he was summoned to meet Edward Gibbon Wakefield, who had been informed that "land for settlement could not be obtained from the natives". (p.

136) He persuaded Flatt to testify to the contrary. Flatt's allegation that "missionaries were acquiring land while reporting none was available" (p. 137) was supported by names and details of holdings. He would later face interrogation and give evidence before the House of Lords in 1838. These historical events are woven into the novel.

Flatt was back in the Bay of Islands with a wife and child at the time of the signing of the Treaty of Waitangi. Stead brings imagination to bear in creating this 1840 section of Flatt's life. Hugh and Jean-Anne study accounts of the signing written by Colenso, Henry Williams, and Reverend Robert Burrows. According to some reports, Hone Heke seems to have approved of the Treaty (which he signed), while, to other listeners and observers, he seemed to have been angered by it. Hugh Grady shows awareness of the Maori inclination to speak figuratively and ironically. Hugh's assessment is that,

> Heke may have spoken with heavy and bitter irony – accepting the inevitable but intending to make his dislike for it plain. ... Is it quite imaginable (Hugh puts it to Jean-Anne) that a proud warrior who wanted above all to confirm his mana in front of the assembly would say to his people, 'We are but children. We are only natives,' in a tone of acquiescence? But on the other hand wouldn't a bitter, angry, even violent tone, suggesting 'This is what *they* think of us', reconcile Colenso's transcript of the words spoken with the impression of aggression and insult his speech made on some who heard it? (p. 222)

Hone Heke's armed confrontations with Europeans five years later drove the Flatt family south to Auckland, leaving their raupo cottage and the gardens Flatt had established. The novel reports that Heke's men "helped settlers get their belongings together" (p. 249) and includes Heke's protest that women and children would not have been harmed, had they stayed.

The Singing Whakapapa shows an appreciation of Maori as complex individuals. Flatt puts his mind to what divides Maori and missionary and what they have in common:

> The 'savage heathens', for example, had proved more savage and heathen than he had ever imagined possible; but they had also been more human, closer, more like kin. The gap

> between the clergyman Brown and the chief Waharoa had been absolute and unbridgeable, and at the same time narrow, so that for Flatt it had constituted not so much a practical problem (his duty had been to serve Brown) as a puzzle to the mind. (p. 128)

The Singing Whakapapa shows that Maori see the world in a way that Europeans find difficult to understand, just as 19th century Maori had difficulty grappling with European assumptions.

Stead's Whakapapa

The central story involves Hugh Grady and his wife Harriet (or Hat) Enverson. It begins with the funeral of a relative and concludes with the birth of a grandchild. The indecisive Hugh, his wife and two sons are fictional characters. Hugh's political views, though, are similar to Stead's. One of his Stead-like observations is that "Young people these days are not educated; they're indoctrinated." (p. 237) Stead's more expansive opinion from *The Writer at Work* is that "literary studies have been press-ganged into the service of social and political causes; and far from resisting this invasion of their space, many teachers of literature have encouraged it."[25]

The Singing Whakapapa, broad in scope and timespan, engages characters in reversals and hardship. The personal challenges faced by Hugh Grady are of a different order from those encountered by Flatt. Stead divides Hugh into a dual personality: Hugo and Wolf. The bold and sensuous Wolf emerges from time to time, displacing the benign and compliant Hugh. With his Wolf persona dominant, the husband and father becomes involved in an affair with student Lydia Lawrence. "Every dog must have his day, and this day, this year, was to be the Wolf dog's." (p. 108) When she discovers the affair, Hugh's wife, a purposeful district court judge, arranges a trip around the world for the family of four. Impressions of London, France, Italy and Sweden are viewed through the filter of Hugh's state of mind, determined by the arrival or non-arrival of word from Lydia. This journey allows the history of another branch of the family tree to take shape. The Gradys travel to Sweden, birthplace of Carl Christianson. Documents are studied and relatives visited. Hugh's grandfather left Sweden as a youth and qualified as a Master Mariner in Britain, Bristol being the city he chose to be his home port. The story that unfolds is that of Stead's grandfather Christian Karlson, who marries John Flatt's granddaughter, Caroline.

The history of these family members is extended through a memoir written by Hugh's mother, relating the events of her early life and telling of her Swedish father and New Zealand-born mother. Her story in *The Singing Whakapapa* is taken directly from that of Stead's mother and her parents, as it would have been related by her and grandmother Karlson, though there will, inevitably, be exaggerations and omissions. The novel's Ethel Elena Grady, née Christianson, is characterised by a "northern European inheritance, with its temperamental swings from short dark winter days to long light summer nights". (p. 23) A reader can only wonder whether such a description would have befitted Stead's mother.

The stories of Stead's forebears invite philosophical reflection. Hugh is the author of a history book named *Without Cause*, which questions the notion that specific 'causes' can be found for the events of history. "What were the causes of – the French Revolution? The First World War? The War of Jenkins Ear? – no, not those, but of Hone Heke's war in the North (And what were the causes of the causes?)" (p. 239) The unsuccessful search for causes has particular significance in a novel that focuses on a family tree, with branches that might have developed differently, but for endless misadventures and opportunities taken or lost. Survival or death is similarly unpredictable and a matter of chance.

> 'The release of a sail' (Ethel Elena wrote) 'may save a ship; the failure to release it might mean its end, and the end of a story. ... Stories are like lives, and are lives. Which of them are permitted to run a full and shapely course is random. Whether they find tellers is also a matter of luck.' (pp. 202-3)

The joy or pain exacted by life's achievements or crises is considered in relation to the swiftness of time's passage. Fifty years is "a mere flash in the pan of history". (p. 19)

A recurrent conundrum is presented in the question, "What is victory, and what is defeat?" (p. 143) Victory or defeat – and for whom – can be asked of the outcomes of the novel's various battles. It can be asked of each of the individuals involved in Hugh's marital upheaval. Whether Flatt's disclosure of illicit land purchases wins him a victory or leads to harm remains in doubt. Ambiguities ensure that the novel's questions continue to be considered long after the book comes to a conclusion.

Although Ken Arvidson[26] judged *The Singing Whakapapa* Stead's best novel to date and Mark Williams offers a generous appraisal in *Landfall*, most critics have failed to appreciate the novel's skilful construction or its depth. Terry Sturm regards *The Singing Whakapapa* as Stead's most under-rated work of fiction.[27] John de Falbe was indignant at what he took to be an unwarranted modesty associated with the publication: "There is a short glossary of Maori words at the back of this novel 'for Australian readers', suggesting that the publisher, or Stead, could not imagine that anyone else might be interested in this brilliant novel because it is about New Zealand history. This is outrageous. Stead is no more provincial than Hardy or Annie Proulx".[28] Stead's reason for including the glossary may have had more to do with his belief that, in 1994, many New Zealanders lacked even a fundamental knowledge of Maori language. The deficiency, at a time of such emphasis on political correctness, is subtly mocked.

Stead may not have engaged fully with Aotearoa/New Zealand's developing cultural awareness, but the title, *The Singing Whakapapa*, can be viewed positively. 'Whakapapa' offers an example of a Maori concept that has been absorbed by a Pakeha writer. Used as a noun, the word signifies a family's comprehensive range of forebears, immediate to distant, including the genetic legacy of strengths, skills or shortcomings passed from generation to generation. Each name spoken rings with the deeds and talents of that person. Several of the Stead relatives who appear in the novel were, in real life, gifted singers and musicians, and his fictional characters Hugh Grady and Jean-Anne Devantier are singers too. Mark Williams notes that, while Stead's title "seems a calculated piece of cultural cheek ... 'singing' ... is also the sound of life, and it looks towards the insistent theme of music in the novel, music as a form of beauty that gives meaning to 'the fluky aggregation of cells that constitute human life'."[29]

Stead's love of music is a significant aspect of his temperament. Given his musical forebears, his sensitivity to music is surely an inherent quality. A musical education, informal apart from boyhood piano lessons, has been a life-long engagement, with Europe providing pleasure and breadth of experience through its concerts and opera. He has described to Curnow what delight he took from attending Wagner's

Ring Cycle in Bayreuth, which he found superior to performances of the same work in Adelaide and London. He was able to appreciate "the terrible beauty of it, the quality of the music with singers and orchestra that are the best in the world".[30] In London, he and Kay have attended many performances at the London Coliseum and Covent Garden, with Stead queuing on one occasion for two hours on a winter morning to secure English National Opera tickets for *Gotterdammerung*.[31] Music is a lure that draws Stead's imagination, and his person, back to Europe.

England, France and Italy provide the main settings for his next novel, *Villa Vittoria*, in which, to quote Paul Millar, "there is nary a sniff of New Zealand".[32]

1 John de Falbe, "Talking About O'Dwyer", *Spectator*, 27 May 2000, p. 39.

2 Steve Braunias, "In for the High Jump", *New Zealand Listener*, 30 July 1994, p. 35.

3 C. K. Stead, "The Treaty, a Contrary View", *Metro* 130, April 1992, p. 131.

4 I. H. Kawharu, *Waitangi*: *Maori and Pakeha Perspectives of the Treaty of Waitangi*, Auckland, OUP, 1989, p. 268.

5 ibid, p. 278.

6 Kawharu, Waitangi: *Maori and Pakeha Perspectives of the Treaty of Waitangi*, p. xii. Had the Maori version been officially recognised, the Treaty could have been considered a partnership from the outset. Instead, the Maori text was ignored in favour of the English version.
To discover the "spirit" or underlying principles of the Treaty, research has investigated exactly what William Hobson promised Maori and what promises were made by the missionaries. Hobson, the British Consul representing the Crown, had assured Maori that Queen Victoria "had a loving and protective concern for Maori". Missionaries claimed that the Treaty was "the personal wish of the Queen" and "her act of love". (Robert and Joanne Consedine, *Healing Our History*, Auckland, Penguin Books, 2001, p. 87) Maori were persuaded to sign the Treaty, assured that, under its terms their land could never be taken forcibly.

7 Ross Stevens, "In Good Stead", *Frontline*, hosted by Susan Wood, TVNZ, 1994.

8 Patrick Snedden, *Pakeha and the Treaty: Why It's Our Treaty Too*, Auckland, Random House, 2005, p. 59.

9 C. K. Stead, "A Short History of New Zealand", *The Blind Blonde with Candles in her Hair*, Auckland, Penguin Books, 1998, p. 165.

10 Camille Guy, "A War of Words", *NZ Herald* 2, 14 December 1989, p. 8.

11 Stephen Stratford, "Blaspheming Against the Pieties: Why the Literati Hate C. K. Stead", *Metro*, April 1990, pp. 79-80.

12 Focusing on tools, R. C. J. Stone has described Maori as "a Stone Age people": "westerners introduced into the country revolutionary products like the common potato and the pig as well as bringing to a Stone Age people new tools of iron, like axes and spades and nails." R. C. J. Stone, *From Tamaki-Makau-Rau to Auckland,* Auckland University Press, 2001, p. 57.

13 Geoff Chapple, "Writer Charges Book Sabotaged", *Sunday Star Times,* 30 January 1994, p. A5.

14 C. K. Stead (ed), *The Faber Book of Contemporary South Pacific Stories*, London, Faber, 1994, pp. xv-xvi.

15 ibid, p. xvii.

16 David Eggleton, "Loaded", *Quote/Unquote*, March 1994, p. 32.

17 Mark Williams, "C. K. Stead and the New Literary Order", *Meanjin* 53, Summer 1994, p. 697.

18 C. K. Stead, *Kin of Place: Essays on 20 New Zealand Writers*, Auckland University Press, 2002, p. 318.

19 John Newton, "The Death-throes of Nationalism", *Landfall*, Autumn 2003, p. 99.

20 C. K. Stead, *Answering to the Language: Essays on Modern Writers*, Auckland University Press, 1989, p. 284.

21 Stead, *Answering to the Language*, pp. 283-4.

22 Kathryn Vivian, "Stead Talks His Way Through Latest Novel", *Sunday Star Times*, 10 July 1994, p. D8.

23 C. K. Stead, *The Singing Whakapapa*, Auckland, Penguin Books, 1994, p. 36. Page numbers in brackets refer to this edition.

24 Peter J. Lineham, *Bible and Society: A Sesquicentennial History of the Bible Society in New Zealand*, Wellington, Bible Society Press/Daphne Brasell, 1996.

25 Stead, *The Writer at Work*, p. 120.

26 Ken Arvidson, "Personal Story of Greater Value than History", *Sunday Star Times*, 10 July 1994, p. D8.

27 Terry Sturm, interview with author, 20 December 2005.

28 John de Falbe, "Talking About O'Dwyer", *Spectator*, 27 May 2000, p. 39.

29 Mark Williams, "*The Singing Whakapapa*, C. K. Stead", *Landfall* 188, Spring 1994, p. 307. Stead's words, "the fluky aggregation of cells..." are from *The Singing Whakapapa*, p. 270.

30 C. K. Stead, letter to Curnow, 26 September 2001, Turnbull Library Papers.

31 C. K. Stead, letter to Sargeson, 11 February 1977, Turnbull Library Papers.

32 Paul Millar, "Nary a Sniff of NZ", *New Zealand Education Review* 2, 25 June 1997, p. 18.

ABOVE: Kay and Karl Stead 1962. Photo: Marti Friedlander

BELOW: The Steads' Tohunga Crescent, Parnell, home since 1963.

LEFT: Supporting Frank Sargeson shortly before Sargeson's death in March 1982.

BELOW: With Janet Frame, 1994.
Photo: Marti Friedlander

BOTTOM: Stead and his friend Barry Humphries – with pavlova.

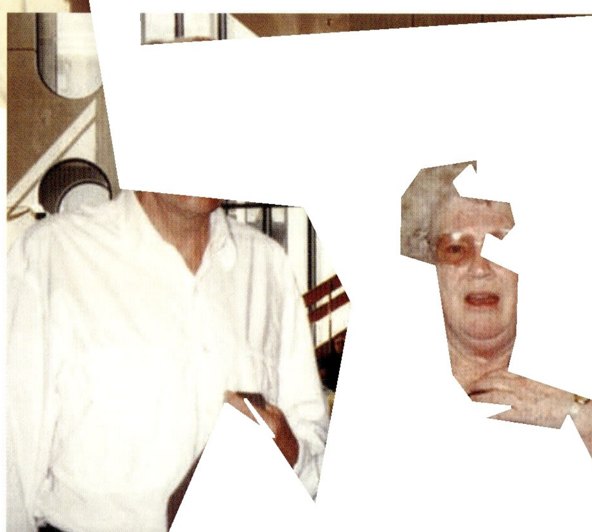

ABOVE: At work in his prefab writing room, 2001.
Photo: *N.Z. Herald* and *Weekly News*

RIGHT: With daughter Margaret at home, Parnell, 1993.

ABOVE: The Trout, Wolvercote, near Oxford, a significant setting in *Talking About O'Dwyer*.
BELOW: Interior of The Trout at Wolvercote.

ABOVE: Stead with his older sister, Norma, at her seventieth birthday party in 2000, and younger sister Frances.

BELOW: Stead with Allen Curnow, 2001.

Above: Kay and Karl at home.

CHAPTER ELEVEN

Tribute and Tribulation

Villa Vittoria

The author of one of *Villa Vittoria*'s finest reviews, appearing in the *NZ Listener*, was Damien Wilkins.

> This is the Stead who can give satisfying, invigorating narrative shape to abstract ideas, who always insists that aesthetic questions rub shoulders with ethical ones, and whose gift for plain talk mixed with passages of great lyrical poise often makes his prose a clean delight. If there's something of the professor in his voice, there's also an instinct for what we might call the "traditional" pleasures of story telling. ...
> *Villa Vittoria* is perhaps his best-made novel.

Having added that the plot "involves a conundrum that feels genuine", Wilkins speaks of Stead's "sure sense of timing" and his "well, *quirks of intelligence*".[1] As a novelist, Stead seems to have redeemed himself in the eyes of this critic, whose positive judgement was borne out by the reading public. Copies produced in Britain sold so rapidly that the book was out of print in five or six weeks, with the next consignment still reprinting.

There is an Australian but no New Zealand character in the novel. A single glance New Zealand's way is occasioned by the sinking of the *Rainbow Warrior* in Auckland. Stead's sceptical attitude to "the pieties, the academic fashions and the intellectual shibboleths of our times"[2] resulted in turbulent years, which may have led him to locate himself, in imagination, in Europe and the US for *Villa Vittoria*. The novel sees Stead turn his attention from New Zealand politics to European political situations in the 1980s and 1990s: the Falklands War, the collapse of a major Italian bank, and the mysterious deaths of Roberto

Calvi and Pope John Paul I. The latter held his position as Pope for just 33 days. Roberto Calvi was found hanging from scaffolding beneath Blackfriars Bridge in London in June 1982. His death, through murder or suicide, was linked to the collapse of the Banco Ambrosiano with its connections to the Vatican and to the unofficial Freemason's Lodge known as P2. In Stead's novel, the Lodge becomes P3. Roberto Calvi is renamed Silvio Calvini and the collapsed bank is called the Banco di Sant' Ambrogio. As Stead explained to journalist Iain Sharp, "I wanted readers who are interested in such things to be aware that the book has a solid factual basis in modern Italian history, but I also wanted the freedom of fiction."[3] Finding that an old university friend had worked as a lawyer on the Banco Ambrosiano scandal rekindled Stead's interest in it. Links to actual events add to the novel's credibility.

Villa Vittoria is not an experimental work. Grounded in the conventions of the thriller, it features elements traditional to the genre: the mafia hit-man, the long-lens camera, the double agent. Danger associated with a project undertaken by Miranda Frayn, one of four main characters, is foreshadowed in the book's opening paragraph. At the Stirling Grant conference in Tigullio, "she was there as a journalist and photographer on an assignment which she knew required discretion, even secrecy, but which she believed to be, if not quite innocent, at least lawful, and certainly not dangerous."[4] Her refusal to take the danger seriously is maintained, adding to tension, until the drama of the final chapter. Another central character, Bruno Strawson, employed by the British secret service, is an expert in international espionage. What Damien Wilkins describes as a "crisply worked plot"[5] has been criticised by others[6] for its use of coincidences. These are essential to the novel's structure, but no coincidence in *Villa Vittoria* strains a reader's sense of the possible.

Villa Vittoria's English settings include a London family home and a country seat, residence of a landed family. In a letter, Stead told Allen Curnow that he would spend a weekend "with our friends the Rileys who have a 17th century schoolhouse", located in Northhamptonshire on an estate with a "splendid country home" and "a croquet lawn and fields full of pheasants and peasants and gamekeepers and woods and shooters round about, and a village a mile or so away across the fields".[7] Stead's Bruno Strawson inherits a 17th century schoolhouse on an estate. His wife and children spend holidays there, enjoying features like those mentioned in Stead's letter. Bruno's family is obliged to call on his cousin, who lives in the estate's grand mansion.

The novel includes a character with views very like Stead's, not Bruno Strawson but an American academic, Steve Jenson. A decade after the 1986 teasing of feminists in *The Death of the Body*, Stead shows himself to be unrepentant. Female academics at the University of London take a stance in *Villa Vittoria*, maintaining that a novel like *The Bostonians* should be taught by a woman, despite there being a male colleague with expertise in the work of Henry James. The male colleague is Steve Jenson. When he eventually decides to quit his academic position, he sends a message to the HOD, saying that his job should be given "to the girls"; he adds, "I was losing my balls in that Department".[8] This is surely a retort that Stead would have relished. He would certainly have endorsed his character's disdain for the terminology of literary theory in vogue at the time; Steve gives expression to views that are stated in Stead's critical essays.[9] The two also share an interest in a famous poet who supported a fascist regime.

The novel's literary figure is Stirling Grant, whose life is patterned on that of Ezra Pound. The name Stirling, with homophone sterling, is a tongue-in-cheek allusion to the worth of Pound. Rapallo, Pound's home for many years, is named Tigullio in the novel. Steve recalls a "Stirling Grant line, 'Say to la Cara, "Amo"'.[10] An affirmation of love, this is a quotation from Ezra Pound's "Canto 76". The significance of Steve's passion for Miranda Frayn is enhanced by an echo of one the world's great love affairs. He quotes Dante's lines spoken by Francesca as she whirls with her lover Paolo in limbo; she remembers her home where the River Po meets the sea. Irony, wit and a sense of humour deflate any hint of sentiment. Steve, his first amorous approach rejected by Miranda, "walked about the room, naked, his semi-erect penis wagging in front of him like a large admonitory finger…".[11] Steve looks foolish when Miranda refuses to become a married man's lover, their situation in contrast with that of Pound and musician Olga Rudge, his mistress. Pound's wife lived near the shore in Rapallo, while, over a period of years, Pound climbed the salita, a pathway up a steep slope, to visit Olga Rudge. Her counterpart in the novel is Albertine Marshall.

As the author of *Pound, Yeats, Eliot and the Modernist Movement*, Stead attended a Pound conference in Rapallo, at which "the various strands of *Villa Vittoria* started to come together".[12] Iain Sharp observed that "Stead gleefully admits that he's fond of playing the kind of game with readers whereby they are lured into identifying characters with historical figures and then are reminded that they are reading a work of fiction not fact."

Facts Relocated in Fiction

European locations predominate in Stead's next novel, *Talking about O'Dwyer*, which developed, in part, from time he spent in Oxford. The story moves from Oxford to Auckland and back, and later includes settings in Croatia, Greece, Crete and the US. Important to his preparation were two visits to Croatia in 1997, after which he wrote,

> Every writer is a shameful scavenger, and one reaches an age where every new experience presents itself for what it is and for what might be made of it. By now all these riches were beginning to merge in my mind with thoughts I'd had long before about a novel that might make something of New Zealand's historical links with Croatia, links which no one growing up in the north can be unaware of. I had recollections of farmland still pockmarked by the grave-like holes made by Dalmatian gumdiggers and of the rusty spade-handled gum spears they left behind. And Kay (like Maurice Gee) had spent her childhood among the orchardists and wine-growers of the Henderson Valley west of Auckland.[13]

The novel's central character is Mike Newall, a New Zealander comparable in age to Stead at the time of writing – somewhat over sixty. He is born and raised in Henderson, home to many fruit-growing, wine-making families from Dalmatia. In the 1930s, during years in which availability of alcohol was restricted, no less than two gallons of wine could, by law, be sold at one time. The notice "LICENSED TO SELL TWO GALS"[14] that the young Mike sees on his way to school, is the very notice that Kay Stead remembers.

Mike tells the story of his own early life and the story of the title character O'Dwyer to an eighty-year-old Oxford don and peer, Bertie Winterstoke, who insists, "Take your time, brother. We're old men, and we have the summer before us." (p. 18) Bertie is past the age of pretence and enjoys directness: "The only thing I miss about marriage … is the adultery." (p. 32) "When you're young the penis has a mind of its own. At my age, it's the bladder." (p. 12) "I don't intend to die, dear boy. Haven't the least intention." (p. 16)

Bertie derives from a particular kind of Englishman Stead has encountered. The surname owes its origin to the Winterstoke Chair of English at the University of Bristol. Bertie's deafness, requiring a huge hearing aid, is a legacy of the war. For the story of how his hearing was impaired, credit is offered to Alan Ross, a British poet and editor, "from whose life", Stead explains in his "Acknowledgements", he "borrowed a brief naval episode". Ross, serving in the navy, was on a destroyer escorting supply ships to the Soviet Union in 1942. He describes the trapping of a man in the hold of his damaged vessel, HMS *Onslow*. Bertie Winterstoke gives an account of such an ordeal, made excruciating by the sustained and piercing sound of steam escaping through a valve.

The novel's opening scene – dinner at high table – draws on Stead's first-hand knowledge of Oxford, gained while a Visiting Fellow at St John's College in 1996 and early 1997, where he enjoyed the archaic and privileged "lush sort of life". Excellent wine accompanied four courses of excellent food. As in the novel, the courses were followed by snuff, port, claret, sauterne, fruit and chocolate. Stead has remarked on the "terrific conversation" involving a "great group of people". While at St John's College, he discussed modern poetry with students, whom he found admirable. He has noted the "truly selective process at Oxford".[15] A house was provided for him and he was able to advance his own writing and research. His poem "The Keys of the Kingdom" reflects familiarity with the buildings of Oxford, their courtyards, keys and gates:

> And this – this is the V2.
> It lets you into the Senior Common Room,
> the Xerox room, the Japanese garden,
> the North Quadrangle by the door from the carpark,
> and also the gardens by the back gate[16]

Stead came to know the town's tree-lined residential streets and squares and its various pubs and restaurants. The home of the imaginary Bertie is one that Stead knew well. It is a replica of New Zealander Dan Davin's home, "a tall dampish brown-brick house with a rather nice back garden that runs down to the canal".[17]

The novel's Mike Newall rises to the rank of Professor of Philosophy and wins recognition internationally in his field of expertise – the work of Wittgenstein,[18] whose proposition from *Tractatus*, "What we cannot speak about must be passed over in silence" (p. 38), becomes significant in the novel. Mike's career is focused on the work of a philosopher whose thinking appealed to Stead. As a senior academic, Mike remarks, "What I now look to Wittgenstein for is not answers but questions..." (p. 125) Stead, too, has a penchant for asking questions in pursuit of accurate information and logical thought.

Mike embraces an opportunity that Stead considered, but did not take. Having gained postgraduate qualifications in Britain, Mike pursues a career at an English university, becoming one of the dons of Bardolph's College, its imaginary name taken from one of Falstaff's drinking mates. Through two characters in *Talking About O'Dwyer*, Stead role-plays two sets of consequences that might follow, should an expatriate take an academic position in Britain. Mike seems content to make Oxford his home. By contrast, Oxford don Donovan O'Dwyer suffers restlessness and a sense of punishment at being unable to return to New Zealand. The dilemma remains unresolved in the poem "Running in Oxford", written in the late 1990s.

> To wrench
> from its fabled lodges
> ordinary 'Oxford'
> and make it real –
>
> would that have been
> a life's work
> worthy
> as any other?
>
> No answer![19]

In the year 2000, Stead admitted to John Campbell that the reason for his youthful determination to return to New Zealand no longer pertained.

> I was lucky enough to have two mentors as a young writer – one was Curnow in the university ... and very deliberately outside it and anti-university was Frank Sargeson and that was why when I finally did go away overseas ... I carried

> with me this determination to come back. I was very much a literary nationalist and over the years I don't feel that any more, but I suppose, with nationalism, you hang on to it while it's important and when it hasn't a function any more, you shake it off.[20]

The more recent *Book Self* reflects a disenchanted view of his youthful literary nationalism, saying that if he has anything to blame Curnow, Sargeson and Brasch for, "it could only be for giving me such a positive idea of what it would mean to 'be a New Zealand writer' – saddling me with a romantic literary nationalism which, in our altered circumstances, is no longer meaningful."[21]

O'Dwyer and Davin

The character O'Dwyer originates from two New Zealanders: Dan Davin and a military man, Lt Col Humphrey Dyer. In his youth Davin was an outstanding Oxford scholar – "a first in Greats", who served in Crete, Greece, North Africa and Italy with the New Zealand Division. After the war he returned to Oxford, where he became academic publisher at Oxford University Press and also the author of poetry and stories. Stead reports, "Of the three or four significant literary drinkers I have known, Dan Davin functioned the best – though I've heard it said in Oxford that his drinking prevented his getting the top job he aspired to in the Clarendon Press."[22] W. H. Oliver, reviewing a biography of Davin, notes that his career has "a persistent subtext [...] a note of failure, frustration and unfulfilment".[23] On 1 October 1990, Stead attended Dan Davin's funeral in Oxford, which led to the idea of beginning *Talking About O'Dwyer* with O'Dwyer's funeral.

Stead's portrayal of O'Dwyer is sympathetic, despite cheerful bad-mouthing by his Oxford colleagues at the novel's opening. "I felt affection for O'Dwyer," Stead has written.[24] Mike Newall's account shows him to be "generous, patient, comforting; and he left the younger man with an open invitation: 'When things get too tough for you, come to us. Don't hesitate. Don't ask. Just come.'" (p. 90) Nevertheless, academic and writer Janet Wilson has accused Stead of denigrating Dan Davin through linking him to O'Dwyer, as a retribution for Davin's negative review of *In the Glass Case*. Stead was indignant, saying that, had he been troubled by Davin's review, he would have "instantly fired off a sharp reply, not brooded about it for fifteen years".[25] Wilson replied that Stead had, indeed, responded to Davin directly. It seems that Stead reacted at the time, then put the matter out of his mind.

The Makutu, Dyer and O'Dwyer

Lt Col Humphrey Dyer, the second source of the character O'Dwyer, also served in Crete. As an officer with the Maori Battalion, he killed a Maori soldier, one of his own men. The story had been told to Stead many years earlier by his friend Rob Dyer, Humphrey Dyer's son. Rob Dyer's account provides the first explanation for the soldier's death, given in Chapter 15 of Stead's novel. A version more difficult to accept is foreshadowed; the truth would be "undoubtedly worse". (p. 185) While carrying out research into the Maori Battalion in the National Archives for *Talking About O'Dwyer*, Stead found and photocopied Lt Col Dyer's notebook. This report of what happened differs from the account accepted by his family. The revised version appears in Chapter 17 of the novel's nineteen chapters. The initial reaction of Rob Dyer was anger at the newly disclosed details. He believed that Stead must have misunderstood the material in the Archives.

The fact that there were two stories meant that Stead could hold something in reserve, creating tension and anticipation. The story, in broad outline, was known in military circles. Michael King heard it from a New Zealand officer:

> Major Humphrey Dyer shot one of his own men as the battalion withdrew from the island under the German onslaught. He did this because the soldier, a Maori private, had stepped on a land mine and was so badly wounded that eventual death was inevitable; attending to him would only endanger the lives of his comrades. When the executed soldier's family heard about the circumstances of the death … they laid a makutu or curse on Major Dyer, and ill fortune had pursued him and his family from that time.[26]

Though he secured confirmation of the military episode, King remained uncertain as to the truth of the makutu or curse. According to King, Rob Dyer considered the curse to be a fact and believed it extended to him as well. King's informant preferred to believe that the makutu idea arose from "a series of misfortunes that had dogged the Dyer family in the years after the war".[27]

A man of early intellectual and sporting promise, Stead's character O'Dwyer shows a steady decline in the course of his career. In this regard, he is quite like Dan Davin, who was characterised by a "successful yet finally anticlimactic career at Oxford, the legendary drinking, the love affairs within a stable marriage, the charismatic quality and the gift for friendship and for inspiring loyalty".[28] The reason for O'Dwyer's failure to fulfil early expectations remains equivocal, caused by the curse or by his own failings – his liking for women, alcohol, and good company in English pubs. The failings could have developed credibly from the trauma in Crete: "he couldn't bear to be alone, and ... any company was better than his own." (p. 89)

The precise reason for the imposition of a makutu on O'Dwyer teases the reader until the book nears its conclusion. Despite being a Pakeha, he is the commander of the Maori Battalion, at a time when senior officers were Pakeha, with Maori leaders still moving up through the ranks. The history of Stead's character Joe Panapa is based on that of the actual soldier shot by his own officer, to whom tribute is paid before the novel begins: "Parata Heta Thompson, killed in Crete 24.5.41". Captain Dyer would have visited Private Thompson's family after the war, to pay his respects, as does O'Dwyer in the novel. The makutu is laid upon O'Dwyer during his visit to Joe Panapa's home marae north of Auckland. Joe Panapa's wife Ljuba tells Mike, "I can't understand why he would have to come to the marae." (p. 180) Mike imagines that O'Dwyer would have been motivated by guilt. However, such a visit would have been obligatory. After the war, the marae of all members of the Maori Battalion who were lost in action were visited by senior officers.

There is one event in the novel that Maori find distasteful.[29] It involves the sprinkling of O'Dwyer's ashes over the grave of Joe Panapa. Of course O'Dwyer, in his ignorance of Maori sensibilities, could have made such a request for the disposal of his ashes. Joe's Maori relative, however, provides a special karakia or prayer to lift the makutu, to be spoken by the character Marica. The novel strays beyond credibility in suggesting that Joe's family would have condoned such interference by providing Marica with an appropriate karakia to be intoned before she scatters the ashes on the grave. Although the intention is to offer conciliation and effect a closure, Maori would consider an intrusion of this kind unacceptable after a man has been laid to rest, especially since the ashes belong to a person with whom

Joe Panapa has no genealogical links. Furthermore, Maori traditions do not favour cremation. No Maori critic has drawn attention to the fanciful nature of the episode. Stead may have lost Polynesians from his potential readership, as John Newton surmised he would.[30]

Despite this detail, *Talking About O'Dwyer* shows appreciation of Maori. Joe Panapa and his two mates are staunch, good-natured, and distinguish themselves in the arena of war. Their droll humour and manner of speech have the right ring. For their individual characterisation, Stead has drawn on his own experience. His Maori cousin Don, younger by a year or so, lived as a member of the Stead household during the war, while his father was fighting overseas. Don's mother, wife of one of the Stead brothers, was the author's favourite aunt. Don claims that the two boys got along well together. Stead has reported that, on the rare occasions when he and Don quarrelled, Don would hurl the word 'Pakeha' at him. Frano Panapa, son of Joe Panapa in *Talking About O'Dwyer*, behaves in the same way, calling Mike a 'Pakeha' when angered, thereby reminding Mike of the racial difference, and imparting the idea that this was, for some reason, a problem. The relationship between Stead and his cousin Don is comparable to the pre-teen phase of the friendship between Frano and Mike.

Croatia and the Novel's Reception

Frano's mother is Dalmatian. In January 1997 the Steads flew to Zagreb for the launch of *All Visitors Ashore*, which had been translated into Croatian. Later in the year Stead returned to Croatia, staying initially with his translator and her aunt in an apartment that provides a model for the one in which Mike stays with the journalist Ira in *Talking About O'Dwyer*. Without experience of this kind it would not be easy for a New Zealander to give a credible impression of a fifth floor apartment above a busy street in Zagreb.

> Grozdana's flat consisted of two bedrooms, one she occupied, the other Ira's bedroom and study, the windows of both looking down on a central city street in which blue trams banged away all through the day and far into the night. There was a very small kitchen with a table just large enough for three to sit at, and with a balcony that looked down over an inner courtyard. The bathroom, with a curtain to protect the privacy of a person using the bath, was also the passageway

> to Ira's room. (p. 35)

In addition, there was a "small room, hardly larger than a cupboard" (p. 36), where the guest was accommodated, and an entrance hall, in which a refrigerator and wardrobe were placed.

Stead claimed that he needed a map in his head before beginning to write. He traveled through the former Dalmatia, a coastal strip along the Adriatic, fifty kilometres wide in the north narrowing to a few kilometres in the south. He visited one of the former Dalmatia's many islands. The following paragraph appears in both his account of travel in the region and in the novel.

> I think we can't have been more than fifty kilometres south of Zagreb when we encountered the first of the war zones – burned-out houses, collapsed roofs pockmarked walls, shell-holes, abandoned crops, tiny villages emptied of their inhabitants. … In one place a very small child standing in the doorway of a burned-out house was the only living creature I saw in a wrecked village.[31]

Stead also stayed in the village of Zaton, near Sibenik. The atmosphere of the place and the sounds of the village night are incorporated into the novel.

> That night Mike slept well, but woke at intervals to a strange conjunction of summer night noises coming in at him through the open windows – a snoring giant in a nearby house, a chiming clock loud enough to suggest that it belonged to the giant, roosters crowing at the moon, the clatter of goat-hooves on cobblestones, and loudest of all, Ana's donkey with its ancient lamentation about the length of its ears and the weight of the loads tomorrow would expect it to carry. (p. 179)

Margaret Walters in the *Times Literary Supplement* concludes that *Talking About O'Dwyer* "achieves real power through the vividness with which it conjures up a particular time and place – whether it is 1930s' New Zealand, contemporary Oxford, war-time Crete or present-day Croatia".[32] Enthusiasm characterises appraisals by other British reviewers. Writing for the *Times Literary Supplement*, Paul Binding reflects, "I don't know why everyone isn't talking about *Talking About O'Dwyer*, C. K. Stead's intricately worked and compelling novel."[33] John De Falbe in the *Spectator* speaks of Stead's "dazzling new novel", and remarks that its "intellectual force is inseparable from its narrative force; the drive towards the core event is gripping." He concludes with unequivocal praise: "It seems incontestable to me that C K Stead is among the very best contemporary novelists." He is comparing Stead with other authors in "the English-speaking world".[34]

By contrast, New Zealand reviewers have been restrained and, at times, disparaging. Iain Sharp's *Landfall* review suggests that the novel "might have worked better as a short story". Despite "some good moments", he ascribes to it a "peculiar air of underachievement".[35] Mark Williams in the *Listener* finds "the narrative elegantly constructed; imagery and phrasing always exact. He makes it look easy, but such lucidity is remarkably difficult to achieve."[36] Lawrence Jones in *New Zealand Books* takes the opportunity to survey several of Stead's novels, searching for Stead's distinctive voice.[37] Overall though, New Zealand commentaries lack the enthusiasm and generosity offered by British reviewers, indicating the persistence of something noted by Kim Hill in 1994; at home in a "small country", "Your books aren't judged like other people's books any more."[38]

Poetry of the 1990s

One of Stead's finest poems to emerge in the 1990s is "Crete", a work begun during the poet's visit to Crete for a commemoration service in May 1998. To recreate events for his novel convincingly, Stead walked over the battleground, observing the foliage and the flowers in bloom and recording his immediate impressions and feelings. "*He learned...*"

> That wild daisies
> can be midnight blue
> and that the Anzac poppy
> blooms also in Crete.[39]

"Crete" captures beauty and antiquity, as well as the horror and tragedy of military engagements, with thousands of deaths and the destruction of buildings, monuments and artifacts, some dating back to Minoan times. The atmosphere of the place, absorbed by Stead, informs *Talking*

About O'Dwyer's intense Crete chapters, where soldiers engage at close quarters on clearly visualised hillsides and ridges, in olive groves and derelict houses. Within the seventeen-part poetry sequence, several poems show people in action: a contemporary local "stands in his skiff"[40] as it skims across the still harbour; in wartime, two enemy soldiers meet in a clearing and one waves the other away; a man is haunted long after the war by a death scream; veterans climb a hill for the commemoration ceremony. In the reflective sections, crosses stand in perfect formation, bats and swallows swoop among the buildings, and impressions of coloured stones and huge ants on the shore bring to mind thoughts of blood and bombardment.

"Crete" was published in the 2000 collection, *The Right Thing*, which includes work written between 1997 and 1999. After *Voices* in 1990, no new book of poetry appeared until *Straw into Gold* (1997), which provides a selection of work from each decade, beginning with the 1950s, and concluding with forty "New poems – the 1990s". Many of the poems from this decade reflect Stead's travels abroad as writer, academic and family man. Holiday trips, conferences and lectures took Stead to Zagreb, Paris, rural France, Tübingen, Stockholm, London and Bristol, as well as to Edmonton, Los Angeles and cities from Lakewood to New York. Most of the destinations provide settings for poems. "Revisiting Bristol", dedicated to Kay, considers identity in relation to place. Stead compares himself and Kay, flying often between England and home, to migratory birds.

> So what's belonging
> unless it's to
>
> one another
> and to our own
> history, the books which
>
> made us what we are
> and those that will
> tell our story?[41]

There are clear links between Stead's fiction and some of his 1990s' poems. The city of Tübingen, one of the settings in *The End of the Century at the End of the World*, is also the setting for Stead's poem

"Ghosts" published in *Straw into Gold*, catching the atmosphere of "a small tavern/ of crooked beams and stairs".[42] The tower imprisoning German poet Hölderlin for thirty-five years appears in the novel and the poem; it overlooks an island in the River Neckar flowing past the city. A bronze figure on the island becomes increasingly visible as autumn leaves fall. Symbol of the paradox of Germany's creativity and aggression, the sculpture represents a composer with many small warriors emerging from his pockets. At the University of Tübingen, Stead was a guest in 1990, lecturing on "Nationalism, Regionalism and the Tradition in Contemporary New Zealand Poetry".

Stead's experience of the university in Lakewood can be traced to 1997, when he presented a lecture at Georgian Court College, on "English in Our Universities".[43] His story "Brightness Falls from the Air" is set on the Jersey Shore, in Lakewood, Brick, and New York. He would have experienced the trips between JFK Airport and Lakewood described in the story. His character travels by stretch limousine, as does the narrator in the poem "Home at Last": "It was the white stretch/ took you/from the town of the Hassidim".[44] This echoes the situation in the story, though the themes of story and poem differ. The poem celebrates the familiarity of the Jersey Shore to a New Zealander who has watched movies located there, while the story, an amusing satire, is concerned with the lure of fame – and its irritating propensity to be achieved after a writer's death.[45]

Two poems from *Straw into Gold* give insight into the psyche of characters from Stead's 2004 novel, *Mansfield*. "Jealousy I" involves the persona of Katherine Mansfield and "Jealousy II" the persona of Virginia Woolf. Long before he began to write the novel, Stead had developed an understanding of the way each character would have regarded the other. The following reaction to Katherine Mansfield is Virginia Woolf's, imagined by Stead:

> I caught us once in a mirror –
>   Katherine with her mask-face
> dark eyes
> quick wit
>
>   Leonard on fire
> admiring

and I
long-faced
lugubrious
superfluous.

No
that I couldn't forgive –
not ever.[46]

Of the eighty-one poems in the two publications of 1990s' poems, only a dozen are located in Auckland. There are, of course, poems in which location does not feature at all as Stead brings a satiric eye to bear on world events and literary figures, or in which he reflects on the art of poetry and the poetic heritage from which he draws and to which he contributes. Most poems of the 1990s seem effortless, with Stead's choice of language bringing action and image as close as possible to the flow of everyday speech. Others feature spoonerisms, puns and play on words: "'Will our movie be made?'" In reply, the narrator hears "the budget/ whistle in its cage".[47] Though two film scripts (for *The Death of the Body* and for *Villa Vittoria*) had been written and revised, the films, instigated by Roger Donaldson, have remained unrealised to date.

The concluding poems in *The Right Thing* anticipate death. "Horation", the book's last poem, wonders what bribe could be offered to "that dry-eyed skuller/ on the darkest river?"[48] The previous poem "Stories" acknowledges "the bat-winged person/ who must come to the door";[49] the third-to-final poem is "Crete", which pays tribute to those "gone beyond call".[50] Stead, as he enters the new millennium, gives thought to mortality.

1 Damien Wilkins, "Books: Get Personal", *New Zealand Listener*, 8 March 1997, p. 50.
2 Andrew Bennett, *Speeches Delivered in Commendation of Honorary Graduates*, University of Bristol, 9-13 July 2001, p. 27.
3 Iain Sharp, "Calvi Financial Scandal Catalyst for Stead Yarn", *Sunday Star Times*, 23 March 1997, p. E: 4.
4 C. K. Stead, *Villa Vittoria*, Auckland, Penguin Books, 1997, p. 9.
5 Wilkins, "Books: Get Personal", *New Zealand Listener*, 8 March 1997, p. 50.
6 For example, Rhonda Cooper, "Map of the Human Heart", *Metro*, June 1997, p.110.
7 C. K. Stead, letter to Curnow, 29 September 1990, Turnbull Library Papers.
8 Stead, *Villa Vittoria*, p. 208.
9 Stead, "English in Our Universities", *The Writer at Work*, Dunedin, Otago University

Press, 2000, pp. 114-126.

10 Stead, *Villa Vittoria*, p. 206.

11 ibid, p. 42.

12 Sharp, "Calvi Financial Scandal Catalyst for Stead Yarn", *Sunday Star Times*, 23 March 1997, p. E: 4.

13 Tina Shaw ed. *A Passion for Travel: New Zealand Writers and their Adventures Overseas*. Auckland, Tandem Press, 1998, p. 21.

14 C. K. Stead, *Talking About O'Dwyer*, Auckland, Penguin Books, 1999, p. 20. Page numbers in brackets in this chapter refer to this edition of *Talking About O'Dwyer*.

15 Brian Edwards, interview with C.K. Stead, *National Radio*, 27 November 1999.

16 C. K. Stead, "The Keys of the Kingdom", *The Right Thing*, Auckland University Press, 2000, p. 33.

17 Michael King, "Vintage Stead", *North and South*, December 1999, p. 128.

18 A further Wittgenstein pronouncement, that "things which look the same are really different", has inspired Stead's poem "Likenesses" in *The Right Thing*, p. 31. His "Ludwig and Jack", published in *Answering to the Language*, is an amusing Pinter-like dialogue between Ludwig Wittgenstein and Jack Kerouac. Each conveys his own philosophy, while paying minimal attention to the ideas of the other. C. K. Stead, "Ludwig and Jack", *Answering to the Language: Essays on Modern Writers*, Auckland University Press, 1989, pp. 272-275.

19 Stead, "Running in Oxford", *The Right Thing*, p. 32.

20 John Campbell, interview with C. K. Stead, *National Radio*, 25 November 2000.

21 C. K. Stead, *Book Self*, Auckland University Press, 2008, p. 35.

22 Stead, *The Writer at Work*, pp. 29-30.

23 C. K. Stead, *Kin of Place: Essays on 20 New Zealand Writers*, Auckland, Auckland University Press, 2002, p. 194.

24 ibid, p. 194.

25 ibid, p. 194.

26 King, "Vintage Stead", *North and South*, December 1999, p. 128. King writes, "I talked to my father's friend Charles Bennett, who had been a Maori Battalion lieutenant at the time of the Crete campaign. To my surprise he confirmed that Dyer had indeed shot the soldier in the circumstances described."

27 ibid. Michael King continues, "Bennett was sceptical about the makutu, however."

28 Lawrence Jones, "Imaginative 'Factionality'", *New Zealand Books*, March 2000, p. 10.

29 Thanks are due to those staff and students of Massey University's Maori Studies Department with whom I discussed this episode.

30 Chapter Ten, p. 149, records that John Newton surmises a loss of Maori readership, as a result of Stead's failure to pay sufficient attention to Maori concepts and values: "The price of this neglect will duly be exacted in the loss of poise, and the loss of at least one portion of his audience." John Newton, "The Death-throes of Nationalism", *Landfall* 205, Autumn 2003, p. 99.

31 Shaw, A Passion for Travel: *New Zealand Writers and their Adventures Overseas*, p. 25.

32 Margaret Walters, "A Soldier's Death", *Times Literary Supplement*, 9 June 2000, p. 22.

33 Paul Binding, "Talking About O'Dwyer", *Times Literary Supplement*, 1 Dec 2000. p. 8.

34 John de Falbe, "Talking About C. K. Stead", *Spectator*, 27 May 2000, p. 9.

35 Iain Sharp, "Review: Talking About O'Dwyer", *Landfall* 199 Volume 8 (1), March 2000, p. 131.

36 Mark Williams, "As I remember", *New Zealand Listener*, 23 October 1999, p. 45.

37 Jones, "Imaginative 'Factionality'", *New Zealand Books*, March 2000, pp. 9-10.

38 Kim Hill, "Nine to Noon", *National Radio*, 6 July1994.

39 Stead, "Crete", *The Right Thing*, p. 81.

40 ibid, p. 80.

41 Stead, "Revisiting Bristol", *The Right Thing*, p. 47.

42 Stead, "Ghosts", *Straw into Gold*, Auckland University Press, 1997, p. 143.

43 Stead, "English in Our Universities", *The Writer at Work*, p. 114.

44 Stead, "Home at Last", *Straw into Gold*, p. 128.

45 Lakewood features also in *Talking About O'Dwyer*. Mike Newall spends a sabbatical there, living in a campus house with his family. In addition the poem, "It Is Only at the Hour of Darkness that the Owl of Minerva Descends", involves the same campus setting, with "a stone Virgin" and "a naked boy" alongside a lake. In the poem, students serve the narrator "hot soup/ and good cheer." C. K. Stead, *Straw into Gold*, Auckland University Press, 1997, p. 131.

46 Stead, "Jealousy 2 (Virginia Woolf, January 1923)", *Straw into Gold*, p. 142.

47 Stead, "Hollywood", *The Right Thing*, p. 63.

48 Stead, "Horation", *The Right Thing*, p. 91.

49 Stead, "Stories", *The Right Thing*, p. 90.

50 Stead, "Crete", *The Right Thing*, p. 87.

CHAPTER TWELVE

"Stead, like Execution, Concentrates the Mind"[1]

The Stories

Stead had been under a certain pressure to produce the novel that became *Talking About O'Dwyer*. In the mid-1990s, Penguin agreed to publish a collection of stories if he would "sign a two-book contract", the second book to be a new novel.[2] *The Blind Blonde with Candles in Her Hair* was published in 1998, most of its nine stories having appeared previously in books or journals: *Landfall*, *Metro*, *Sport*, *Chelsea Hotel*, the *London Magazine*, *The Faber Book of Contemporary South Pacific Stories*, and *The Inward Sun* (a book of tributes to Janet Frame). The collection's opening story, "Concerning Alban Ashtree", appeared first in the *London Magazine* in 1984; "The Last Life of Clarry" appeared in *Metro* in 1989. The others were published in the 1990s.

The first, fifth and ninth stories concern the same fictional poet – Alban Ashtree, with settings in Alberta, Auckland and America's Jersey Shore. The other six stories are set in California, London, Oxford, New Zealand, Sweden and Sydney. Common to most is the proximity of love and death, symbolised by the blind blonde with candles in her hair, who features in "Uncle Bjorn and the Saint of Light". She belongs to an ancient St Lucia ritual acknowledging death with the passing of the old year, and renewal of life out of the depths of winter. To a greater or lesser degree, this central image has relevance to each of the stories. There is a fragile poise, after which either renewal or death will take precedence. Death is an ever-present threat in "A Short History of New Zealand". Energy is renewed after pauses or intervals; each reprieve could be regarded as a new life. The three Alban Ashtree stories contemplate the significance of the poet's possible death in an avalanche. While news of his death brings to life his reputation as a poet, discovery that he is still alive could spell the death of that reputation.

The figurative love-death of copulation is one expression of the theme. In several stories, sexual favours are given freely to men who accept them with pleasure. Those for whom sexual activity becomes impossible are at risk of losing their lives. Clarry in "The Last Life of Clarry" knows he must be gravely ill, "Because the big fella won't stand up any more".[3] Uncle Bjorn in "Uncle Bjorn and the Saint of Light" approaches the age of eighty without a young woman at his side. His response is to walk through the Arctic snow to his death. To these men, sexual activity is vital to their concept of 'life'. (Mike Newall in *Talking About O'Dwyer* gives a wry explanation for the failure of his marriage: "She'd turned off the life-support".[4] This, without doubt, terminated the life of the marriage.) Sexual activity – the need for it, its quantity and quality – is significant in several stories. In "Sex in America", for instance, the two characters come together to watch a hotel fire from a window, the woman standing on a set of telephone directories. Their sexual experience intensifies as flames rise and lives are at risk.[5]

The withholding of generous sex is at issue in "Figures of Speech". A character named Carlo recounts what happened to him in his twenties, chiefly in London, in the late 1950s. He was unable to consummate a relationship with the woman of his choice, though he claims that, "There were times when we shared a bed – chastely, as she intended, but not (how shall I put it?) absolutely, or infallibly, or entirely. Let it be left there; because the important, or significant, truth is that we were never lovers in the wholehearted, fullblooded sense; and that was because she did not want us to be."[6]

"Figures of Speech" provides a number of parallels between the lives of Stead's characters and the history of Sylvia Plath and Ted Hughes. Stead creates a character reminiscent of Sylvia Plath, named Claudia Strange.[7] Claudia's ideal man in the story appears as Jack Gibbs, "six foot three, handsome, broad-shouldered, strongly built…".[8] Her desire for such a man echoes Sylvia Plath's similar craving. Ted Hughes was the embodiment of Plath's ideal, being, as her journal records, "that big, dark, hunky boy, the only one there huge enough for me".[9]

Carlo, in contrast with Jack, is one of Stead's many thin, six-foot tall characters. Because he is "*skinny*",[10] Claudia does not take his love for her seriously. Carlo is disconcerted to find that Claudia carries a small handgun in her handbag. Stead creates a relationship between a man and such a woman, not only in the story, but in one of the 1990s poems: "Reality is Like …". There the narrator speaks of his love for Scorpia. The poem conveys terror, "not so much of a bullet/ as of a woman".[11] Poem and story explore the powerful and erotic proximity of love and death that recurs in *The Blind Blonde with Candles in Her Hair*. The poem's Scorpia is a counterpart to Sylvia Plath, born under Scorpio, whose behaviour matched the Scorpio stereotype; she was intense, passionate and jealous.

Claudia and Jack are not writers but scientists, Jack advancing his research and professional success through Claudia's discoveries. Their marriage pursues a disastrous course, comparable to the Plath-Hughes marriage: time spent in America, return to England, one child (rather than two), the husband's affair, the wife's suicide. Carlo is the friend and observer of a woman whose work wins acclaim after her death and who comes to be championed by feminists.

For the purpose of the story, Stead imagines his way into the psyche of Plath, a literary figure he describes elsewhere as "brilliant, tough but erratic, given to extremes of gloom and ecstasy".[12] Her final poems, he maintains, have strengths she "achieved without trying".[13] Fascination with Plath is intimated in a poem addressed to "Sylvia" that first appeared in 1994, in the *London Review of Books*. It begins, "Ten days after he was, you were born",[14] in which "he" refers to Stead, born 17 October, while Plath's birthday was 27 October 1932. Playing on Plath's famous statement, "Dying is an art. I do it exceptionally well," the poem concludes with the line, "Living is an art. He does it as well as he can."[15] Stead's insight into Plath's life anticipates the sensitive understanding of a fellow writer that he brings to *Mansfield*.

The Writer at Work

After completing *Talking About O'Dwyer*, and thus fulfilling his contract with Penguin, Stead assembled critical essays for a publication that became *The Writer at Work: Essays* (2000). Only one article appears here for the first time. Most were written and published during the 1990s. Exceptions are two reviews from 2000, two from 1989 and a conversation with Harry Ricketts dated 1985. The book includes reviews for the *London Review of Books*, the *Times Literary Supplement, Landfall*, and *New Zealand Books*, articles for *Merian*, *Metro* and *Landfall*, interviews that were first published in books or journals, and papers presented to conference and other audiences.

Impressive in range, the book discusses work by writers from New Zealand, Britain, Australia, and the US.

The Introduction refers to various disputes in which Stead had been embroiled. Fearless in his questioning, he has sometimes been amazed at the outcome of his critical scrutiny. "I expressed public doubts about government policy in relation to Maori issues and issues of gender equity, and all at once the roof fell in on me." He maintains that "the statements of mine which gave most offence all seem moderate in tone and rational in argument."[16] Despite this claim, Philip Mead, writing for the *Times Literary Supplement*, is unsympathetic. He finds Stead to be out of step with his time.

> The reality is that, while Stead has been in his foxhole, lobbing grenades, history has swept on. He appears in this collection like the legendary Japanese soldier, lost in the jungle for twenty years, who emerges in a post-modern world, still with the idea that the war is raging. (...) But the complex, vigorous, post-colonial realignments of New Zealand culture that Stead wants to contest with his insistence on an old orthodoxy of imperial relations had been going on for nearly thirty years ... It seems inconceivable to Stead that the cultural future of New Zealand may already lie with Maori/Pakeha convergence, or that Hone Tuwhare is as important a figure in the history of New Zealand language as Allen Curnow.[17]

Mead refers specifically to Stead's 1990 lecture, "Nationalism, Regionalism and the Tradition in Contemporary New Zealand Poetry". In Mead's view, Stead has not recognised or valued the integration of Polynesian sensibility and creativity into the increasingly rich, diverse literature of New Zealand. Conversely, Maori writers have broadened their perspectives through strengthening their knowledge and experience of European traditions.

Another British reviewer, Karl Miller, reads Stead's position differently. It seems to him that "respect for the Maori contribution to life in New Zealand – a contribution to which he is far from indifferent or hostile, as his recent novel bears witness – is demanded and enjoined. It's the demanding and enjoining he objects to."[18] Refusal to bow to pressure is certainly one of Stead's attributes. As Miller confirms, Stead is not disrespectful toward Maori in his novels. Mead, on the other hand, focuses on attitudes conveyed through the critical text, *The Writer at Work*.

A series of "Reviews and Reminiscences" comprise the first section of the text. Rather than addressing publications being reviewed, Stead is sometimes inclined to offer his opinion of the book's subject. This is the case with "Lady Chatterley's Glover", ostensibly a review of Ogilvie's life of Glover, but providing an account of Stead's recollections of the poet, his wit, his drinking, and his chequered career. Similarly, Stead's review of the life of Ngaio Marsh by Margaret Lewis offers Stead's own informative commentary on Marsh. By contrast, Michael King's *Frank Sargeson: A Life* remains, throughout the review, at the centre of Stead's attention. It receives from Stead a tribute for "on the whole" capturing "the true Sargeson flavour"[19] and for allowing Sargeson to speak for himself wherever possible. While Stead's own interaction with Sargeson leads him to adjust a number of details, he gives the biographer full credit, saying, "The broad picture that King has given is right."[20]

A review of Keith Sinclair's autobiography provides the key to Stead's attitude to revisionist historians. An article by Stead, originally for *Metro*, places them among the foolish citizens who fail to notice the nakedness of the Emperor in the popular fable. Historians have not rushed into print to record indignation, or to protest at Stead's reference to "the kind of history which predominates at the moment, in which the Maori view is given the high moral ground". Sinclair's publication is, according to Stead, "the only one which offers anything like a balanced and rounded account of our history, and goes any distance towards doing justice to all".[21] Revisionist historians have been disinclined to argue these issues with C. K. Stead – poet, novelist and critic of literature.

Since Sinclair's day, countless assumptions have been discredited through careful investigation into primary sources – and through the discovery of material in the Archives that the older historians failed to look at. Many studies could illustrate the point, one of which is Hazel Riseborough's, *"The Taranaki Report": Background Papers for the Taranaki Raupatu Claim*.[22] If Maori have secured the moral high ground, it has resulted from research instigated by Waitangi Tribunal claims – recent historical research, in other words, that has had to stand up to scrutiny and cross-examination by the Crown. Stead has stated that, "The duty of the historian is not so much to get the story right as to compensate for what are considered to have been the wrongs of the past".[23] Whether or not readers share Stead's opinion, they could anticipate a frosty response among colleagues in the field of history to comments that call their professional integrity into question.

While affirming that his primary concern is "English language and its literatures", Stead claims to be "temperamentally predisposed to doubt official statements and policies".[24] He is ready to argue in Part Four of *The Writer at Work*, "Thinking Aloud – Thinking Allowed" that his intention has always been to stimulate debate and discussion. His view is that "the effect of Women's Studies and Black Studies has been to put women and blacks into academic ghettos, leaving them uncertain whether they have really done well or profited from an official bias."[25] In his opinion, 'positive discrimination' can never be reconciled with 'equal opportunity'. Given the strengthening position of Maori and ethnic minorities in skilled employment and positions of responsibility – a workforce increasingly representative of New Zealand's mix of cultural groups in other words – the practice of positive discrimination has decreased in the past ten or twelve years.

Stead's best reviews, whether of New Zealand writing or "in the world",[26] provide precise analysis of language use in the works under discussion. Rather satisfying is his critique of Paul Theroux's biography of V. S. Naipaul, exposing as invention Theroux's story of a New Zealand couple with "extreme New Zealand accents", who visit Naipaul's home. Stead notes that 'w*ee*nd' for 'wind' is Australian, and that the couple's turns of phrase indicate American or Australian speakers. Grains of truth amid inaccuracies allowed Stead to discover the identity of the visitors transformed by Theroux – Professor Michael Neill of Auckland University, educated at Harrow and Sandhurst, who has "one of those neutral international accents",[27] and Chinese academic, Pek-Koon.

The Secret History of Modernism

Stead has always resisted invitations or inclinations to pursue a career outside New Zealand. His fascination with the prospect, explored imaginatively in *Talking About O'Dwyer*, recurs in *The Secret History of Modernism*, which considers the lure not of an overseas academic position but the pursuit of a writing career abroad. Having sailed to England about the time Stead made the journey, his character Laszlo Winter embarks on a PhD, studying, not at the University of Bristol, but at the University of London – before tossing aside his PhD prospects and choosing to become a writer. In a discussion-interview, Stead admitted to Fleur Adcock, "I always wanted to write fiction and couldn't really write it substantially until I left the university ... If I had been really daring I could have done that much earlier here in London."[28]

The *Secret History of Modernism* is narrated by Laszlo, a character of Stead's age who finds himself suffering from writers' block. Stead encountered such a problem after completing *Talking About O'Dwyer*. Laszlo imagines the satisfaction of "silence and anonymity", a future with "No more bruising public attention. No more wounding reviews."[29] Nevertheless, he continues to search for a story, which will become "a light for my darkness, a flame for my fuse. ... One had to be open – to the world, to suggestion. One had meekly to hold out one's cloth cap and hope Chance would drop a coin in it." (p. 8) Laszlo's earnest belief in the value of story telling is likely to be in accord with Stead's.

> Without stories everything flew apart and became shapeless, nameless, meaningless; and the more we learned about ourselves and our place in the dreadful exploding-and-dying universe we now know we inhabit, the more essential they became. Stories were the saviours of our sanity. (p. 4)

With the creation of Laszlo, Stead was on his way into the novel. He was later able to say to an audience gathered to hear his address in the Maidment Theatre, at the University of Auckland, "I made writers' block the key to my own door."

> By the end of the first chapter I'd created a character, a voice and a situation. Laszlo Winter was not C. K. Stead but clearly he was in some ways a projection of myself with the same temperament and stylistic inclinations, amused by the same kinds of jokes, given to similar behaviours good and bad, and currently facing the same problem: how to begin a new novel. Laszlo finds his subject by an accident, which is also taken from my own experience right at this time. A German academic with whom I'd had distant connections many years before visited Auckland and got in touch with me. I met him and with the ruthlessness of a needy author I borrowed him, renamed him Otto Stilz and put him straight into the novel.[30]

What develops is a reflective fictional memoir. At the conclusion, Laszlo is ready to turn his material into a novel, a resolution very like Moravia's at the end of *Conjugal Love*. A writer approaching seventy, Laszlo moves easily from present to past, returning to the present at intervals, generally to comment on the episodes he is assembling. He notes the importance of the novel's "scenes" which form "discrete but interlocking narratives" (p. 18) and reflects on his particular point of view, governed as it is by his home base in Auckland, in a country at a southern extreme and on the outer edge of many world maps, contributing to the "maximum insignificance" (p. 49) of his perspective. Rather than be demoralised, he chooses to consider this a liberation. As a mature writer, he decides that "Imagination, after all, is a master key, and all (all!) you need, in order to use it, is confidence and intelligence." (p. 213)

Stead has remarked that he likes *The Secret History of Modernism* very much, saying that it suits his temperament. More specifically, it has allowed him to include experiences he relished in London in the late 1950s. His enthusiasm for the city at that time is apparent in "Pictures in a Gallery Undersea" and parts of "Walking Westward". Characters in the novel frequent the places he came to know well: the Reading Room in the British Museum, its Manuscript Room, its annexe out at Colindale, a bedsit in Kensington, Russell Square, the Lyric Hammersmith where Patrick McGoohan played Robespierre. He could also include his colonial reaction to England: "what had existed for us only in books was now all around us, able to be seen and touched. The unreal had become real, but without quite losing its unreality." (p. 74) Laszlo and his friends are "members of a generation living at a time when the British Empire was transforming itself into the Commonwealth and London was still the centre of the English-speaking world."[31]

Australia, home to Laszlo's friend Samantha Conlan, provides other significant settings: Beecroft, seventeen miles from the heart of Sydney, a sheep station on the Tableland four hundred miles to the north, Pearl Beach on the Pacific Coast, and a settlement in the Blue Mountains. These are all familiar places to Stead, through visiting Kay's relatives in Beecroft, through his residence in Armidale on the Tableland, from which he and Kay travelled to other parts of the country, and through time spent at an Australian Writers' Retreat in the Blue Mountains in 1999, to which he was invited ahead of the reissue of *The End of the*

Century at the End of the World by HarperCollins Australia. For Stead, place is always significant, helping create atmosphere and contributing to the mood that characters reflect.

The mature Laszlo, his writing underway, can enjoy a residence and environs in France, as guest of the fictional Otto Stilz. The place near Uzès, well known to Stead, was until recently home to his friend Tony Axelrad, with its own swimming pool, and not far from "the Pont du Gard, that remarkable Roman triple aquaduct". (p. 156) In the neighbourhood, Laszlo, like Stead himself, could anticipate French food and wine while walking "along beaten clay lanes between freestone walls, through vineyards, small orchards, olive groves, fields of wheat and fields of sun flowers". (p. 158)

Critic Merle Rubin for the *Los Angeles Times* has indicated appreciation of Stead's comprehension of "the century's history".

> Stead interweaves three strands of narrative: the reflections and peregrinations of middle-aged Laszlo; the mildly comic adventures of young Laszlo and his friends; and the harrowing story of the Goldsteins ... Much of the poignancy of this novel resides in the contrast between the leisurely cultivated lives of Laszlo and his friends and the brutal, unthinkable realities that the equally cultivated Goldsteins were forced to confront just one generation earlier.[32]

A love affair between Freddy Goldstein and Samantha Conlan motivates Samantha's investigation into the lives of the Modernist poets. Unlike her friends Laszlo and Rajiv, she is not a student at London University, but is independently engaged in a project she calls *The Secret History of Modernism*. It was Freddy who asked her to explain how it was that "all the great Modernist writers of that period had been fascists". She finds that, while the premise is not entirely true, it is "nearly true". (p. 227) The 'real' secret history lies in the link between the lives and mindset of writers like T. S. Eliot and the totalitarian regimes in Germany and Italy, regimes that were strengthened in reaction to an impression of past decadence, softness and lack of rigour.

There was belief in "a new discipline in writing and in thought, and also in social and political life". Samantha concludes that, if "undiluted", the philosophy of "steel and sinew and will" manifests itself as "a poison". (p. 227) The story of Freddy Goldstein is located during years of terror in Germany, Holland and Palestine. The tragic history of his Jewish family during the Nazi era, conveyed in three chapters in the novel, provides a significant political and historical dimension. As Norman Bilborough points out, Freddy's tragic family history in *The Secret History of Modernism* is "a story that is so frequently told in different forms that it's almost a cliché. Yet it's a moving story; it's the most moving narrative in the book."[33] Substantial and compelling, Freddy's story could have become the focus of its own novel.

The political dimension is linked to a literary dimension. Laszlo, Rajiv and Samantha, researchers into Shakespeare, Yeats and Eliot, discuss and compare the relative merit of the supreme Modernist poem "The Waste Land" and Eliot's later work of religious affirmation, "The Four Quartets". As a mature writer looking critically at his novel, Laszlo discusses its many poetry quotations with his wife Louise: "Of course it's too literary. I know that." (p. 228) She reassures him, citing the example of Moravia. Laszlo believes Moravia would have pleased Italian and French readers. "And I, unfortunately, am – well you know what I am and who I'm writing for. There's a difference." (p. 229) Despite Laszlo's misgivings, the words of Eliot, Yeats, Shakespeare, Marvel, Marlowe and Milton add to the work's philosophical thought.

Reference to New Zealand literature is oblique, with a caricatured Maurice Shadbolt making a brief appearance as Dick Flinders, "a man with a moustache, a pipe and darkly horn-rimmed glasses" (p. 125), a response to Shadbolt's 1965 caricature of Stead as the balding academic and poet Derek Flinders in *Among the Cinders*. Reviewers did not chastise Shadbolt for mocking Stead, but Stead's Dick Flinders has been described as "a denigrating portrait of Shadbolt, and unnecessary."[34] Stead's intuition into the way his caricature might be received is reflected in the scolding Laszlo is given by Oxford student Margot Derry. She rebukes him for a tone that is "sneering, sardonic, superior" (p. 125) when he speaks of Dick Flinders.

Stead considered some years later that the title, *The Secret History of Modernism*, lacked immediate appeal to readers. Sales and other forms of recognition were not in accord with the praise the book earned from reviewers in Ireland, England and Scotland – in the *Dublin Sunday Tribune*, *The Irish Times*, *The Spectator* and *Scotland on Sunday* – characterised by Stead as "the best reviews I've ever had in the UK ... really extravagantly positive reviews."[35]

Among the matter-of-fact New Zealand reviewers, Lawrence Jones entitled his article, "Not the Master's Best but Still a Good Read".[36] Peter Wells found the work "casual to the point of sauntering".[37] The novel allows time for witty and amusing observations, like Laszlo's reflection on his lack of initiative with women: "my thoughts about Heather tended to be florid, and she, a professional, must have recognised this as surely as a motor mechanic recognises, when he glances under the bonnet of a car, that the engine is overheating." (p. 105) There is time to describe the America's Cup Challenge, a topic not essential to the book's central concerns or progress.

> The challenge races had been much closer and more exciting than those of the final. They'd been sailed in higher winds and rougher seas, with injuries, protests, hysterical helmsmen, near and actual collisions, split spinnakers and torn sails, a broken mast, even a boat cracked amidships and bent upward at either end like a banana, the crew diving overboard as it threatened to sink. (p. 9)

The Secret History of Modernism played a significant part in preparing the way for *Mansfield*. Laszlo reads the chapter "Only Connect!" from Samantha's research assembled for her "*Secret History*" (p. 159). He finds an account of a late evening walk by Katherine Mansfield and T. S. Eliot after an actual dinner party that both had attended without enjoyment. In *Mansfield*, the encounter is not merely reported; the novel opens with a sustained dialogue between Stead's Katherine and Eliot that rings with credibility, signalling the novelist's remarkable insight into the character and psyche of these literary figures.

Stead's interest in the project he found for Samantha rekindled his interest in Mansfield's life and her interaction with the friends and writers she knew. To recreate imaginatively that life and those interactions led him to offer, according to Alberto Manguel, "the most delicious, exquisitely prepared, delicately spiced Katherine Mansfield *dans son jus* that one could ever wish for."[38]

1 From Michael King's dedication, "To C. K. Stead", in *Tread Softly, for You Tread on My Life*, Auckland, Cape Catley Ltd, 2001.

2 Letter to Curnow 19 May 1997, Turnbull Library Papers.

3 C. K. Stead, "The Last Life of Clarry", *The Blind Blonde with Candles in Her Hair*, Auckland, Penguin Books, 1998, p. 61.

4 C. K. Stead, *Talking About O'Dwyer*, Auckland, Penguin Books, 1999, p. 30.
5 Stead, "Sex in America", *The Blind Blonde with Candles in Her Hair*, pp. 119-120.
6 Stead, "Figures of Speech", *The Blind Blonde with Candles in Her Hair*, p. 137.
7 Stead has chosen names for his characters with the same rhythm as the names of Plath and Hughes: Sylvia Plath/Claudia Strange; Ted Hughes/Jack Gibbs.
8 Stead, "Figures of Speech", *The Blind Blonde with Candles in Her Hair*, p. 141.
9 Sylvia Plath, *The Journals of Sylvia Plath*, New York, Anchor Books, a Division of Random House, 1998, first published 1982, p. 111.
10 Stead, "Figures of Speech", *The Blind Blonde with Candles in Her Hair*, p. 128.
11 C. K. Stead, *Straw into Gold*, Auckland University Press, 1997, p. 138.
12 C. K. Stead, *The Writer at Work*, Dunedin, University of Otago Press, 2000, p. 170.
13 ibid, p. 171.
14 C. K. Stead, *The Right Thing*, Auckland University Press, 2000, p. 72.
15 ibid, p. 73.
16 Stead, *The Writer at Work*, p. 12.
17 Philip Mead, "The Veteran's Cadre: C. K. Stead", *Times Literary Supplement*, 4 January 2002, p. 23.
18 Karl Miller, "Talking About Stead", *Landfall* 205, May 2001, p. 177.
19 Stead, *The Writer at Work*, p. 55.
20 ibid, p. 58.
21 ibid, p. 53.
22 Hazel Riseborough, *"The Taranaki Report": Background Papers for the Taranaki Raupatu Claim*, Waitangi Tribunal, 1989.
23 Stead, *The Writer at Work*, p. 119.
24 Stead, *The Writer at Work*, p. 13.
25 ibid, p. 220.
26 ibid, a phrase from the 'Contents' page.
27 ibid, p. 192.
28 ibid, p. 248.
29 C. K. Stead, *The Secret History of Modernism*, London, The Harvill Press, 2001, p. 16. Page numbers in brackets in this chapter refer to this edition.
30 C. K. Stead, "One Thing Leads to Another", speaking as Distinguished Alumnus, opening speaker in the Distinguished Alumni Series, in the Maidment Theatre, University of Auckland, introduced by Emeritus Professor Mac Jackson, 3 March 2008.
31 Christopher Moore, "Approach With Care", *The Press*, 16 February 2002, p. 17.
32 Merle Rubin, *Los Angeles Times*, 1 September 2002.
33 Norman Bilborough, The Secret History of Modernism", *New Zealand Books*, June 2002, p. 7.
34 ibid, p. 7.
35 C. K. Stead, "It's Not Wishful Thinking", Writers and Readers Week, Wellington Festival, Embassy Theatre, introduced by Elizabeth Alley, 14 March 2008.
36 Lawrence Jones, "Not the Master's Best but Still a Good Read", *Otago Daily Times*, 19 January 2002. p. B 48.
37 Peter Wells, "Bang, Bang, Bang", *Landfall* 203, May 2002, p. 163.
38 Alberto Manguel, *The Spectator*, 5 June 2004, p. 44.

CHAPTER THIRTEEN

"The Wicked Wisdom of Europe"[1]

Stead's Katherine

The novel *Mansfield,* published in 2004, allowed Stead to interact creatively with a captivating literary figure: "She has always fascinated me, in that the fiction was really only beginning when she died. But she left this mass of letters and journals that are packed with flashes of brilliance and wit."[2] *The End of the Century at the End of the World*, published twelve years earlier than *Mansfield*, includes discussion of a work of fiction about Mansfield written by Stead's imaginary author Hilda Tapler; she has her heroine survive tuberculosis and return to New Zealand. Even earlier, Stead made a study of all Mansfield's work, publishing, in 1977, extracts from her journals and diaries. An instructive introductory essay begins the work, and biographical notes link the different sections.

An early draft of *The Secret History of Modernism* included a chapter in which Mansfield featured.

> 'It was too obviously a tangent,' so it got dropped and set aside. Nonetheless, 'it just presented itself as a great subject for a novel. ... The biographer, if it's a good biography, is giving you a factual thing, which really is surface. But what did people actually say to one another? What did she see when she looked out the window? The biographer goes up to the limit of what is known, and will speculate a wee bit beyond and then has to stop. The fiction writer has to pretend to know everything.'[3]

In a niggardly review of *Mansfield*, Kim Hill remarks, "There's not a great deal of imagination required of the author, given the reliance on the wealth of material that Katherine and others associated with her left behind".[4] Alberto Manguel, for *The Spectator*, views Stead's achievement differently:

> It may be supposed that being the editor ... of *The Letters and Journals of Katherine Mansfield* had destined C. K. Stead to the writing of this novel. I don't think so. It is one thing to know the material of your subject in scholarly detail, to have read all her work, to have the dates and names and places of her biography at your fingertips; it is quite another to bring her to life as a sentient, complex and believable person. Stead's Mansfield may or may not be true to the documentary truth, but she is as large as life and twice as natural.[5]

The Prologue's conversation between Stead's Katherine and T. S. Eliot sets the tone. It is a fact that she and Eliot left a party, at which Captain Robert Graves was present. What the two said as they walked along the Embankment on a summer evening is not recorded in journal or diary, but Stead has imagined a discourse in keeping with the character of each. On finding that Eliot uses Apteryx, the Latin name for a kiwi as his pen name, Katherine remarks, "Apt. Tricks. It's good. It suits you".[6] She is spontaneous and confident in conversing with another expatriate, while Eliot is initially reticent, but sensitive to her presence and remarks.

Stead's ability to identify with Mansfield has allowed him to infer credible physical, emotional and mental reactions to traumatic events encountered and endured by his Katherine in the three years – winter 1915 until winter 1918 – encompassed by the novel. He describes these years as "the period of her greatest involvement with the most interesting people in her life. Subsequent to that, she becomes much more absorbed with her battle with her health."[7] He chose to avoid writing about a dying woman. Instead he concludes the novel with Katherine's discovery that she is suffering from tuberculosis and her resolve to work, to finish the book she is writing and then perhaps another, in the knowledge that death from this disease may take several years.

Mansfield is a third person narration, but each chapter brings into focus a particular character, coming close to his or her consciousness. Katherine is at the centre of seven chapters and the Epilogue. Two chapters are written from Fred Goodyear's point of view, and four other chapters have different central figures: Leslie Beauchamp, Jack Murry, Frieda Lawrence, Dora Carrington. The novel also provides particular insight into the perspectives of D. H. Lawrence, Virginia and Leonard Woolf, Bertrand Russell, T. S. Eliot, and Lady Otteline Morrell. Mansfield is placed in her time among her contemporaries. In Stead's words, "I didn't want it just to be Mansfield. I wanted it to be a bigger picture in the historical and moral sense."[8]

Affinity

Following a 2004 interview with Stead, journalist Margo White concluded that the novel offers "Stead's version of the woman, which he agrees is partly about Mansfield and partly about him".[9] His presence in the novel is not obvious, but there is an affinity, perceived or subconscious, between Stead and Mansfield. The two writers have in common a feeling for the French language and the endeavour to master it. Both were awake to their situation as colonials, with Stead alert to the taunts and the condescension suffered by Mansfield. Coming from coastal cities in New Zealand, both writers grew up with abundant sky and water and "ample light", which has led to a highly developed "visual sense".[10] Impressions of life at home and life abroad have been thrown into sharp relief by a sensitivity to contrast apparent in the work of both.

Stead's Katherine describes her mind as "stored with all the meticulous detail of childhood memory, the store seemingly unlocked by the kind of shock foreign places and new love can deliver". (p. 114) Like the original Mansfield, Stead's Katherine is keen to experience foreign places and discover new love, which will not only unlock memories, but will increase the breadth of understanding that her art requires. Passion for life and devotion to art are features of temperament that Stead and Mansfield share.

Stead's Katherine, questioning and critical, describes herself as "a citizen of nowhere. ... what I'm taught here I don't always accept or believe. Nothing ever seems gospel, you know?" (p. 176) Stead is just as sceptical, whether in Europe or New Zealand or elsewhere. When he has his Katherine observe France, he brings the awareness of a dispassionate outsider. "Notre Dame ... seemed horrible, the forests of candles in its murmuring-echoey interior deeply sinister, its smell the smell of death, but faded, cold, as if death itself had died there a long time ago. The disappointed God, His tormented Son, the Son's grieving

Mother, the variously wounded, tortured or suffering saints, looked down at her." (p. 24) Fred Goodyear is another sceptic, his rational thinking in keeping with views expressed in Stead's 1993 essay "What I Believe".[11] Fred dismisses the belief that God has His "hand ready at the Wheel of Fate". (p. 187) He is quite sure that "There would be no finality, no great explanatory outcome, no revelation of a Divine Plan. ... The pretences and deceptions of childhood were over. There was no Omnipotent and Loving Father ... – only Generals and Politicians, men and machines, destruction and death." (p. 187)

Stead has described Mansfield as "a high-spirited pagan for whom the notion of art had replaced traditional religion as the source and receptacle of the highest truths and the finest achievements of humankind".[12] The belief that "the highest truth" can be found in "art" finds expression in *The Singing Whakapapa*. When Hugh Grady's sister, Aida Norma,

> came home from school upset because some Plymouth Brethren schoolmates had said *their* names came, as all names should, from the Bible, she was instructed to explain that *hers* came from 'Grand Opera'. Hugh is sure their mother thought this would settle the matter. That the Bible might be more sacred than the works of the great European composers was not a proposition she would have entertained.[13]

The name of Stead's older sister, Norma Nellie, carries similar musical connotations, with *Norma* the name of a Bellini opera, and Dame Nellie Melba one of the great opera singers in her time. The fictional Mrs Grady and the actual Olive Stead would have found ultimate truth in art, the art of music.

Mansfield was described by Otteline Morrell as being "as aware of herself as a writer as Queen Victoria was of being a Queen".[14] Since his teen-age years, Stead, too, has regarded himself as a writer first and foremost. He could relate to Mansfield's intermittent frustration when her writing failed to flow freely. His Katherine speaks of fluency that comes and goes, as if it were an entity with a life of its own.

> How can one's talent, one's fluency, one's *will* to *write* (because that is what it amounts to) so desert one, and so return? Like a very large and noisy prodigal son, missing, wept over, searched

> for and unresponding. For a whole year all correspondence "returned to sender". And now back again, as loud and alive as ever, as healthy and pushy, brooking no questions about reasons for departure or reasons for return. Mind your own business and take dictation! She minds it, and takes it. (p. 207)

Stead could respect Mansfield's intuitive sense of the 'rightness' achieved by her finest stories: "She lays before us as few writers have done, the psychic state, the inner condition, of the artist whose material is language."[15] She valued immediacy, authenticity and depth, qualities that Stead has valued in his own work. The linguistic range of both writers has been extended through breadth of reading, and by re-reading at intervals the supreme exponents – Shakespeare and Dickens.

Mansfield's writing reveals her chameleon quality, a characteristic she notes in her *Journal*, when she reflects on the difficulty of being "True to oneself. Which self? Which of my many – well really, that's what it looks like coming to – hundreds of selves?"[16] Stead, as a many-faceted personality himself, could relate to this aspect of Mansfield's character. Margo White has written "of Stead's various complexities and contradictions". She continues:

> "I considered framing this feature around 'Catullus of Nine Tails' or 'Seven Deadly Steads' or the 'Six Faces of Stead' but when I mentioned this to his wife, Kay, she said, 'No, it wouldn't work because there are more than six faces.'"[17]

Mansfield's ability to adopt different roles is clear in her letters as well as her stories. In his Introduction to *Letters and Journals: Katherine Mansfield*, Stead quotes Middleton Murry in a letter to Violet Schiff, saying that Mansfield "tended to assume a personality to please a correspondent. I suppose we all do it in some degree. But in her it was very pronounced."[18] The novel shows Katherine to be an inspired letter writer, shaping each letter to accord with the interests, understanding and status of the recipient.

As Stead has explained in relation to *All Visitors Ashore*, adopting the persona of an historic figure or someone an author has known requires a deep interest in that person. Observation and imagination combine as the writer gradually eases into enacting the character. Self is forgotten – and yet part of the writer's self is invested in the characterisation. Stead's Katherine reflects on a comparable process. She thinks about her own writing based on actual people, who "became separate from their originals in real life, became independent – aspects, perhaps, of her self – herself shared out and divided and made many, like the loaves and fishes ...". (p. 47)

"How it's done ... I have no idea"

Manguel has tried to find the source and secret of Stead's achievement in creating "a moving, comprehensible, convincing fictional narrative" from the "jottings of [Mansfield's] documented voice in journals and letters". Having asked himself how it was done, he reflects:

> I must confess, I have no idea. A dearth of adjectives, an extraordinary accuracy of description merely through the use of verbs and nouns, the right intuition of when to comment and when to leave good enough alone, a taste for the right anecdote and a certain Mansfieldean humour that permeates the entire story from choice beginning to measured end.[19]

Stead had absorbed from Mansfield's writing a feeling for those details that would catch his Katherine's attention. Chapters in which Katherine is the central character ring with language use like Mansfield's: "it was a winter sun and the trees knew better than to take the least notice of it. They were dead to the world ...". (p. 12) The description of Virginia Woolf offers another example: "She was cat-like, a particularly well-bred, long-faced feline, with nice fur and perfect cat manners, capable of purring and rubbing up against one, but with sharp unscrupulous claws." (p. 207) Sometimes there is humour in a story that unfolds with feigned solemnity. When Otteline Morrell confides that her husband is responsible for two pregnancies, one involving his wife's personal maid and the other his secretary, Katherine reflects that "This was carelessness with a certain grandeur. From one point of view you could see it as a triumph, as easily calling for champagne as for weeping and gnashing of teeth." (p. 211)

Stead brings his novelist's scrutiny to bear on relationships among people who feature in Mansfield's life. In the novel, Leslie Beauchamp's view of his parents is in keeping with available evidence: "the Mother, apparently so frail and indecisive, the father such a Pa-man, so commanding and brusque, and yet the reality, when you knew how the family worked, entirely otherwise – she up on the bridge steering the ship, he down in the engine room shovelling coal." (p. 58)

Stead takes an interest in the closeness of Mansfield and her brother Leslie. The night before Leslie departs for France with his regiment, Stead's Katherine goes to his attic room: "let me lie down on your bed Bogey, like I used to when you were really my little brother." (p. 67) After Margo White raised with Stead the possible implication of incest, he replied, "Well, there are things there, which I quote, which are difficult to interpret any other way. I mean, I don't *know*, I haven't got the faintest idea... but the intensity was really strange. She wrote things like 'you're in my body now' and when he died she wrote 'Jack and I can no longer be lovers'."[20]

Stead's characterisation does allow other readings, however. The words "you're in my body now" could hark back to Mansfield's poem "To L.H.B. (1894-1915)", which tells of a dream in which poisonous berries are plucked by Leslie, who "stands/ Waiting for me with berries in his hands.../ 'These are my body sister, take and eat'."[21] The berries are symbolic of death. In her depressed state after the loss of Leslie, Mansfield writes, "I am just as much dead as he is. The present and the future mean nothing to me."[22] These words can indicate a time of shock in which she could not countenance the thought of Jack as her lover.

Sometimes Katherine's words from her journal are transferred directly into *Mansfield*.[23] Other episodes have her letters as their source. In his 1977 Mansfield book, Stead published for the first time an "extraordinary [letter] written May 1916 to Koteliansky recounting a quarrel between the D.H. Lawrences".[24] Mansfield's lengthy and vivid account of fighting between Frieda and Lawrence provided Stead with material to recreate conversation, shouting, and lively interaction when the two couples were living in adjacent houses in North Devon.

Stead retains the essence of what he learnt from Mansfield's *Journal*, though he changes the emphasis on occasion. Having arrived in a French town for an assignation with Francis Carco, Mansfield must convince two officers that her visit is legitimate. Her *Journal* describes the confrontation, in which one officer looks at her passport and says, "It won't do at all," before his colleague "dismissed the objection, stamped it and let me go".[25] Stead's novel makes much more of Katherine's encounter with authority. She is interrogated and invents an uncle, an aunt, and a reason for travel. As she and Carco drive away from the station in a cab, "The doors flapped like elephant ears. Katherine reached for one, Carco for the other, and they slammed them shut." (pp. 38-9) The latter by Stead is somewhat crisper than Mansfield's account: "we tore away with both doors flapping and banging. 'Bonjour, ma cherie,' said F. and we kissed each other quickly and then clutched at the banging doors. They would not keep shut…".[26]

Puritan Naïvety

While Alberto Manguel commends *Mansfield*, Ali Smith in the *Times Literary Supplement* undercuts her appreciation of Stead's "poignancy and elegance of form" by alleging "a failure of nerve when it comes to the figure of Mansfield herself". Smith considers "that Fred Goodyear might have made a more sympathetic centre for this novel".[27] She notes that almost all Katherine talks about is sex, especially to female characters. Distasteful to Smith is an impression that Katherine is limited by an on-going need to relate to a man. Smith writes, "even with Lawrence urging her to 'learn to be alone' for her art … Stead insists 'she believed, felt she had no choice except to believe, that there could be a man … her perfect man!'"[28] Within the psyche of the actual Mansfield, a moral and cultural legacy of her New Zealand upbringing endured, even though she appeared to reject it in favour of what Mark Williams has termed "the wicked wisdom of Europe". Stead could not ignore or change this feature of his Katherine's personality without damaging the character's historic integrity. Mansfield's ingrained belief that there must be an ideal man for her to marry was part of what Williams calls "the puritan naïvety of New Zealand".[29] It was reinforced in Mansfield's case from pre-school age, when she and her sisters played with a beautiful dolls' house in which there were parents and children.[30]

As a woman in her twenties, and even earlier, Mansfield broke a major taboo. Instead of abiding by the puritan ideal of chastity before marriage, she embraced defiantly "the notion that the artist must go in pursuit of 'experience', and that governed her sexual behaviour".[31] Breadth of experience need not, Mansfield reasoned, be incompatible with eventual marriage and parenthood. In the novel, Katherine often imagines herself as a mother and visualises her own small child.

Katherine's affair with Francis Carco, which she later calls "a wartime episode" (p. 57), quickly over and set aside, is unsurprising in the context of the experiential liberty that Mansfield – and Stead's Katherine – allowed herself. Margo White, in discussion with Stead, noted Katherine's "surprising lack of remorse" after the affair, the fact that she seemed "undaunted by any notion that she may have caused Murry grief". White considered this behaviour to be "untypical in a woman". Stead replied that the behaviour of his imaginary character "fits in with the [historical] evidence. Mansfield wrote about the Carco affair in a story and in her journals. 'And there wasn't ever the merest hint that she was worried about Jack's feelings. So while I agree that it may not be typical of women, it is not untrue of her'."[32]

To Mark Williams, Stead's Katherine is "an imagined version" of Mansfield, which could never be "biographically exact."[33] Stead's impressions, though, do concur with evidence that throws light on her character and temperament. Stead has understood the need to create a Katherine who was affected by social values and constraints of late nineteenth-early twentieth century New Zealand, even when she considered herself to be acting in defiance of them. He shows the enduring influence of this conditioning on a young woman who dared to embrace Europe's "wicked wisdom".[34] Mansfield's boldness, her willingness to engage in new experience, won Stead's admiration: "She remains one of the most brilliant and extraordinary of modern women."[35]

Honours and Accolades

The first decade of the new millennium secured a new measure of admiration for the extraordinary achievements of C. K. Stead. New Zealanders became aware that the University of Bristol had honoured him in July 2001, conferring the degree Doctor of Letters, *honoris causa*. "The doctoring was generously done," Stead wrote to Curnow. "The Orator seemed to have read everything I had written and took his time over the oration."[36] The pleasure Stead felt finds expression in "Applause (Bristol University 12.7.01, with thanks to Andrew Bennett)". Stead listened to his "life in summary", so positive in every detail, that, he observes, "it could be my funeral." He was gratified to have been rewarded "only for being myself".[37] Professor Andrew Bennett was the Orator who addressed "Mr Vice-Chancellor" in offering a lengthy citation applauding Stead's career in literature:

> whatever form his writing takes and within whatever forum, Professor Stead achieves a clarity of vision and elegance of prose which many aspire to but few can achieve. [...] His work has been published in New Zealand, England and the United States and has been translated into many European languages. Edgy and lyrical, acerbic and witty, intellectually incisive but also visceral and bawdy, disarmingly direct and often intricately plotted, international in focus but always grounded in his country of birth, the poems and novels are always provocative, always challenging and above all, always pre-eminently readable.[38]

Also in 2001, Stead reported to Curnow that he was to receive the King's Lynn Poetry Award: "a rather strange thing; you get 1000 pounds – to spend a week there and a week in a port served by King's Lynn in its heyday, and write a poem or poems about the experience, to be published and read at the following year's festival."[39] Stead wrote thirteen poems. At the final session of the King's Lynn Poetry Festival, poets were invited to read from and discuss the work of their favourite poet. He chose Allen Curnow.

Earlier recipients of this award had linked King's Lynn with other lands – the Netherlands, Portugal and Iceland. Stead took up the challenge by relating King's Lynn to the Pacific region: "Although there may not have been ships that sailed from King's Lynn to the Pacific, its seamen certainly did – most notably James Burney (younger brother of Fanny Burney and son of the musician Charles Burney) and George Vancouver".[40] Notes accompanying each poem appear at the end of *Dog*, the collection in which "King's Lynn and the Pacific" forms the first of three poetry sequences. The following is a reflection from one of the poems, all of which are grounded in historical accuracy, telling of journeys, courage, privation, ambition:

> There is, it seems, more than one
>
> *real* world, and while you are in one
> the other goes on without you.[41]

Stead has managed better than most to keep abreast of events in different parts of the world. In recent years, invitations to speak at conferences and festivals have taken him to many cities abroad and in New Zealand. In 2000, he spoke at writers' festivals in Melbourne, Hay-on-Wye, Auckland, and Toronto. In 2003, he addressed the Vancouver Writers and Readers Festival, and in the same year contributed as an invited guest to literary festivals in Calgary, Banff, Sydney and Eaglereach NSW. Such engagements provided interaction with other writers. *The Red Tram* includes the poem "My Fellow Writers at Eaglereach", a work showing the resilience and stoicism of participants from five different countries, all of whom had suffered in the past but who are enjoying discussions, reminiscences, and laughter.

Success in New Zealand in the early years of the new millennium included the placement of *Talking About O'Dwyer* as runner up in the fiction category of the Montana New Zealand Book Awards in 2000. Stead was again a Montana Award finalist in 2005 in the novel category with *Mansfield* – and also in the poetry section for *The Red Tram*. Success of a different kind was achieved that year when he received a Michael King Fellowship, a prize of $100,000 to advance three literary projects – the novel that would become *My Name Was Judas*, publication of a selection of letters written to him by Sargeson and Curnow, and a collected edition of his poetry.

An award of even greater prestige followed in 2007, when Stead received the highest honour in the land, limited to twenty living individuals. He was admitted to the Order of New Zealand for services to New Zealand literature, in recognition of the quality and range of his literary work, and as the culmination of many successes and accolades, including a CBE in 1985 and New Zealand Book Awards for *Quesada* in 1978, *All Visitors Ashore* in 1985 and *The Singing Whakapapa* in 1995. Before 2007, his most prestigious achievement had been his election in Britain in 1995 to the status of Fellow of the Royal Society of Literature, an honour that only one other New Zealander shares – poet Fleur Adcock.

1 Mark Williams, "Stead's Mansfield", *Landfall*, Spring 2004, p. 199.

2 Nicholas Wroe, "Writing in the Dark", *The Guardian*, 10 March 2007. Retrieved August 2007http://www.guardiah.co.uk/books/2007/mar/10/featuresreviews.guardianreview35.

3 John McCrystal, "The Teddy Bear Within", *Dominion Post*, 24 April 2004, p. E:8.

4 Kim Hill, "She Said, He Said", *New Zealand Listener*, 8 May 2004, p. 50.

5 Alberto Manguel, "Leaving Fingerprints Behind", *The Spectator*, 5 June 2004, p. 44.

6 C. K. Stead, *Mansfield*, London, Vintage, 2004, p. 5. Page numbers in brackets in this chapter refer to this edition.

7 McCrystal, *Dominion Post*, 24 April 2004, p. E: 8.
8 ibid, p. E: 8.
9 Margo White, "Interview: Karl Stead", *Metro*, May 2004, p. 103.
10 C. K. Stead, *In the Glass Case*, Auckland University Press/Oxford University Press, 1981, p. 30.
11 C. K. Stead, *The Writer at Work*, pp. 200-6.
12 C. K. Stead, *Answering to the Language: Essays on Modern Writers*, Auckland University Press, 1989, p. 151.
13 C. K. Stead, *The Singing Whakapapa*, Auckland, Penguin Books, 1994, p. 23.
14 Stead, *Answering to the Language*, p. 160. Stead cites a remark made by Otteline Morrell in *Dear Lady Ginger: An Exchange of Letters between Lady Otteline Morrell and D'Arcy Cresswell*, ed. Helen Shaw, Auckland University Press, 1983, p. 120.
15 ibid, p. 160.
16 C. K. Stead (ed.), *The Letters and Journals of Katherine Mansfield: A Selection*, London, Allen Lane, 1977. Published simultaneously in paper-back by Penguin Books, p. 173.
17 Margo White, "Mr Congeniality", *Metro*, August 2005, p. 60.
18 Stead ed., *The Letters and Journals of Katherine Mansfield*, p. 16.
19 Manguel, *The Spectator*, 5 June 2004, p. 44.
20 White, "Interview: Karl Stead", *Metro*, May 2004, p. 103.
21 Stead ed., *The Letters and Journals of Katherine Mansfield*, p. 73.
22 ibid, p. 62.
23 Stead, *Mansfield*. An example of words transferred to the novel from Mansfield's Journal: "She reads what she has written in her notebook, and goes on, 'Oh, I want for one moment to make our undiscovered country leap into the eyes of the old world.' " (p. 103) Several more lines from the journal follow, in which she promises to recall every detail as a "sacred debt" to Leslie.
24 Stead ed., *The Letters and Journals of Katherine Mansfield*, p. 22.
25 ibid, p. 51.
26 ibid, p. 52.
27 Ali Smith, "Pioneer and Tangi", *Times Literary Supplement*, 4 June 2004, p. 22.
28 Smith, *Times Literary Supplement*, p. 22. Smith's word "insists" may be an overstatement. Stead simply attributes the belief to his Katherine, a reflection of the belief held by Mansfield.
29 Williams, "Stead's Mansfield", *Landfall*, Spring 2004, p. 199.
30 Mansfield's story, "The Doll's House", indicates her disillusionment by 1921, at age 32, when it was written. In focus is just one doll that can be identified as a puppet-like wife and mother, despite the occupants of the dolls' house being parents and two children.
31 Stead, *Answering to the Language*, p. 151.
32 White, "Interview: Karl Stead", *Metro*, May 2004, p. 103.
33 Williams, "Stead's Mansfield", *Landfall*, Spring 2004, p. 198.
34 ibid, p. 199.
35 Stead, *Answering to the Language: Essays on Modern Writers*, p. 168.
36 C. K. Stead, letter to Curnow, 18 August 2001, Turnbull Library Papers.
37 C. K. Stead, "Applause", *Dog*, University of Auckland Press, 2002, pp. 21-2.
38 Andrew Bennett, *Speeches Delivered in Commendation of Honorary Graduates*, University of Bristol, 9-13 July 2001, p. 27.
39 C. K. Stead, letter to Curnow, 7 May 2001, Turnbull Library Papers.
40 Stead, "Notes", *Dog*, p. 65.
41 Stead, "The Puzzle", *Dog*, p. 17.

CHAPTER FOURTEEN

In the Limelight

The Launch of *My Name Was Judas*

While writing *Plume Of Bees*, I arranged a detour from Germany to London to attend the launch of *My Name Was Judas*. I had been lecturing and meeting with students of English researching New Zealand literature at German universities. Having never before been to the launch of any of Stead's books, let alone a launch in London, I was keen to experience at first-hand a small part of his literary history.

An affable, relaxed Karl Stead appeared on the sixteenth floor, the penthouse of New Zealand House. According to his custom as host, High Commissioner Jonathan Hunt greeted arriving guests individually. New Zealand wines and delicacies – mussels, bite-sized pieces of tender lamb and kumara – were provided by the publisher Harvill Secker. It was a dignified evening event, sparkling with conversation as seventy people mingled, imbibed and admired patterns of lights, viewed from windows facing south, east and west.

In his address the High Commissioner welcomed members of the Stead family (Kay and Karl, daughter Margaret and her husband Guy Clayton), conveyed the best wishes of New Zealand's Prime Minister Helen Clark, paid tribute to Stead's distinguished career as a novelist and poet, and acknowledged him as a fellow Aucklander. Geoff Mulligan spoke for Harvill Secker, praising the immensely readable new novel, which convincingly recreates the ancient world. Stead was the third speaker, casually smart in an open-necked mid-grey shirt and suit of deeper grey. He explained a reluctance to address Jonathan Hunt as Your Excellency. "He used to be a student of mine, you see." The High Commissioner had been in one of Stead's tutorial groups at Auckland University in 1960.

The novelist shared with an attentive gathering the story of his new novel's inception. It was the difficulty of creating D. H. Lawrence as a character in *Mansfield* that led to the idea of writing about Judas and Jesus. In discussing with Kay his problem in characterising the messianic Lawrence, he remarked that it would be rather like depicting Jesus of Nazareth. To his astonishment, the notion of a novel with Jesus as a character wouldn't leave him. He discussed his preoccupation with Paul Morris, Jewish Professor of Religious Studies at Victoria University, whose reply spurred him to begin writing: "These are our stories. They must be constantly retold." Stead began researching the life and times of Jesus and Judas, knowing that Jesus would need to be observed by someone who knew him well. Judas seemed ideal. Since nothing of the boyhood of either is indicated in the Gospels, a boyhood friendship could underpin their adult relationship. Stead spoke of writing swiftly and surely, submitting a section as part of his application for the Michael King Award, then continuing to write until the book was finished. A draft was sent to the Religious Studies Department at Victoria University to ensure the accuracy of fundamental facts.

Since arriving in London, Stead had been in demand, he said, for a series of newspaper interviews and for radio interviews with the BBC. A Christian radio station wanted to speak to him a second time, though he had not expected his novel to be of special interest to Christians. No copies of the book were on sale at the launch. Neither were they available in a Christian bookshop I came upon the following day, but I found a handsome hard-backed copy at Blackwells. Though the first-person narrator is Judas, it was Stead's voice I could hear as I read – the clear, light voice that had presented part of Chapter Four so effectively at the launch.

The Debater

It was Stead himself who remarked, "I suppose you could say Judas (of the novel) is the type of person I am, and Jesus is the kind of Messianic character, very different from myself."[1] Stead enjoys teasing and misleading readers into drawing parallels between himself and his characters. Back in 2001, Professor Andrew Bennett noted in Stead's writing the recurrence of "a Stead-like figure as its focus and protagonist".[2] Judas is another such figure. The lean appearance of Stead's Judas provides an obvious, though superficial, likeness to Stead. Giotto's fresco "The Kiss of Judas" shows a round-faced man, who, one imagines, would be rotund under his cloak, whereas Stead's Judas is told he is too thin. "It doesn't look right. You have nothing spare to come and go on."[3] The Judas who narrates the novel is a man of seventy. It helped, Stead has remarked, to draw on his own experience: "of course I'm in my 70s now and I suppose you have to be that old to know how it feels."[4] In this work and in his other fiction Stead seems at ease when he enters the persona of characters his own age and with his own physical shape, the same ability to walk easily, a similar relish for good food, without fear of gaining weight.

More importantly, intellectual qualities are shared by Judas and Stead. Scepticism is a feature of Stead's temperament. The betrayal of Jesus by Judas in the novel takes the form of his "refusal to affirm" what he "couldn't believe". (p. 171) It becomes clear that Judas, who does not believe in the divinity of Jesus, is an atheist. Stead's personal view has been somewhat more precisely defined. In an essay, "What I Believe", he has described his intellectual stance as, "subtly, but I think significantly, different from both atheism and agnosticism. The atheist denies God exists; the agnostic doesn't know. For me the word 'God' lacks a referent; lacks objective meaning; and consequently uncertainty about, or denial of, God's 'existence' are equally without meaning."[5]

Judas has a fine memory and considerable linguistic skill. Stead, too, is a man of superior intellect, skilful with words. He has confidence in his own judgement and assessment. Judas plays the debater very effectively, reasoning the miracle of the empty tomb into the realm of political expediency; temple priests, who would not have wanted Jesus honoured through burial in such fine style, would have removed the body. The miracle of the loaves and fishes is reasoned into the realm of exaggeration. Judas subjects the story to cross-examination: "Was the fish served raw? Was there nothing to drink? When the meal was eaten there were supposed to be twelve baskets of leftovers, but where had the baskets come from? Who had brought them and for what purpose?" (p. 143) According to Ptolemy, formerly the disciple Bartholomew, some of the poor among the crowd had brought too little food. It is a crowd of "three or four dozen" – not five thousand – but, Ptolemy maintains, "'numbers don't matter.'" He claims that, if those with plenty will share, there will be sufficient for everyone, as Jesus has demonstrated. When Judas replies, "'That's politics ... Nothing to do with miracles,'" the retort of Ptolemy is clever indeed: "'when you persuade people to share their possessions, that's more than politics. That's a miracle.'" (p. 145)

In his preaching, Judas concentrates on those aspects of Jesus' teaching that he could believe in, avoiding ambiguous parables and explaining himself by saying, "My own preference – a reflection of my own temperament – was for clarity. I liked where possible to be understood." (p. 183) Stead also places a high value on clarity, concluding the Introduction to both *Answering to the Language* and *The Writer at Work* with the very words he assigns to Judas: "I am not interested in arcane dialogue. I would like, where possible, to be understood."[6]

Stead and Judas were introduced to belief in God as young children. For Stead, Bible stories and prayer were features of his Sunday School education. Scepticism in both author and character developed over time, with caution governing their behaviour as boys. Judas's attitude to God, as a young man, shows his conduct still to be governed by religious upbringing and ritual. Later, though, Judas considers that signs offering confirmation of the existence of God have been absent from the time of Jesus' death. Having watched the crucifixion of Jesus and heard his cry, "Lord God in heaven, why have you forsaken me?" (p. 230), Judas claims, "It's how I know there's no God. If there had been one, and He had ordained this end for His faithful son and servant, He would at that moment surely have died of shame." (p. 231) He reasons, "if there is a God ... He's silent and has remained so throughout these forty years when, Jesus assured us, we would see the fiery chariot, the divine wrath, the choosing of the elect, and the end of time." (pp. 211-212) Stead, also, has noted the Almighty's failure to provide a sign of His existence, declaring, after observing the US's contribution to slaughter in Iraq as part of Operation Desert Storm in 1991, "we were privileged to watch the President praying, invoking a God who, if He were listening and still in business, ought to have responded with a thunderbolt or a plague of locusts."[7]

Stead would have felt an affinity with Judas as he developed this character's reasoning and shaped his retorts. Though similar in type to Stead, Judas emerges as a distinct individual, whose friendship with Jesus is understandable and whose place among the disciples is cleverly motivated.

My Name Was Judas and the Auckland Festival

"Once, *My Name Was Judas* would have been a controversial book. Now we can read it as the compelling story of what might have happened to Judas, Jesus and the disciples." This is the view of Tom

Aitken of the *Times Literary Supplement*, who finds the novel "lucid and humane". He admires Stead's "understanding of how stories come into being and how they may be modified under pressure of hindsight. How does a small crowd become 5,000? How does Judas's embrace of a friend in distress become a kiss that will echo down the centuries?"[8]

Stead discussed the novel before a well-disposed audience of several hundred at the Auckland Writers and Readers Festival in May 2007. He acknowledged that some readers disliked the novel, citing a reviewer for a Presbyterian publication who refused to read beyond Chapter 15, though the book has twenty-two chapters. Her appraisal is indignant: "In the Gospels, Mary and Jesus enjoy an ideal mother-son relationship. But here, Stead sets us right; in fact Jesus hated and resented his mother – with no explanation as to why."[9] Stead told his listeners that he replied to the editor, listing every biblical exchange between Mary and Jesus. "When you look at the Bible, there are very few interactions, but all are negative."[10] He based his understanding on the few snippets that exist in the Gospels.

To the festival audience Stead affirmed the importance of the setting in all of his writing. Failure to visit the Holy Land was contrary to his usual practice of experiencing locations at first hand. Nevertheless, one of the remarkable features of his book is the skill with which he creates a sense of time and place. To achieve this, he carefully researched the terrain and vegetation of the Holy Land. The situation was enlarged upon in an interview for the *NZ Herald*:

> "I would have liked to have gone to Israel and visited the sites, but the novel sort of rushed on me and I was writing it so fast. I made inquiries but it was too late really.
>
> But I did read a lot of descriptive and pictorial stuff and I did a lot of hunting and managed to get in a second-hand bookshop *Travels in the Holy Land*, a book of travels in that region in the 19th century. Very little had changed over the centuries..."[11]

Stead's recreation of Israel and Jerusalem is so convincing that *Spectator* reviewer Jane Gardam assumed that he must have "used his recent awards to visit the Holy Land, for the beauty of Galilee, its atmosphere and light, and the looming presence of Jerusalem are some of the best things in the book".[12] Sam Phipps of the *Glasgow Herald* was also impressed with the novel's setting, but his appreciation is more wide-ranging:

> Among Stead's many achievements is a convincing historical, political and physical backdrop. The landscape, the rival Jewish factions, the complex attitudes to the Roman occupation are all sketched in subtle, absorbing tones. But above all, this is an exploration of the power of language. And his creation of a coherent, rival story – clever, moving and sometimes witty, with fully human characters – is nothing short of a revelation.[13]

According to Stead's own judgement, the novel's approach to the Gospels and the Christian message is "respectful on the whole". He told the Festival assembly that Dean Randerson of the Anglican Church made reference to the book in one of his sermons and provided Stead with the text of it. The Dean made it clear that Stead had erred, "… though I thought *he* did, factually," Stead added, raising a laugh.

Also shared with the audience was Stead's delight at the timing of other publications featuring Judas. He had finished writing the novel before the release of an English translation of the *Gospel According to Judas*, discovered in the 1970s. Stead considered this a bonus and believed it brought the story of Judas to public attention. The Gospel suggests that Jesus foresaw and sanctioned his own betrayal; furthermore, Judas did not commit suicide and he did not regard Jesus as the long-awaited Messiah. Another bonus for Stead came in the form of a book that appeared four months after the publication of Stead's novel. Supposedly narrated by Benjamin Iscariot, the son of Judas, it was written by Jeffrey Archer in collaboration with one of the world's leading biblical scholars, Francis J. Moloney. Based on the information revealed in the newly translated Gospel, Archer's book was, Stead told his listeners, "great for publicity. I got a lot of extra publicity from this lucky accident."

Judas the Sceptic

Stead explained to the festival listeners that he "wanted something that would take the novel beyond the prosaic, the literal and the mundane – but without taking it into the supernatural. Poetry is my 'beyond'." Judas is the composer of crisp verses that conclude each chapter, giving pithy or wry insight into the key events. One of them suggests that children embrace religious belief through ritual and fear.

> I hear jackals
> barking in the night.
> They take me back
>
> to a childhood
> when every shadow
> wore a shadow
>
> that housed a
> ghost. The desert was
> alive with the dead,
>
> fear ruled the
> roost, commanding prayer
> and penance, and two
>
> small boys shook
> in their beds begging
> God to forgive them
>
> for what they
> were unsure, only knew
> they were guilty. (pp. 24-5)

The thirteen syllables of each verse form a small code – the twelve disciples plus Jesus. Satire is a feature of the poetry. The poem at the end of Chapter 4 begins, "In the beginning/ was the word, the/ sentence, the text"; three verses later it concludes with a clever conceit, saying of Jesus, "He was his own/ first convert, able/ to see himself/ / burning, bathed/ in the white fire of/ the noun and the verb." (p. 48) Each of the twenty-two idiomatic, yet disciplined, poems rewards careful thought.

As for the prose, Judas the narrator employs a crispness that is possible only when effective verbs give pace to the narrative. Often the prose achieves the intensity of poetry: "His voice echoed out over the stony field and seemed to shake the cypress points so that bats flew out in a silent black shower and flickered over our heads." (p. 198) Or, "Ptolemy, kneeling in the dust beside a mule sucking noisily in the water trough, prayed, his voice silent, his lips moving, the soles of his big battered sandals turned, like his blind eyes, upward into the midday light." (p. 85)

My Name Was Judas offers insight into Stead's preoccupations and idiosyncrasies. It is Stead's rational disposition that masterminds Judas's critical investigation into the biblical beliefs and miracles. Stead's Judas observes and questions Jesus. Knowing that a thinker may accept the figurative, rather than the literal, Jesus tries to dispel the incredulity of Judas by encouraging him to view strange or miraculous stories as parables. Among readers of this novel, faith may remain strong for those who choose to accept without doubt the words spoken by Jesus. Others may examine critically old beliefs or find fresh justification for disbelief. A mythical or figurative interpretation provides a further choice. It takes Stead's ironic temperament to keep all the options in view and viable.

"I was forever noticing differences, evaluating, criticising, awarding pluses and minuses. That was my way, my temperament." (p. 113) This is Judas's way and Stead's way, too. Two versions of the death of Judas are well known. Stead, the man of reason, has concluded that, while both could not be correct – one involving suicide by hanging and the other resulting from a fall on to a ploughshare – both could be *in*correct. Hence, Stead provides another option. His Judas is still alive at 70, having changed his name to Idas of Sidon.

Stead's "godless gospel" and *Dog*

Stead's questioning is consistent, whether in poetry, essays or *My Name Was Judas*. Judas finds it impossible to view Jesus as the "Son of God the Creator", though he considers him to be intelligent, charismatic and an outstanding orator. "At the core of the novel is Judas's denial that Jesus was anything more than a great man."[14]

Philip Matthews subtitles his review of *My Name Was Judas* "The godless gospel of C K Stead". Referring to several of Stead's poetic satires, he mentions "Lucifer Dictates his Reply": "Stead as Lucifer mocks God, author of the Bible, within a kind of divine literary spat ('No one ever wrote/ A longer novel/ Or a worse one.')"[15] It is something of a misrepresentation to quote this poem without referring to the one it replies to. In "Letter to the Enemy" a narrator assumes the role of God, speaking of joy taken and care invested in His creation of Auckland and its inhabitants. These are humorous poems that show Stead's delight in adopting and enacting opposite positions.

There is no doubt, though, that Stead's poetry and fiction sustain an impious attitude to God, called Dog by characters Mike Newall and his friend Frano in *Talking About O'Dwyer*. Mike, secretly excited by a classmate's observation that "god was only dog spelt backwards," contemplates even then that "'god' might in fact signify nothing at all". The boys test the consequences of singing "'Dog save our gracious King', or 'Dog defend New Zealand'",[16] but find themselves untouched by divine retribution. The joke, which gives them endless amusement, recurs in the poetry collection *Dog*. In the time of Captain James Cook and George Vancouver, "the Beginning hadn't begun/ and the Word was Dog."[17] "Psalm" addresses Dog, but, since the language has an elevated, biblical ring, the word also alludes surreptitiously to God: "Dog the heavens call him/ whose Bark and Bite alike/ shall be praised forever...".[18] Curnow, who "called himself 'an old man/ who wouldn't say his prayers'", is honoured by a poem that includes tribute to his "Dog", by which he is "towed at last/ /headlong into the westerly".[19] The poem is one of the volume's two elegies to Curnow.

Those poems in *Dog* focused on religion apply a tongue-in-cheek logic to biblical concepts, playing with ideas such as the virgin birth and the nature of Heaven and its location. "Who'd ever been there/ and come back to report? – apart from the One/ and look what happened to Him!" A peevish voice disputes the notion that Jesus is the Son of God: "He was not. I am." In contemporary business jargon, the narrator boasts of "my Father's chain of Mansions".[20] These satirical poems, which subject religious dogma to scrutiny, provoke critical thinking and amusement among readers inclined to question religion.

Interrogation of religious concepts occurs again in *The Black River* (2007). A sceptical response to the Bible is summed up in the narrator's rejection of "the whole fat lie of it/ the hypocrisy/ the honey –".[21] It is not surprising to find in the poem "S-T-R-O-K-E" the proposition that, "god is dying in the desert of the mind/ no god no god".[22] In the third of a sequence called "Four Poems", the concept of eternity is questioned; it is suggested that "we made Him in our image/ it can't be for ever,"[23] with the fourth of the "Four Poems" claiming that "an eternity"[24] needs to be related to something tangible to be understood, like incarceration at Guantanamo Bay. Considered logically, "world without end"[25] seems nightmarish. "Heaven was it/ or hell?"[26] In *My Name Was Judas* Stead's own exasperation is surely echoed by Judas the rational man, who reacts against an emphasis on "talk of what might be waiting for us beyond the grave – empty promises and threats that divert attention from the horror of what men do to one another in the real world." (p. 144)

Stead saves his reverence for the detail and diversity of nature. He takes particular delight in Auckland's weather, shorelines, seascapes and foliage. Colours, sounds and textures are defined and savoured.

> On the bank, flax spears
> convert to flowers
> and the jet-feathered
> tangata whenua
> (white wobble at throat)
> beaks into them.[27]

The sun assumes the attribute of a deity "walking on water" in a life that "goes/ godlessly on",[28] reiterating a thought from an earlier poem, "Good Morning", which shows the sun, "the oldest of the gods/ alight in the mangroves". The poem advises, "enjoy his hands on your face."[29] Elsewhere a biblical text, Isaiah 40:8 – "The grass withers, the flower fades; but the word of our God stands forever" – is transformed into secular appreciation of the power of the word:

> The grass withers
> the flower falls
> but the lordship of the word
> is for ever.[30]

Note: For an account of the launch of *My Name Was Judas* according to Stead's journal entry, see C. K. Stead, *Book Self*, Auckland University Press, 2008, pp. 339-341.

1 Belinda McCammon, "New Zealand Author Prepared for Trouble Over Judas Book", *Wairarapa Times*, 13 October 2006, p. 7.

2 Andrew Bennett, from an address to 'Mr Vice-Chancellor' at the conferring of the degree Doctor of Letters on Professor Karl Stead, 12 July 2001. *Speeches Delivered in Commendation of Honorary Graduates*, University of Bristol, 9-13 July 2001, p. 26.

3 C. K. Stead, *My Name Was Judas*, London, Harvill Secker Press, 2006, p. 74. Page numbers in brackets in this chapter refer to this edition.

4 McCammon, *Wairarapa Times*, 13 October 2006, p. 7.
5 C. K. Stead, *The Writer at Work: Essays*, Dunedin, University of Otago Press, p. 200.
6 Stead, *The Writer at Work*, p. 13.
7 ibid, p. 204.
8 Tom Aitken, "The Boyhood of Jesus", *Times Literary Supplement*, 1 December 2006, p. 23.
9 Juliette Bowater, *SPANZ*, "Book Review", Issue 30, March 2007, p. 14.
10 C. K. Stead. This is the first of several statements that are quoted directly from Stead's address at the Auckland Writers and Readers Festival, 24 May 2007.
11 Linda Herrick, "Judas, A Man of Reason", *NZ Herald*, 7 October 2006, p. 30.
12 Jane Gardam, "The Uninteresting Survivor", *The Spectator*, 25 November 2006.
13 Sam Phipps, "First Editions: *My Name was Judas* by C K Stead", *Glasgow Herald*, 18 November 2006.
14 McCammon, *Wairarapa Times*, 13 October 2006, p. 7.
15 Philip Matthews, "Stead and the Heretics: The Godless Gospel of C K Stead", *New Zealand Listener*, 21 October 2006, p. 43.
16 C. K. Stead, *Talking About O'Dwyer*, Auckland, Penguin Books, 1999, p. 55 and p. 56.
17 C. K. Stead, "In Principio", *Dog*, University of Auckland Press, 2002, p. 6.
18 Stead, "Psalm", *Dog*, p. 20.
19 Stead, "His Round", *Dog*, p. 27.
20 Stead, "Creation etc", *Dog*, p. 31 and p. 33.
21 C. K. Stead, "Embarrassment", *The Black River*, Auckland University Press, 2007, p. 42.
22 Stead, "S-T-R-O-K-E", *The Black River*, p. 70.
23 Stead, "Four Poems: 3", *The Black River*, p. 13.
24 Stead, "Four Poems: 4", *The Black River*, p. 14.
25 Stead, "Theology", *The Black River*, p. 35.
26 ibid, p. 34.
27 C. K. Stead, "The Season, Tohunga Crescent", *The Red Tram*, Auckland University Press, 2004, p. 6.
28 Stead, "Auckland", *The Black River*, pp. 4 and 5.
29 C. K. Stead, "Good Morning", *The Right Thing*, Auckland University Press, 2000, p. 2.
30 Stead, "Horae Secularae: *Vespers* (London)", *The Red Tram*, p. 46.

CHAPTER FIFTEEN

The Black River Poet and the Stead Phenomenon

The Years of *The Red Tram* and *The Black River*

Words are what Stead held fast to after a stroke in May 2005. In a small notebook he recorded words, thoughts and impressions even though he was unable to read: "it was like writing in the dark."[1] After his recovery the fragments were shaped into a long poem, from which the following is a sample:

> words have given me access
> to the inside
> of the inside
> of the mind
>
> whose mind?
> mine
>
> the mine of the mind[2]

The poem "S-T-R-O-K-E", dated May-June 2005, forms the second of two sections comprising *The Black River*. Poems for section "*One*" were written later, between July 2005 and September 2006. Mortality is a central theme, with the title's "Black River" an allusion to the River Styx that flows between the realms of the living and the dead.

In "S-T-R-O-K-E", the hospital has a presence and Stead's medical condition is described: "the little river/ in the dark interior/ blocked or broke –".[3] The word "JUMP" recurs, recalling the sport of his youth that required for success the discipline of Zen. After the stroke, his mind demands concentration, memory and focus, asserting itself, refusing to be suppressed. "JUMP" also signals a pause, a leap to the next verse, a new start. It becomes the poem's concluding word.

Immediately after the stroke Stead's visual perception was affected so that the ocean seemed vertical, rather than horizontal. This condition and his inability to read were temporary setbacks, however. His writing, walking, swimming and travelling abroad have since been resumed with undiminished vigour.

The theme of death, central to *The Black River*, features also in the previous poetry volume, *The Red Tram*. "Africa: An Autobiography" conflates, with abundant poetic licence, the narrator's life story as he moves from childhood to boyhood (aware as he looked at the harbour from a hilltop of the need to travel) to adulthood to "Love" (which "is no end of trouble") to children and then to "Death", which carries a bag "marked 'Africa'".[4] This continent lies to the west. The poem's journey through life to death echoes, in summary, a theme from "Walking Westward".

Three poems celebrate Karekare, each concerned with death: the sale of a dead man's bach; the "death wish"[5] of fresh-water streams that plunge to the ocean; and the death of twelve whales cast up on the shore. Poems recall Allen Curnow, and there is an elegy to Janet Frame. "Letter from the Mountains" is dedicated "to Lt. Col. John Mulgan, 1911-1945". The emphasis on death gives point to the final line of "Rapallo: An Economy": "Live as well as you can."[6]

Not all the poems are serious; *The Red Tram* includes several that are satirical and amusing. "The Tree: A Story" dramatises, in mock-heroic manner, a dispute between neighbours: "Every time he looks at my tree, a branch turns red/ and sheds more leaves." "The Writer", "The Neighbour", "The Cat", "The Police Officer", "The Thrush" and "The Judge" all provide a different account of alleged tree poisoning and a scuffle. Although "found not guilty"[7] of assaulting his neighbour, the Writer appears in a questionable light, remembered by the police for having "given us no end of trouble in '81";[8] he is also the target of the cat's indignation and scorn. Other comical sections in the volume are less successful. Terry Locke remarks that a small poem in a sequence called "Sentry Duty" "would have a place in an old-style capping magazine".[9]

Unlike *The Red Tram*, *The Black River* includes nothing flippant. None of its poems could be dismissed as "negligible squibs",[10] Mark Houlahan's description of some minor pieces from *The Red Tram*.

Humour in *The Black River* poem "C.K."[11] is self-ironical in a volume that is serious in tone and profound in its implications. The poetry shows a clarity and economy of expression that makes for direct communication. For example, the poet imagines speaking to the ferryman at the wharf on the River Styx, where he hears of his mother's much earlier crossing. Though "reluctant to go", she "stood in the prow/ no tears/ and never looked back".[12] As in *The Red Tram*, several poems in *The Black River* speak of or to those who have died. Most tender is a poem that honours Stead's sister Norma, who died of multiple sclerosis.

> Small boys avoid big sisters but mine in age
> against all the odds in that battle with her
>   body proved that grace could win.[13]

The poet sometimes addresses himself, with "Into Extra Time" looking ahead to his own death, but finding that words are still working in his head, keeping him awake and alive. "Black River Blues" considers his life as a poet after his death:

> Will you sing when you're gone away
> down to the end of the ever
> to row on the black river
>
> – will you? [14]

Stead regards poetry as "a reflection of your temperament, your very self, set free in language".[15] Poetry has conveyed different aspects of his protean temperament at different stages of his life. Written after the shock of the stroke, *The Black River* bespeaks the condition of a man in his seventies with matters of importance on his mind. The collection shows, in three "Art of Poetry" pieces, that a Stead poem is composed of words that embody clear images.

>   'My
> theory', I say
>
> 'is the warblers
> working, the stilts up

on their stilts, the

'world looking hard
at the word and the
word at the world.'[16]

The principle is reiterated in "S-T-R-O-K-E": "the rose/ should not mean/ but be/ /the rain also".[17] *The Black River* earned the following comment from Nelson Wattie: "This book marks a climax in the growth of clarity and openness (of voice) in Stead's work. He has achieved a spare, diamantine style..."[18]

Rapallo Uzès London Oxford

Other important themes in *The Black River* are related to history and memory. Stead's long poem "History" brings together tragic and poignant moments from Italy's past, opening with reflections from playwright and novelist Pirandello and poet Ungaretti, and moving through a series of moments, settings or events between 1940 and 1948. Stead creates his historical pattern by including attacks during World War II, memories of Italian deaths, and details from Ezra Pound's life. The poem then leaps ahead to 2004, with Stead and his friend Massimo Bacgialupo at anchor off Rapallo in the yacht "*Vagabonde III*/ indifferent that once/ Ezra sailed in her". The poet seems to be busy writing above a "greenly transparent"[19] sea, in an atmosphere of calmness and ease that forms a sharp contrast to the poem's suffering and fraught politics.

Rapallo and the neighbourhood of Uzès are two of Stead's favourite destinations in Continental Europe. He has spent up to eight weeks in one or both places every year during the past dozen years. The countryside near Uzès in the Rhône Valley, not far from the Mediterranean coast, is home to Stead's friend Tony Axelrad, who translated *The Death of the Body* into French. The Steads and Axelrads have holidayed together, or, alternatively, Tony Axelrad has fulfilled assignments elsewhere in Europe, at the Hague, for example, leaving the Steads in charge of his family's property three kilometres from the town of Uzès. In the nearby village of St Maximin, the Axelrads bought another home to which the Steads were welcomed from 2004. "Versions of Two Poems by Victor Hugo" from *The Black River* have as dedication, "for Tony Axelrad". Both are sensitive pieces, the first involving a journey to a grave and the second anticipating death.

> But what a black hole that dark sapphire has become!
> How can I now, so late, learn to distinguish
> Night itself from the blue-robed angel of death?[20]

During the European summer of 2006 Stead attended the New Zealand Studies Association conference in Paris in June, at which he was the opening keynote speaker, his topic, "The Sweetshop Window: One New Zealand Writer's Engagement with French Language and Literature". In November the Steads flew to London for the launch of *My Name Was Judas*, and, in 2007, C. K. flew from Auckland to Zagreb to attend the launch of the book translated into Croatian. Colombia was his mid-year destination. Later in the year the two Steads flew to Italy, so that the author could take up a Bogliasco Fellowship in Genoa for up to forty-eight days, a residency that allowed him to focus on completing *Book Self*, a collection of critical essays, reminiscences, personal interviews and journal entries.

Between the overseas trips were visits to New Zealand destinations, Dunedin, for example, where he gave the Michael King/Hocken lecture in October 2007: "Fifty Years Ago: Some Images of the Young Poet and his Elders, Brasch, Curnow, Sargeson". The number of journeys and engagements in eighteen months testifies to the stamina of C. K. Stead.

London is a regular European destination for both Steads, home to daughter Margaret, a son-in-law and two grandchildren. The poem "ii. Bella" speaks of Stead's youngest grandchild:

> Isabella
> is a-born
> in London.[21]

Arrival back in Auckland returns the couple to the home of Oliver, father of two, and Charlotte, mother of three of the Stead grandchildren.

London, today a place where Stead meets family, friends, colleagues and publishers, was once associated with a sense of loss. He felt torn away from the city in 1959, returning to New Zealand after spending less than the time required to complete his PhD, less, in fact, than the two-year entitlement of the Michael Hiatt Baker Scholarship and without a time extension that could have been arranged. To his considerable satisfaction, a Nuffield Fellowship took him back to London in 1965. The greater parts of 1972 and 1977 were spent in Europe, but it was not until the 1979-81 Senior Research Fellowship that trips abroad could begin and end according to his own inclinations. "Already, during those three years on the research fellowship, a pattern had been established of nine or ten months of the year at a desk in Auckland and two – occasionally three (and once six) – abroad in England and Europe and sometimes North America."[22] The writer could view New Zealand with a clarity provided by distance and contrast, and observe other countries with the innocent eye of a man from elsewhere.

Oxford, *The Black River* discloses, remains for Stead an unfulfilled dream.

> but in youth
> how tempting
> if a door had opened
> a word been said
> to step inside a moment
> and wake middle-aged
> drowning in honey.[23]

Had he been tempted, invited to enter Oxford in his youth, he might have become a comfortable middle-aged don at the centre of his academic world. The image, "drowning in honey", is one of luxuriance and gradual stultification. Implicit in the image is an absence of the tension and irritation that provoked and stimulated Stead to become an acclaimed writer and critic, triumphing as an international man of letters while living in the remotest corner of the Western world.

The Phenomenon

Tension and irritation in New Zealand have followed from Stead's forthright literary and social criticism. In reviewing several possible explanations for the author's extraordinary unpopularity in 1990, Stephen Stratford, in a *Metro* article, examined the apparent reluctance on Stead's part to praise writers of his own generation – finding fault with the work of Shadbolt and Edmond and publishing little or nothing about O'Sullivan, Gee, Campbell or Ireland. Stead protested that he had never sought to be comprehensive, nor could this be considered his responsibility. Furthermore, Stratford's proposition that Stead may have attempted to promote himself by ignoring some writers and exposing the shortcomings of others[24] is less than convincing. Had this been his intention, he would also have noted the risk to himself when calling into question the quality of writing by fellow New Zealanders. That he would have given any consideration to such matters is unlikely.

Stead's international reputation as a literary critic has led him to pay scant attention to the judgment of his compatriots. Who else in New Zealand could claim authorship of a critical text as successful as *The New Poetic*, praised by L. C. Knights and Seamus Heaney, and continuously in print since 1964? Stead could disregard petulant New Zealand opinions of *In the Glass Case* and *Pound, Yeats, Eliot and the Modernist Movement*, when both texts were acclaimed by British academics.[25] He developed abiding confidence in his own critical judgment. As a celebrated critic with the prestige of a university professor, he has included negative comments in reviewing work by Hulme, Ihimaera, Fairburn and Edmond. His stated intention has been to encourage New Zealanders to appraise more stringently "the words on the page"[26] – to lift standards of writing and criticism in this country. Here, the best of Stead's literary criticism is unsurpassed. His exemplary standard, however, has been marred at times by loss of patience and by a blunt honesty that has impacted as condescension.

For Stead, honesty has always been paramount. There is an example in *My Name Was Judas* in which Judas cannot refrain from replying truthfully to a question posed by Jesus, although he reflects, "I knew even as I spoke that silence would have been better".[27] Stead's inclination has always been to speak out. In acknowledging Stead's staunch belief that "if you think something is true you should say so," Stratford remarks, "His saying so has been little tempered by tact or even an awareness of the possibility of causing offence." The journalist has noted the author's failure "to consider how what one may wish to say will be received".[28]

In an interview with Dennis McEldowney, Stead was prepared to concede that controversy "can't be totally unconnected with me; it must come partly from my temperament."[29] Having thought of clever quips, he likes to share them. Some appear in his poetry, the line about the poet Healy, for instance: "When the Dimple's gone he goes –".[30] Others appear in personal correspondence, like the remark to Allen Curnow that "Alan Loney wasn't the Black Mountain he was the Black Molehill."[31]

Stead believes his remarks to be mild-mannered and reaction to them excessive. Stratford has noted the author's surprise "when people express hurt at what he considers reasonable judgments – indicating a degree of naïvety astonishing in such a formidably intelligent man".[32] The observation calls to mind an episode from *My Name Was Judas* in which Judas as a boy provokes rage and hurt in Jesus by relating an item of gossip: his father may have been a Roman soldier named Panthera. Judas was quite unprepared for the impassioned reaction of Jesus.

> I'm not sure how I came to think Jesus wouldn't be upset if I repeated this story. Perhaps I thought that if I brought it up casually, as if it was nothing special, it would seem I believed it couldn't be true. Or (more likely) it was just carelessness, the lack of forethought, of a child.[33]

The experience of Judas – provoking an unexpected degree of wrath in response to words spoken casually or mildly – has been encountered by Stead on many occasions. The reaction has been made visible with the image of a plume of bees: "You had trailed a plume of demons over the land." The encounter with the bees has become, within the context of his life, "a mythic story".[34] Knowing how one's words will affect readers or listeners is one aspect of sensibility. It is not always or inevitably possible, however, to predict how others will react, any more than the existence or behaviour of the swarm of bees could have been foreseen.

Critical commentary and analysis were an important part of Stead's academic role. Sargeson, in 1959, foresaw that Stead's university career would be in conflict with his career as an author of poetry and fiction; he imagined the university would sap a good deal of Stead's creative energy. And it did. It must be conceded, though, that Stead's pursuit of excellence would have inclined him toward literary criticism even without his university position. In combining the talents of poet and critic, he was following a tradition: "The greatest critics in English were, all of them, poets – Sir Philip Sidney, Dr Johnson, Wordsworth ... Coleridge, Matthew Arnold, T. S. Eliot".[35] From the outset Stead has sought a place in the unfolding story of New Zealand's literature, not only as a writer of prose and poetry but also as a shaper and sharpener of the nation's aesthetic awareness.

"A very antic quality"[36]

Stead has used his wit and critical judgment to play the maverick, provocateur, protester, aesthete and entertainer. A feature of his temperament, vital to the novelist, is an ability to adopt different rolcs. Charlotte speaking of his "antic quality" was referring to his talent for role-play, as well as his capacity for fun and verbal jokes.

Adopting a role generally involves choice, but Stead, in 2000, found that a "new identity as an apostate"[37] had emerged with the subversion of his left-wing liberal reputation. He reflects in *Book Self*, 2008, on his lack of personal caution, recalling some fine counsel from James Joyce – "Silence, exile and cunning". Stead comments, "I thought, and still think, it's the perfect formula for writerly self-protection, although I have myself failed on all three fronts."[38] He has never been inclined to use cunning and has been far from silent. Exile, for him, has been limited to a few months of escape from New Zealand's "repressive intellectual climate"[39] in each of the past thirty or so years.

In Europe, Stead is at ease and very much at home in the midst of the literary community there, as his journal entries in *Book Self* reveal: "I get more satisfactory reviews in England than I do here ... Over here reactions to my fiction get mixed up with reactions to me and to my role outside fiction."[40] He has found "publishing outside New Zealand ... a kind of protection. I never feel safe on the New Zealand literary scene."[41] Usually published simultaneously in Britain and New Zealand, Stead's work is available in other English-speaking countries and has been translated into many languages. *My Name Was Judas* has already appeared in Croatian, French, Hungarian, Polish, Portuguese, Romanian and Spanish.

Justin Clemens, University of Melbourne, who reviewed *Collected Poems 1951-2006*, provides testimony that Stead's work receives generous attention in Australia.

> If Stead is prepared to sink his fangs into almost anything – Sappho and Catullus, childhood memories, inadmissible desires, personal terrors, national bloodshed – and suck out their vital essence to deposit as black letters in the vials of his book, he also ruminates on the fact that every great book is a tomb. If it is, it is one he will inhabit for some time to come, surviving life by means of his poetic powers.[42]

This comment, paying particular attention to Stead's legacy as a poet, invites a contrast with W. B. Yeats who contemplated his own legacy at the age of sixty and was surprised, on re-reading his work, "at what he saw as the revelation of his own bitterness".[43] If one looks for bitterness in Stead's writing during the years of public opprobrium, it is nowhere to be found. His reaction has been to out-debate his detractors and to make a good many hard-hitting points, flinging taunts like the following: "Unlike our present editors, Curnow was never embarrassed by the notion of excellence, or by the fact that talent is undemocratically distributed."[44]

When Kay Stead was asked by journalist Michele Hewitson to comment on her husband's temperament, she said,

> "Most people go along on a more ordinary plane, you see, and one reason why he has trouble is that the literary community operates at a much lower level than he does, so there's a million reasons for him to bridle."
> And, "Of course, he's hyper-sensitive himself. He whacks back really hard and often he's right ... but he does whack hard." [45]

Stead's rejoinders and provocative remarks, however, form just one facet of his character. The poetry Stead has written is of far greater significance in disclosing his complex personality – its depth and diversity. Dougal McNeill, reviewing Stead's *Collected Poems: 1951-2006*, observes that "it is in the poetry as it gathers, that one senses the centre of his intellectual commitments and ambitions for language, and it is here where the richest readerly experiences are to be found".[46] McNeill addresses directly the matter of Stead's personality, as he casts eye and mind over the poetic achievement of five and half decades:

> Where does this leave the famed "presence of a particular person, a personality" that Stead demands from literary criticism, and that some readers are supposed to dislike in his work? There's plenty of personality here, in these poems that sometimes toy with the idea they might be "models" of their author or acts of self-creation ("I sentence myself"). ... The discipline of verse-work, the unruliness of inspiration, means that there's more Karl than C. K.[47] – to use the division one of

> the poems themselves suggests – in these pages than in those of Stead as a critic, and certainly less of the thrawn, pugilistic stance that makes *Book Self* such an odd collection.[48]

The collected poems are infinitely richer in yielding clues to the essence of the man and writer than his critical commentaries or defensive repartee.

Book Self shows Stead, the unrepentant critic, still "presenting a counterblast to slovenly contemporary arguments."[49] His thinking, the stance he has taken in the past five decades, has not changed, but attitudes toward him seem to include a greater measure of tolerance and good humour. Nelson Wattie's review acknowledges Stead's "absence of popularity in certain quarters", but shows appreciation of a book that "is entertaining, sometimes illuminating, but also uneven"; it has, at its centre, "a series of brilliant essays".[50] Even more enthusiastic is Iain Sharp who finds the collection "always lively and engaging", its ideas articulated with "outstanding lucidity". Stead's stance, as described by Sharp, seems more than reasonable: "battles have arisen because he won't stand for literature being judged by criteria other than excellence, such as race, gender, political affiliation or social standing."[51]

In the year 2007 Stead's address at the Auckland Festival, according to the local *NZ Herald*, was judged a highlight. That year he received a more tangible honour from his own city when he was made a Distinguished Citizen of Auckland. Recognition was further enhanced in 2008; he was presented with one of the University of Auckland's Distinguished Alumni Awards. Stead has also attracted appreciative audiences in other parts of the country in recent years. During Wellington's Writers and Readers Week, March 2008, Stead featured on two occasions, once joining Ian McEwan and Uwe Timm to address the theme, "Don't Mention the War", an hour that concluded with Stead's reading of three short poems from his sequence "Crete". The previous day he was the speaker in a session chaired by Elizabeth Alley. Her introductory remarks indicated approval for Stead's challenging ways:

> Karl Stead has entered into a good many debates over the years and thank goodness he has. He doesn't mince words and his opinions are frank and reinforced by his authoritative knowledge gained in his many years of experience on the

> battlefield of literature. We don't always like what he says but most of us would greatly respect his point of view.[52]

When he takes the stage these days, Stead shows skill in self-deprecation. He entertained his Maidment Theatre audience in Auckland by detailing the paradoxical success and failure of *The Secret History of Modernism*, a novel that "sank without trace" at home. The Distinguished Alumnus chose to share extracts from reviews that had not appeared in New Zealand, reading one extravagant quotation after another from papers and periodicals before pausing mid-way to say, "Only a few more!" Then followed words of even higher commendation. In a country where modesty is revered, the catalogue was outrageously amusing, especially when capped by the remark, "I'd never written a better book to worse effect."[53]

Also in March 2008, Stead was asked by Kathryn Ryan on Radio New Zealand's "Nine to Noon" just how well New Zealanders apply criticism to social issues. He said there was fear of open debate here. A fire alarm interrupted the interview, allowing Stead to adopt the self-ironic pose his listeners have come to enjoy. "I've got into a lot of trouble because I tend to be very frank and undiplomatic so it doesn't surprise me when the studio goes on fire! I think, here we go again. You can't trust this guy!"[54]

Being frank and undiplomatic in New Zealand has not affected Stead's standing in Britain. There he is applauded for the intellectual rigour of his literary criticism, and for his talent as poet and novelist; the Stead 'phenomenon' signifies extraordinary achievement, rather than a reputation that extends between negative and positive extremes. British critic and biographer Roger Lewis, in reviewing Stead's latest novel, awards it five stars and writes of "the brilliance and plausibility of C. K. Stead ... who, on the basis of *My Name Was Judas,* must surely be a prime candidate for the Nobel Prize".[55]

New Zealanders are coming to appreciate C. K. Stead's idiosyncrasies and to relish his divergent views. As old differences are forgotten or lose their sting, he wins increasing respect, respect as an uncompromising critic, a consummate novelist and a poet who makes language his own musical instrument.

1 C. K. Stead, *The Black River*, Auckland University Press, 2007, p. 68.

2 Stead, "S-T-R-O-K-E", *The Black River*, p. 69.
3 ibid, p. 73.
4 C. K. Stead, "Africa: An Autobiography", *The Red Tram*, Auckland University Press, 2004, p. 41.
5 Stead, "Karekare", *The Red Tram*, p. 50.
6 Stead, "Rapallo: An Economy", *The Red Tram*, p. 69.
7 Stead, "The Tree: A Story", *The Red Tram*, p. 11. In *The Singing Whakapapa*, pp. 235-6, District Court Judge Harriet Enverson describes a similar situation, in which a man, whose position corresponds to that of the Writer, is defended in court by his two daughters, both lawyers.
8 ibid, p. 12.
9 Terry Locke, "Review: The Red Tram", *English in Aotearoa 58*, April 2006, p. 73.
10 Mark Houlahan, "All Aboard, Including Ovid", *Dominion Post*, 4 December 2004, p. E 10.
11 The poem "C. K." is discussed in the Introduction, pp. 8–9
12 Stead, "Elegy (24.1.06)", *The Black River*, p. 19.
13 Stead, "My Sister and M.S.", *The Black River*, p. 60.
14 Stead, "Black River Blues", *The Black River*, p. 36.
15 Michael Harlow, "Craft Interview with C. K. Stead", *Landfall*, December 1983, p. 454.
16 Stead, "The Art of Poetry (i)", *The Black River*, p. 3.
17 Stead, "S-T-R-O-K-E", *The Black River*, p. 70.
18 Nelson Wattie, "The Old Guard", *The Dominion Post*, 28 April 2007, p. 18.
19 Stead, "History", *The Black River*, p. 58.
20 Stead, "Versions of Two Poems by Victor Hugo (for Tony Axelrad)", *The Black River*, p. 61.
21 Stead, "S//CRAPBOOK", *The Black River*, p. 22.
22 C. K. Stead, *The Writer at Work: Essays*, Dunedin, University of Otago Press, 2000, p. 10.
23 Stead, "Oxford", *The Black River*, p. 6.
24 Stephen Stratford, "Blaspheming Against the Pieties: Why the Literati Hate C. K. Stead", *Metro*, April 1990, pp. 74 and 76.
25 Part of K. K. Ruthven's critique of *Pound, Yeats, Eliot and the Modernist Movement* appears in the Introduction, p. 10, *Plume of Bees*, and part of Dan Davin's critique of *In the Glass Case* appears in Chapter 6, p. 99 in this text.
26 C. K. Stead, *Kin of Place: Essays on 20 New Zealand Writers,* Auckland University Press, 2002, p. 300. Referring to the support Lauris Edmond had received from Roger Robinson, Stead concludes his essay with the words, "Enough of this clubby stuff! It is time to look hard at the words on the page."
27 C. K. Stead, *My Name Was Judas*, London, Harvill Secker Press, 2006, pp. 173-4.
28 Stratford, "Blaspheming Against the Pieties", *Metro*, April 1990, p. 78.
29 Stead, *The Writer at Work*, p. 243.
30 C. K. Stead, "Sonnet 19", *Walking Westward*, Auckland, The Shed, 1979, p. 28.
31 C. K. Stead, letter to Allen Curnow, 6 January 1981, Turnbull Library Papers.
32 Stratford, "Blaspheming Against the Pieties", *Metro*, April 1990, p. 78.
33 Stead, *My Name Was Judas*, p. 38.
34 C. K. Stead, "Bald Caesarion", *Dog*, Auckland University Press, 2002, p. 48.
35 C. K. Stead, *Book Self*, Auckland University Press, 2008, p. 3.
36 Charlotte Grimshaw, interviewed by Deborah Coddington, *North & South*, July 1999, p. 28.

37 Stead, *The Writer at Work*, p. 13.
38 Stead, *Book Self*, p. 112.
39 C. K. Stead, interview with the author, 29 August 2005.
40 Camille Guy, "A War of Words", *NZ Herald* 2, Dec 14, 1989, p. 8.
41 Stead, *The Writer at Work*, p. 245.
42 Justin Clemens, "Kiwi Poet With His Eye on Here and Beyond", *The Australian*, 20 December 2008.
43 C. K. Stead, *Answering to the Language: Essays on Modern Writers*, Auckland University Press, 1989, p. 29.
44 ibid, p. 135.
45 Hewitson, "Swimming Against the Tide", *Canvas*, 24-25 April 2004, p. 20.
46 Dougal McNeill, "Steadfast: *Collected Poems 1951-2006*", *New Zealand Books*, Autumn 2009, p. 5.
47 Stead, "C. K.", *The Black River*, pp. 63-4. Quoted in full on the first page of this book's "Introduction".
48 McNeill, "Steadfast: *Collected Poems 1951-2006*", *New Zealand Books*, Autumn 2009, p. 5.
49 Iain Sharp, "A Bracing Blast from the Past", *Sunday Star Times*, 30 March 2008, p. C8.
50 Nelson Wattie, "Self Evident", *New Zealand Listener*, 26 April 2008, p. 38.
51 Sharp, *Sunday Star Times*, 30 March 2008, p. C8.
52 Elizabeth Alley, chairing Stead's discussion "It's Not Wishful Thinking", at Writers and Readers Week, Wellington Arts Festival, 14 March 2008.
53 C. K. Stead, "A Writer Reflects", opening address in the Distinguished Alumni Series, chaired by Emeritus Professor Mac Jackson, Auckland, Maidment Theatre, 3 March 2008.
54 C. K. Stead, interviewed by Kathryn Ryan on "Nine To Noon", *Radio New Zealand National*, 7 March 2008.
55 Roger Lewis, "This Judas is More Betrayed Than Betrayer", *Sunday Express*, 24 December 2006.

Bibliography

Publications by C. K. Stead

Note: The University of Auckland's New Zealand Literature File provides a comprehensive list of publications – books, articles, reviews, poems – by C. K. Stead, as well as an extensive list of critial articles on his work: http://www.nzlf.auckland.ac.nz/author/?a_id=151
With such a resource on line, C.K. Stead's BOOK PUBLICATIONS ONLY are indicated here.

Novels

Smith's Dream. Auckland : Longman Paul, 1971.
— Auckland : Longman Paul, 1973. Author's note concerning altered ending.
— Auckland : New House Publishers, 1993.

All Visitors Ashore. London : Harvill, Auckland : Collins, 1984.
— London : Picador, 1986.
— Auckland : Godwit, 1994. (Godwit series no.3).
— London : Harvill Press, 1995.
— *Svi Posjetitelji na Obalu!* Zagreb : Nakladni Zavod Matice Hrvatske, 1997. Croatian translation.
— *All Visitors Ashore.* London : Harvill, 2001. (Harvill Panther). Released in U.K. 2002.

The Death of the Body. London : Collins, 1986.
— *Kroppens dod.* Oversattning, Carin Svensson. Stockholm : T. Fisher, 1990. Swedish translation.
— *The Death of the Body.* London : Harvill, 1991. (Harvill paperback edition.)
— *Je ne suis pas ce corps.* Roman traduit de l'anglais par Anthony Axelrad. Paris : P.O.L., 1993. French translation.
— *A morte do corpo.* Lisboa, Edicoes Asa, 1993. Traduzido do Ingles por Ana Luisa Faria. Portuguese edition.
— *Der Tod des Korpers : Roman.* Aus dem Englischen von Silvia Morawetz. Frankfurt-am-Main : Fischer, 1994. German translation.
— *The Death of the Body.* London : Harvill Press, 1999.

Sister Hollywood. London : Collins, 1989.
— New York : St Martins Press, 1990.
— Anstey, Leicestershire : Ulverscroft, 1991. (Ulverscroft large print edition.)

— London : Harvill ; New York : HarperCollins, 1994.
— Frankfurt-am-Main : Fischer, 1998. German translation.

The End of the Century at the End of the World. London : Collins Harvill, 1992.
— Auckland : Flamingo [an imprint of HarperCollins], 1999.

The Singing Whakapapa. Auckland : Penguin Books, 1994.
— Wordplay Audio Books, 2001. (Print edition, Penguin, 1994). "This Wordplay Audio Book was published jointly by The Library Supply Company Limited and the Royal New Zealand Foundation for the Blind, by arrangement with Penguin Books, C.K. Stead and Graeme Wilson."

Villa Vittoria. Auckland : Penguin Books, 1997.

Talking About O'Dwyer. Auckland : Penguin Books (NZ), 1999.
— London : Harvill, 2000. Slightly amended text.
— London : Harvill, 2002. (Harvill Panther).
— *Makutu.* Prevela Ljiljana Scuric. Zagreb : Meandar, 2001. Croatian translation, 2000.
— *Makutu.* Aus dem Englischen von Silvia Morawetz. Berlin, Zu Klampen!, 2001. German translation, 2000.
— *Makutu ;* prevod Dusanka Zabukovec ; [spremna beseda Igor Maver]. Ljubljana : Cankarjeva zalozba, 2006. (Moderni klasiki ; 31). Slovenian translation of *Talking About O'Dwyer.*

The Secret History of Modernism. London : Harvill, 2001. Paperback edition, released in NZ, 2001.
— London : Harvill, 2001. Hardback edition. [Publication date 2001, but issued in U.K. January 24 2002].
— *The Secret History of Modernism.* London : Vintage. 2004. Paperback edition.

Mansfield : a novel. London : Harvill, 2004.
— Auckland : Vintage (Random House), 2004.
— *Mansfield* : a Novel – a Variation of Love and Friendship. C.K. Stead. Translated by Ginsaku Osawa, Tetsuro Tajima. Tokyo : Bunka Shobo Hakubunsha (Publisher), 2007. Publishing details transliterated from Japanese language. Text in Japanese.
— *Srce Nema Nista s Tim Katherine!* S engleskoga prevela Iva Uszcumlic-Gretic. Zagreb : Edicije Bozicevic, 2007. Croatian language edition of *Mansfield.*

My Name Was Judas. London : Harvill Secker, 2006.
— Auckland : Vintage, 2006.
— *Mon nom etait Judas.* Christian Karlson Stead. Roman traduit de l'anglais par Francoise Fauchet. [Paris] : City Editions (Collection Citadelle), 2007. French language edition of *My Name was Judas.*
— *Zvao Sam Se Juda.* Prevela s engleskog: Ljiljana Scuric. Zagreb : Profil, 2007. Croatian language edition of *My Name was Judas.*
— *Judas volt a Nevem.* Forditotta Bajsz. [Budapest] : Ringier, 2007. Translation into Hungarian of *My Name was Judas.* 247 p.
— *Meu nome era Judas* .Traducao Debora da Silva Isidoro. Sao Paulo : Arx, 2007. 239p. Portuguese language edition of *My Name was Judas.*

— *Mi Nombre fue Judas*. Una novella de C.K. Stead. Traduccion de Rita da Costa. [Barcelona] : Grijalbo, 2007. 286p. Spanish language edition of *My Name Was Judas*.

Poetry

Whether the Will is Free : Poems 1954-62. Hamilton, N.Z. : Paul's Book Arcade, 1964.

Crossing the Bar. Auckland University Press, 1972.

Quesada : Poems: 1972-1974. Auckland : The Shed, 1975.

Walking Westward. Auckland : The Shed, 1979.

Poems for the Eighties: New Poems. Wellington : Wai-te-ata Press, 1979.

Geographies. Auckland University Press, 1982.

"SCORIA", from *Geographies*. Reading arranged and directed by Dell Boldt for Radio New Zealand, the Concert Programme, with convenor Elizabeth Alley. First broadcast October 15 1983.

Poems of a Decade. Dunedin : Pilgrims South Press, 1983.

Paris : A Poem, by C.K. Stead : illustrated by Gregory O'Brien. Auckland : Auckland University Press : Oxford University Press, 1984.

Three Poems for Kendrick Smithyman. Auckland : Dept of English, University of Auckland, 1987.

Between. Auckland University Press, 1988.

Voices. Wellington : GP Books, 1990.

'Voices : The Poems of C.K. Stead'. Produced by Ross Jolly for National Radio [dramatic readings of poems from *Voices*, with soundtrack]. First broadcast on National Radio, Waitangi Day February 6 1991.

Straw Into Gold : Poems New and Selected. Auckland : Auckland University Press ; Todmorden, Lancs. : Arc, 1997.

The Right Thing. Auckland University Press, 2000.

— Todmorden, Lancs. : Arc Publications, 2000. This edition is as above, except for the addition of 'I've Seen the Future and It's OK' [Cal in Santa Monica]; and the omission of 'Even Newer English Bible'. The last poem in the Auckland University Press edition, 'Horation', is titled 'Horatian' in the Arc edition.

King's Lynn and the Pacific. Published by the King's Lynn Poetry Festival, King's Lynn. 2003. Printed by Lown and Capps Printers, King's Lynn, Norfolk. (The Fourth Annual King's Lynn Award for Merit in Poetry 2001). Casebound edition, signed by the author, 50 copies.

— Published by the King's Lynn Poetry Festival, King's Lynn, 2003. Paperback edition.

Dog. Auckland University Press. 2002.

— Todmorden, Lancs. : Arc Publications, 2004.

The Red Tram. Auckland University Press, 2004.

The Black River. Auckland University Press, 2007.

Collected Poems 1951–2001, Auckland University Press, 2008.

Stories

Five for the Symbol. Auckland : Longman Paul, 1981.

The Blind Blonde with Candles in Her Hair. Auckland : Penguin, 1998.

Literary Criticism

The New Poetic. London : Hutchinson, 1964.

— *The New Poetic : Yeats to Eliot.* New York : Harper & Row, 1966. (Harper Torchbooks : The Academy Library).
— *The New Poetic : Yeats to Eliot.* Harmondsworth, Mddx. : Penguin Books, 1967. (Pelican Books).
— London : Hutchinson University Library, 1975.
— New York : AMS 198, 1981.
— Philadelphia : University of Pennsylvania Press, 1983.
— Rev. ed. Philadelphia, Penn. : University of Pennsylvania Press, 1987.
— *The New Poetic.* New edition. London : Athlone Press, 1998.
— London : Continuum, 2005.
In the Glass Case : Essays on New Zealand Literature. Auckland : Auckland University Press, 1981.
Pound, Yeats, Eliot, and the Modernist Movement. Basingstoke, Hampshire : Macmillan, 1986.
— New Brunswick, N.J. : Rutgers University Press, 1986.
— Basingstoke, Hants. : Macmillan, 1989 (Paperback).
Answering to the Language : Essays on Modern Writers. Auckland : Auckland University Press, 1989.
The Writer at Work : Essays. Dunedin : University of Otago Press, 2000.
Kin of Place : Essays on 20 New Zealand Writers. Auckland : Auckland University Press, 2002.
Book Self: The Reader as Writer and the Writer as Critic. Auckland : Auckland University Press, 2008.

C. K. Stead as Editor and/or Author of Introduction

New Zealand Short Stories. Second Series, selected with an introduction by C.K. Stead. London : Oxford University Press, 1966. (Worlds Classics, no.613).
New Zealand Short Stories : Second Series, edited by C.K. Stead. Wellington : Oxford University Press, 1976.
— [*Along Rideout Road*] *: New Zealand Short Stories : Second Series*, selected with an introduction by C.K. Stead. Auckland : Oxford University Press, 1989.
Shakespeare : Measure for Measure : a Casebook, edited, with an introduction by C.K. Stead. London : Macmillan, 1971.
The Letters and Journals of Katherine Mansfield : a Selection, edited by C.K. Stead. London : Allen Lane, 1977.
— Harmondsworth, Mddx. : Penguin Books, 1977. (Penguin Modern Classics)
— Auckland : Random House, 2004. (A Vintage Book).
Collected Stories of Maurice Duggan, edited and introduced by C.K. Stead. Auckland : Auckland University Press : Oxford University Press, 1981.
The Gramophone Room : Poetry and Fiction, selected by C.K. Stead and Michael Gifkins. Auckland : Auckland University Press, 1983. Introduction by C.K. Stead.
The New Gramophone Room : Poetry & Fiction; selected by C.K. Stead, Elizabeth Smither, Kendrick Smithyman. Auckland : Dept of English, University of Auckland, 1985. Includes Preface by C.K. Stead.
The Faber Book of Contemporary South Pacific Stories. edited by C.K. Stead. London : Faber & Faber, 1994.
Werner Forman's New Zealand. Photographs by Werner Forman; introduction and captions to the photographs by C.K. Stead. London : Harvill ; Auckland : Whitcoulls, 1994.

Secondary Material

Books and Articles Consulted or Cited

Aitken, Tom. "Antipodean Dogfights", *Times Literary Supplement*, 22 February 1991.
— "Auckland Affairs", *Times Literary Supplement*, 11 December 1992.
— "The Boyhood of Jesus", *Times Literary Supplement*, 1 December 2006.
Arvidson, Ken. "The Biography of a Culture", *New Zealand Listener*, 27 February 1982.
— "Personal Story of Greater Value than History", *Sunday Star Times*, 10 July 1994.
— "Stead Muses on Life's Experiences", *Waikato Times*, 18 March 2000.
Berry, Reginald. "*Stead's Dream*", *Landfall*, September 1987.
Bilborough, Norman. "*The Secret History of Modernism*", *New Zealand Books*, June 2002.
Binding, Paul. "*Talking About O'Dwyer*", *Times Literary Supplement*, 1 December 2000.
Blake, Maggie. "Stead's Dream a Nightmare", *Auckland Star*, 17 October 1983.
Bowater, Juliette. *SPANZ*, "Book Review", Issue 30, March 2007.
Braunias, Steve. "In for the High Jump", *New Zealand Listener*, 30 July 1994.
— "C K, 70", *New Zealand Listener*, 11 January 2003.
Chalker, John. "Review of *Pound, Yeats, Eliot and the Modernist Movement*", *The Year's Work in English Studies* 67, Oxford, 1986.
Chan, Stephen. "No Stainless Steel Poet", *New Argot*, May 1974.
Chapple, Geoff. "Writer Charges Book Sabotaged", *Sunday Star Times*, 30 January 1994.
Coddington, Deborah. "Family Ties: In Good Stead", *North & South*, July 1999.
Cooper, Rhonda. "Map of the Human Heart", *Metro*, June 1997.
Consedine, Robert and Joanne. *Healing Our History*, Auckland, Penguin Books, 2001.
Cox, Nigel. "Leading with His Chin", *Quote/Unquote*, July, 1994.
Davin, Dan. "Reviews", *Review of English Studies*, February 1984.
de Falbe, John. "*Talking About O'Dwyer*", *Spectator*, 27 May 2000.
Edmond, Murray. "The Terror and the Pity of 1984: Mervyn Thompson's *Coaltown Blues*", *Landfall*, Issue 209, May 2005.
Eggleton, David. "The Things that Matter", *New Zealand Listener*, 19 February 2005.
— "Loaded", *Quote/Unquote*, March 1994.
Eliot, T. S. "The Waste Land", *The Waste Land and Other Poems*, London, Faber and Faber, 1930.
— "Little Gidding V", *Four Quartets*, London, Faber and Faber, 1951.
Feinstein, Elaine. "When Hearts Need to Be as Hard as Nuts", *London Times*, 28 August 1986.
Frame, Janet. *An Angel at my Table: An Autobiography*, Auckland, Hutchinson, 1984.
Francis, Richard. "Artist as a Young Man", *Times Literary Supplement*, 26 January 1996.
Fuller, Roy. "Special Notices", *The London Magazine*, July, 1964.
Gardam, Jane. "The Uninteresting Survivor", *The Spectator*, 25 November 2006.
Gifkins, Michael. "I Am Not This Body", *New Zealand Listener*, 25 October 1986.
Gordon, Ian. "Poet and Audience", *New Zealand Listener*, 14 August 1964.
Grimshaw, Charlotte. Interviewed by Deborah Coddington, "Family Ties: In Good Stead", *North & South*, July 1999.
Guy, Camille. "A War of Words", *NZ Herald*, 14 December 1989.
Hamilton, Ian. "Fairburn and Dr Stead", *Comment*, September 1967.
Harlow, Michael. "Craft Interview with C. K. Stead", *Landfall* Volume 37 (4), December 1983.
Herrick, Linda. "Judas, A Man of Reason", *NZ Herald*, 7 October 2006.
Hewitson, Michele. "Swimming Against the Tide", *Canvas*, 24 April, 2004.

Hill, Kim. "She Said, He Said", *New Zealand Listener*, 8 May 2004.
Houlahan, Mark. "All Aboard, Including Ovid", *Dominion Post*, 4 December 2004.
Jackson, Kamala. "C. K. Stead: Poet, Novelist, Academic, Activist and Aucklander on His Origins", *Metro*, February 1985.
Jones, Lawrence. *Barbed Wires and Mirrors: Essays on New Zealand Prose*. Dunedin, University of Otago Press, 1987.
— "Imaginative 'Factionality'", *New Zealand Books*, March 2000.
— "Not the Master's Best But Still a Good Read", *Otago Daily Times*, 19 January 2002.
Kawharu, I. H. *Waitangi: Maori and Pakeha Perspectives of the Treaty of Waitangi*, Auckland, OUP, 1989.
King, Michael. *Frank Sargeson: A Life*, Auckland, NZ Viking, 1995.
— *Wrestling with the Angel*, Auckland, Viking, 2000.
— *Tread Softly, for You Tread on my Life*, Auckland, Cape Catley Ltd, 2001.
— *The Penguin History of New Zealand*, Auckland, Penguin Books, 2003.
— "High Accomplishments", *Metro*, December 1989.
— "Ethnic Cleansing", *Metro*, January 1993.
— "Vintage Stead", *North and South*, December 1999.
Lewis, Roger. "This Judas Is More Betrayed than Betrayer", *Sunday Express*, 24 December 2006.
Lineham, Peter J. *Bible and Society: A Sesquicentennial History of the Bible Society in New Zealand*, Wellington, Bible Society Press/Daphne Brasell, 1996.
Locke, Terry. "Review: *The Red Tram*", *English in Aotearoa 58*, April 2006.
McAllister, Janet. "Friends and Foes", *NZ Herald*, 9 July 2005.
McCammon, Belinda. "New Zealand Author Prepared for Trouble over Judas Book", *Wairarapa Times*, 13 October 2006.
McCrystal, John. "The Teddy Bear Within", *Dominion Post*, 24 April 2004.
McNeill, Dougal. "Steadfast: *Collected Poems 1951-2006*", *New Zealand Books*, Autumn 2009.
McNeish, James. "Letter to the Editor", *Landfall* Volume 21 (2), June, 1967.
Malcolm, Wilf and Nicholas Tarling. *Crisis of Identity? The Mission and Management of Universities in New Zealand*, Wellington, Dunmore Publishing Ltd, 2007.
Manguel, Alberto. "Leaving Fingerprints Behind", *The Spectator*, 5 June 2004.
Marshall, Owen. "Power of Language to Influence Beliefs", *Dominion*, 3 October 1992.
Matthews, Philip. "Stead and the Heretics: The Godless Gospel of C. K. Stead", *New Zealand Listener*, 21 October 2006.
Mead, Philip. "The Veteran's Cadre: C. K. Stead", *Times Literary Supplement*, 4 January 2002.
Mellors, John. " His Master's Voice", *London Magazine*, November 1986.
— "Obsessions and Illusions", *London Magazine*, Oct/Nov 1989.
Millar, Paul. "Nary a Sniff of NZ", *New Zealand Education Review* 2, 25 June 1997.
Miller, Karl. "Talking About Stead", *Landfall*, Issue 205, May 2001.
Moore, Christopher. "Approach with Care", *The Press*, 16 February 2002.
Moore, Toby. "C. K. Stead: *Sister Hollywood*", *Times Literary Supplement*, 11 August 1989.
Moravia, Alberto. *Conjugal Love*, London, Martin Secker and Warburg Ltd, 1951; first published 1949.
Needham, John. "Letter of Reply to C. K. Stead", *Comment*, September 1979.
Newton, John. "The Death-throes of Nationalism", *Landfall*, Issue 205, May 2003.
O'Brien. Greg. (text), Robert Cross (photographs), "C. K. Stead: The Pigeon and the Clock",

Moments of Invention, Heinemann Reed, 1988.
Oliver, W. H. *Comment 15*, April 1982.
O'Sullivan, Vincent. *Long Journey to the Border*, Auckland, Penguin Books, 2003.
Quinn, Kenneth (introduction and selection). *Approaches to Catullus*, New York, Barnes and Noble, 1972.
Phillipson, Allan. *C. K. Stead and Three Modes of New Zealand Poetry*, The University of British Columbia, July, 1997. Thesis submitted in partial fulfilment of requirements for Doctor of Philosophy. Electronic resource retrieved May 2006 from http://www.collectioncanada.gc.ca/obj/s4/f2/dsk3/ftp04/nq25137.pdf
Phipps, Sam. "First Editions: *My Name Was Judas* by C K Stead", *Glasgow Herald*, 18 November 2006.
Plath, Sylvia. *The Journals of Sylvia Plath*, New York, Anchor Books, a Division of Random House, 1998, first published 1982.
Radice, Betty (ed.). *The Poems of Catullus*, Harmondsworth, Penguin Books, 1966.
Reilly, Colleen. "Keeping Us on Our Toes", *Dominion*, 5 October 1991.
Ricketts, Harry. "Sylvia, Meet Horace", *New Zealand Listener*, 1 April 2000.
Riseborough, Hazel. *"The Taranaki Report": Background Papers for the Taranaki Raupatu Claim*, Waitangi Tribunal, 1989.
Robinson, Roger and Nelson Wattie (eds.). *The Oxford Companion to New Zealand Literature*, 1998.
Roger, Warwick. "Face to Face: C. K. Stead", *North and South*, May 2004.
Rubin, Merle. "A Sheltered Life in a Century of Turmoil", *Los Angeles Times*, 1 August 2002.
Ruthven, K. K. "*Pound, Yeats, Eliot and the Modernist Movement*, C. K. Stead", *Landfall* Volume 40 (4), December 1986.
Scott, Dick. *Dick Scott: A Radical Writer's Life*, Auckland, Reed Publishing, 2004.
Sharp, Iain. "Calvi Financial Scandal Catalyst for Stead Yarn", *Sunday Star Times*, 23 March 1997.
— "Review: Talking About O'Dwyer", *Landfall* 199 Volume 8 (1), March 2000.
— "A Bracing Blast from the Past", *Sunday Star Times*, 30 March 2008.
Shaw, Helen (ed.), *Dear Lady Ginger: An Exchange of Letters between Lady Otteline Morrell and D'Arcy Cresswell*, Auckland, Auckland University Press/Oxford University Press, 1983.
Shaw, Tina (ed.). *A Passion for Travel: New Zealand Writers and their Adventures Overseas*. Auckland, Tandem Press, 1998.
Shrapnell, Norman (cited by Bernard Orsman), "Critics Flatter NZ Novelist", *New Zealand News UK*, 19 September 1984.
Smith, Ali. "Pioneer and Tangi", *Times Literary Supplement*, 4 June 2004.
Snedden, Patrick. *Pakeha and the Treaty: Why It's Our Treaty too*, Auckland, Random House, 2005.
Stead, C. K. "Professor Stead's Work in Menton and London", *Ariel*, June 1973.
— "A Room Much Maligned", *New Zealand Listener*, 18 May 18 1974.
— "Voiture d'Occasion, *Islands* Vol. 3 (1), Autumn 1974.
— "Suffenia the Poet", in *New Writing 7*, Carmen Callil and Craig Raine (eds.) London, Vintage, in association with the British Council, 1998.
Stone, R. C. J. *From Tamaki-Makau-Rau to Auckland,* Auckland University Press, 2001.
Stratford, Stephen. "Blaspheming Against the Pieties: Why the Literati Hate C. K. Stead", *Metro*, April 1990.
Tolerton, Jane and Joy Tonks (compilers). "Oh To Be a Writer, a Real Writer!" *Winners of the Bank of New Zealand Katherine Mansfield Short Story Award*, Wellington, Victoria

University Press, 1999.
Vivian, Kathryn. "Stead Talks His Way Through Latest Novel", *Sunday Star Times*, 10 July 1994.
Walters, Margaret ."A Soldier's Death", *Times Literary Supplement*, 9 June 2000.
Wattie, Nelson. "The Old Guard", *The Dominion Post*, 28 April 2007.
— "Self Evident", *New Zealand Listener*, 26 April 2008.
Wells, Peter. "Bang, Bang, Bang", *Landfall* 203, May 2002.
Wevers, Lydia. "Parallel Clichés of Tinsel Town", *Dominion Sunday Times*, 22 October 1989.
Whigham, Peter. (translation and introduction). *The Poems of Catullus*, Harmondsworth, Penguin Books, 1966.
White, Margo. "Interview: Karl Stead", *Metro*, May 2004.
— "Mr Congeniality", *Metro*, August 2005.
Wilkins, Damien. "The Self-loathing of a Stead Novel", *New Zealand Books*, 27 December 1992.
— "Books: Get Personal", *New Zealand Listener*, 8 March 1997.
Williams, Mark. *Leaving the Highway: Six Contemporary New Zealand Novelists*, Auckland University Press, 1990.
— "Our Most Trenchant Critic", *The Dominion*, 4 November 1989.
— "C. K. Stead and the New Literary Order", *Meanjin* 53, Summer 1994.
— "*The Singing Whakapapa*, C. K. Stead", *Landfall*, Issue 188, Spring 1994.
— "As I Remember", *New Zealand Listener*, 23 October 1999.
— "Asking the Hard Questions", *New Zealand Books*, March 2001.
— "Stead's Mansfield", *Landfall*, Issue 208, November 2004.
Wroe, Nicholas. "Writing in the Dark", *The Guardian*, 10 March 2007. Retrieved August 2007.http://www.guardian.co.uk/books/2007/mar/10/featuresreviews.guardianreview35
Young, David. "Tenants of Fiction", *New Zealand Listener*, 13 October 1984.

Letters Lodged and Filed as Turnbull Library Papers

Curnow, Allen. Letter to Karl Stead, 5 August 1982.
Stead, C. K. Letter to Allen and Jeny Curnow, 24 May 1983.
Stead, C. K. Letters to Allen Curnow
— 10 July 1956.
— 6 January 1981.
— 26 March 1981.
— 27 July 1981.
— 29 September 1990.
— 19 May 1997.
— 7 May 2001.
— 18 August 2001.
— 26 September 2001.
Stead, C. K. and Kay Stead. Letter to Frank Sargeson, 1 May 1956.
Stead, C. K. Letters to Sargeson
— 27 July 1956.
— 8 August 1956.
— 5 October 1956.
— 9 June 1957.
— 18 October 1957.

— 3 June 1958.
— 18 August 1958.
— 7 November 1958.
— 23 January 1963.
— 16 November 1964.
— 22 March 1972.
— 27 March 1972, begun 22 March.
— 28 March 1965.
— 4 May 1972.
— 13 June 1972
— 22 July 1972.
— 21 December 1972
— 11 February 1977.

Addresses and Interviews Cited

Alley, Elizabeth. Interview with C.K. Stead on "SCORIA", *Concert Programme*, 15 October 1983.

Bennett, Andrew. An address to 'Mr Vice-Chancellor' at the conferring of the degree Doctor of Letters on Professor Karl Stead, 12 July 2001. *Speeches Delivered in Commendation of Honorary Graduates*, University of Bristol, 9-13 July 2001.

Campbell, John. Interview with C. K. Stead, *National Radio*, 25 November 2000.

Edwards, Brian. Interview with C. K. Stead, *National Radio*, 3 December, 1994.

— Interview with C. K. Stead, *National Radio*, 27 November 1999.

Hill, Kim. "Nine to Noon", interview with C. K. Stead, *National Radio*, 6 July1994.

Ryan, Kathryn. Interview with C. K. Stead, "Nine To Noon", *Radio New Zealand National*, 7 March 2008.

Stead, C. K. Interview with author, 28 August 2005.

Stead, C. K. An address delivered at the University of Alberta, Edmonton, Canada, 16 February 1982.

— An address at the Auckland Writers and Readers Festival, introduced and chaired by Emeritus Professor Terry Sturm, 24 May 2007.

— "One Thing Leads to Another", speaking as Distinguished Alumnus, opening speaker in the Distinguished Alumni Series, in the Maidment Theatre, University of Auckland, introduced and chaired by Emeritus Professor Mac Jackson, 3 March 2008.

— "It's Not Wishful Thinking", Writers and Readers Week, Wellington Festival, Embassy Theatre, introduced by Elizabeth Alley, 14 March 2008.

Stevens, Ross. "In Good Stead", *Frontline*, hosted by Susan Wood, TVNZ, 1994.

Sturm, Terry. Interview with author, 20 December 2005.

Worsfold, Josephine. Interview with author, 2 February 2006.